# Warman's

# 101

## GREATEST

# Baby Boomer Toys

| Item | Page | Item | Page | Item | Page |
|------|------|------|------|------|------|
| Addams Family Game | 163 | Chatty Cathy | 30 | Give-A-Show | 92 |
| American Plastic Bricks | 141 | Colorforms | 179 | Go to the Head of the Class | 134 |
| American Skyline | 143 | Cootie | 73 | Gumby | 105 |
| Atomic Mobile Unit | 120 | Davy Crockett's Coonskin Cap | 55 | Honey Wheat Dinosaurs | 126 |
| Auburn Cars | 148 | Dick Tracy Squad Car | 98 | Hoppity Horse | 182 |
| Aurora Monster Kits | 88 | Dream Pets | 158 | Hot Wheels | 50 |
| Barbie | 12 | Easy-Bake Oven | 34 | Howdy Doody Puppets | 60 |
| Bash! | 168 | Eldon's Big Poly | 165 | Hula Hoop | 54 |
| Batman Toys | 78 | Erector Sets | 145 | Japanese Battery Toys | 128 |
| Beany-Copter | 82 | Etch A Sketch | 93 | Johnny Astro | 171 |
| Billy Blastoff | 172 | Flintstones Push-Button Puppets | 162 | Klackers | 173 |
| Bop Bags and Punchos | 197 | Flip Your Wig! Game | 76 | Krazy Ikes | 198 |
| Bozo | 185 | Frisbee | 36 | Lamb Chop | 194 |
| Bubble-Topped Coupe | 102 | Fury Frame-Tray Inlay | 118 | Liddle Kiddles | 86 |
| Bugs Bunny Magic Pictures | 196 | Game of Life | 170 | Life-Size Kitchen | 138 |
| Buzzy Bee | 202 | G.I. Joe | 26 | Lincoln Logs | 144 |
| Captain Video Aliens | 114 | Girder & Panel | 142 | Little People School Bus | 201 |

| Item | Page | Item | Page | Item | Page |
|---|---|---|---|---|---|
| Lone Ranger | 130 | Rin Tin Tin Paint By Number | 116 | This Little Piggy | 203 |
| Magic Rocks | 186 | Robert the Robot | 62 | Tinker Toys | 190 |
| Marx's Modern Farm | 66 | Rock 'em Sock 'em Robots | 80 | Tom Corbett | 113 |
| Matchbox | 32 | Roy Rogers Cap Gun | 63 | Tonka Trucks | 68 |
| Mickey Mouse Club Toys | 70 | Silly Putty | 187 | Tootsietoys | 150 |
| Monopoly | 136 | Slinky | 58 | Tru-Action Electric Football | 152 |
| Mouse Trap Game | 42 | Slot Cars | 166 | Trolls | 48 |
| Mr. Machine | 84 | Space Patrol Ray Gun | 108 | Twister | 81 |
| Mr. Potato Head | 18 | Space People | 104 | View-Master | 191 |
| Musical Teddy Bear | 200 | Speed King | 146 | Vinyl-Faced Bear | 176 |
| Mystery Date | 169 | Spirograph | 85 | Vinyl Squeakers | 178 |
| PEZ | 180 | Spoonmen | 127 | What's My Line? | 111 |
| Play-Doh | 199 | Sputnik | 122 | Winky Dink Magic Television Kit | 96 |
| Pogo | 183 | Spy Toys | 160 | Wooly Willy | 193 |
| Prehistoric Times | 124 | Super Ball | 159 | Yogi Bear Score-A-Matic | 192 |
| Rat Fink Charms | 156 | Tammy | 44 | Yo-Yo | 181 |
| Renwal Dollhouse Furniture | 140 | Thingmakers | 38 | | |

©2005 Mark Rich
Published by

kp books
*An Imprint of F+W Publications*

**700 East State Street • Iola, WI 54990-0001**
**715-445-2214 • 888-457-2873**

Our toll-free number to place an order or obtain
a free catalog is (800) 258-0929.

Library of Congress Catalog Number: 2005930195

ISBN: 0-89689-220-4

Designed by Kim Schierl
Edited by Dan Brownell

Printed in United States of America

# CONTENTS

INTRODUCTION .................... 7

CHAPTER ONE: THE TRIUMPH OF
THE STYLE DOLL ............ 10

1. Mattel's Leading Lady: Barbie ........................ 12

2. Everyone's Favorite Vegetable: Mr. Potato Head ........... 18

CHAPTER TWO: ... AND THE TRIUMPH
OF TELEVISION: HITS OF THE SIXTIES .......... 24

3. Seeing Action: G.I. Joe ...................... 26

4. Just Pull the Chatty Ring:
Chatty Cathy and Her Friends ...................... 30

5. Rolling in Realism: Matchbox Cars ..................... 32

6. Light-Bulb Inspirations: The Easy-Bake Oven ............. 34

7. From Flying Saucer to Frisbee ...................... 36

8. Thingmakers ...................... 38

9. Mouse Trap! ...................... 42

10. The Typical Teen: Tammy ...................... 44

11. From Under the Bridge: Trolls ...................... 48

12. Greased-Wheel Revolution: Hot Wheels ................... 50

CHAPTER THREE:
FADS AND FAVES OF THE FIFTIES ................ 52

13. Dateline 1958: Hula Hoop ...................... 54

14. The Unexpected TV Hit:
Davy Crockett and His Coonskin Cap ..................... 55

15. It's Slinky! ...................... 58

16. *Howdy Doody* Puppets ...................... 60

17. Robert the Robot, the Mechanical Man .................. 62

18. Bang, You're Dead! ... The Roy Rogers Cap Gun ........ 63

19. Marx's Modern Farm ...................... 66

20. Sandbox Workhorses: Tonka Trucks ...................... 68

21. *Mickey Mouse Club* Toys ...................... 70

22. The Game of Cootie ...................... 73

CHAPTER FOUR: FLIP YOUR WIG! ...
MORE FAB SIXTIES HITS ............ 74

23. The Beatles Flip Your Wig Game ...................... 76

24. Into the Bat Suit, Batman! ...................... 78

25. Red Rocker, Blue Bomber: Rock 'em Sock 'ems! ....... 80

26. Twister ...................... 81

27. The Beany-Copter ...................... 82

28. Mr. Machine ...................... 84

29. Spirograph ...................... 85

30. Locket Dolls: Liddle Kiddles ...................... 86

31. Models of Midnight: Aurora Monster Kits ................ 88

32. Give-A-Show ...................... 92

33. Doodle Dialing: Etch A Sketch ...................... 93

CHAPTER FIVE: WINKY DINK AND YOU ........ 94

34. Interactive TV: *Winky Dink* Magic Television Kit ....... 96

35. Dick Tracy Squad Car ...................... 98

36. The Bubble-Topped Coupe ...................... 102

37. Space People ...................... 104

38. Gumby ...................... 105

39. Zap, You're Disintegrated! ...
The Space Patrol Ray Gun ...................... 108

40. TV Make-Believe: *What's My Line?* ...................... 111

41. Visionary Toys: *Tom Corbett* ...................... 113

42. *Captain Video* Aliens ...................... 114

43. Paint By Number: *Rin Tin Tin* ...................... 116

44. Frame-Tray Inlay: *Fury* ...................... 118

45. Atomic Mobile Unit ...................... 120

46. Sputnik, the Magnetic Satellite ...................... 122

47. Prehistoric Times ...................... 124

48. Honey Wheat Dinosaurs ...................... 126

CONTENTS

49. Spoonmen ..................... 127

50. Lights! Sound! A-C-T-I-O-N!: Japanese Battery Toys. 128

51. *The Lone Ranger* and the Plastic Old West ............. 130

**CHAPTER SIX: REAL-LIFE MAKE-BELIEVE..... 132**

52. Go to the Head of the Class .................. 134

53. The Road to Millions: Monopoly ........................ 136

54. The Life-Size Kitchen ................ 138

55. Furnishing Dollhouses the Renwal Way ................. 140

56. Suburban Builder: American Plastic Bricks ............ 141

57. Girder & Panel ................................... 142

58. Architect's Training Ground: American Skyline ....... 143

59. Pioneer Builder: Lincoln Logs .................. 144

60. Erector Sets ................................ 145

61. The Hard-Plastic Highway: Speed King ................. 146

62. The Vinyl Passing Line: Auburn Cars ...................... 148

63. Tootsietoys ............................... 150

64. Tru-Action Electric Football ...................... 152

**CHAPTER SEVEN: BASH! WOW! ...
MORE SIXTIES AND SEVENTIES TOYS.......... 154**

65. Rat Fink Charms ..................... 156

66. Dream Pets ......................... 158

67. Super Ball .............................. 159

68. Spy Toys .............................. 160

69. Cartoon Crazy: *The Flintstones* Push-Button Puppets 162

70. TV Make-Believe: *The Addams Family* Game ......... 163

71. Plastic Powerhouses: Eldon's Big Poly ..................... 165

72. Slot Cars ............................ 166

73. Bash! ... The Decade of Loud Games ...................... 168

74. Romantic Games: From Ben Casey to Mystery Date 169

75. The Road to Happiness: The Game of Life ............. 170

76. Johnny Astro ........................ 171

77. America's First Boy in Space: Billy Blastoff ............. 172

78. Klackers ........................ 173

**CHAPTER EIGHT: SQUEAKERS
AND SQUEALERS ...................................... 174**

79. Vinyl-Faced Bear: From Chubby Tubby to Yogi ........ 176

80. Vinyl Squeakers ........................ 178

81. Vinyl Stick-Ons: Colorforms ................ 179

82. Plastic-Age Candy Dispenser: PEZ .................. 180

83. The Yo-Yo ......................... 181

84. Hoppity Horse ....................... 182

85. Comics-Page 'Possum: Pogo ................. 183

86. Recording Star: Bozo! ..................... 185

87. The Mountains of the Moon: Magic Rocks ......... 186

88. Silly Putty .......................... 187

**CHAPTER NINE: TINKERS AND WHISKERS... 188**

89. Tinkertoys ........................ 190

90. The World's Fair Stereoscope: View-Master ............. 191

91. Yogi Bear Score-A-Matic ...................... 192

92. The Magic Whiskers of Wooly Willy ....................... 193

93. Lamb Chop ........................ 194

94. Crayon Magic: Bugs Bunny ........................ 196

95. Bop Bags and Punchos ...................... 197

96. Krazy Ikes ......................... 198

97. Play-Doh ......................... 199

98. The Musical Teddy Bear ...................... 200

99. The Little People School Bus ...................... 201

100. Buzzy Bee ....................... 202

101. This Little Piggy ...................... 203

**BOOMER TOY VALUES............................. 204
(LISTED ALPHABETICALLY BY MANUFACTURER)**

**ADDITIONAL READING............................. 206**

**INDEX ........................................ 207**

# INTRODUCTION

THE 1954 *Woolworth's New Christmas Book* had everything a child could want: coloring books, records, activity sets, dolls, trucks, blocks, cap guns and trains. It showed more than 150 toys, many of them new to the season. The toy ads were slipped between the pages of a comic-book story featuring Phineas the Pelican and the two children of a circus ringmaster. The toys were what the children really looked at, though.

Every one of those toys was fated to become some child's favorite in that 1954-55 season of Eisenhower, the Red Scare, *The Lord of the Rings*, *Lolita* and the Bikini Atoll hydrogen bomb explosion. They were five-and-dime favorites—every single one of them—to some child, somewhere.

Or open the *Ward's Christmas Book* of a year later. While Woolworth's beguiled the child with comic-book reading material, Ward's took the hardcore approach. It presented an overwhelming number of neatly arranged photographs, with blocks of carefully organized descriptions arranged in columns.

What those photographs showed, and those blocks of tiny text described, were all the latest and greatest treasures of American childhood. Four pages of "Gifts from Your Davy Crockett Trading Post." Annie Oakley, Superman, Hopalong

Cassidy, Lone Ranger and Tonto outfits. An inflatable version of the Lone Ranger's Silver. Chemistry sets, steam engines, Revell's old-time auto kits, Ideal's Take-Apart toys, gas-powered airplanes, Lincoln Logs, Tinkertoys, paint-by-number sets, toy guitars, drum kits, a Marx farm play set with tin barn and plastic animals, a Davy Crockett Alamo play set, toy telephones, a plastic bubblegum bank, plastic cowboys and Indians, Gund's plush Mickey Mouse, Sun Rubber Donald Duck cars, Disneyland games, Playskool floor trains, Pony Boy guns, a Rin Tin Tin Cavalry Set, a Coca-Cola dispenser, Krazy Ikes, plastic and china tea sets, doll houses, Fisher-Price's Buzzy Bee and Jolly Jumper Frog, Slinky Dog, toy vacuum cleaners and sewing machines, a hard-plastic Pet Shop delivery truck with tiny plastic dogs, doctor and nurse kits, doll buggies, toy chests, Lone Ranger and Space Ranger flashlights, Structo, Marx, and Wyandotte trucks, made-in-Japan remote-control cars, the Electric Robot with Baby, the Dick Tracy Police Station with squad car, steel Action Cars, wind-up tractors, K.O. Joe punching-toy, Foto Electric Football, Lionel and Marx electric trains, tricycles, scooters, the Dennis the Menace Mischief Kit, Monopoly, Clue, Sorry and even a Davy Crockett canvas-covered coaster wagon.

How could any of them not have been someone's favorite toy, and not to just any one single child but to many thousands among the millions of Boomer children? How could such things in those private, secret moments alone in the playroom not have been treasured and placed closer to the heart than parents, siblings or best friends?

And then take the *Sears Toy Book* of 10 years later. Over 200 glossy pages—many in kid-riveting color—of toys arrayed

on their pages in such a way that the children gazing there would lose their souls forever. Those 200 pages held over 1,500 items. Somewhere in this country, at least one person will stand up for each item in that fabulous catalog and will tell you how that particular item belongs on anyone's list of 101 great toys of their time.

That toy was the greatest ever, they would say. They will stand up for that toy, and they will be right to do so. How could they be wrong, after all? They were there. They saw, they yearned, they held, they played. If they did not play with their own toy, they played with a friend's. If they never played with it in their own grubby hands, then they carried TV ads and jingles in their minds for years and played with the toys in their heads.

Children like to make lists. And then, grown-up, they think, "Yes, I remember. *That* was my favorite toy." Then they realize they are thinking of a time when they were 8. Right then, *that* toy was, indeed, their favorite. But if they think hard about it, they can remember another time when they fixated on something quite different. And before they know it, they set up a long line of toys, like toy soldiers marching down a hallway to the idyllic playrooms of the past. And each of those toys was, at one time or another, *the* favorite. Each of them was number one.

In the list that follows, I had to make choices. I gave weight to the novelty, popularity and significance of the toys, but did not give as much weight to current collector interest.

This book aspires to provide an indirect history of Boomer children by presenting their playthings—those things that ended up dirtied and broken and discarded, things that were thrown out by the hundreds of millions each year of those many years of growing up. Each of the toys in this book presents a window on those children born from World War II through the early 1960s.

In a way, the Boomers were two different generations linked by their birth within that postwar period. Statisticians can point to a single bell-shaped curve that looks like a blacked-out mound on their graph paper. It is that great mountain that represents the birth of many millions of children within a time span of nearly 20 years—a span longer than typical for a generation. Yet the shape of that bell curve is irresistible to historians. That shape itself is what gives this generation cohesion.

The Boomers themselves accept it. Millions of former children point to that mountain and say that is where they came from. In terms of the kind of childhood they led, however, it was an immense period of time. The first wave of children born in 1946 were given the first small cardboard, metal, wood, paper and plastic toys of the postwar era to play with, along with various hand-me-downs from the 1930s and early '40s. And the last wave of children, born during the swiftly passing years of the Kennedy administration, were playing with toys into the 1970s. So while the generation includes people born over a period of nearly 20 years, the toys of that generation appeared over a span of 25 years or more.

Think of the toys from 1948 through the early 1950s: plastic-mesh Christmas stockings full of plastic Dillon-Beck and Banner toys, the Space People, plastic Marx flatbed trucks carrying loads of real Lifesaver candies, cardboard Keystone gas station play sets, imported Mobo riding horses, big Wyandotte fire engine riding toys, black rubber Auburn farm tractors, little Dowst Tootsietoy cars with black-rubber tires, etc.

Then think of the toys from late 1960s, when Lesney's Matchbox cars were so popular, Mattel's Liddle Kiddle

miniature dolls appeared, and stores were full of bags of MPC plastic toy soldiers, Super Balls, Frisbees, trolls and Marx Big Wheel plastic trikes, the low-slung noise-producers designed for the very youngest sidewalk hotrodders.

Consider even the toys of that foggy period when the next generation was being given toys that some of the last Boomers played with, too, such as Mattel Hot Wheels die-cast performance cars, Mego's superhero figures, and Chein's Tweaky Toy little plastic people.

From the toys clutched by two-inch hands in 1947-50 to the toys for larger, more adept hands in 1969-74, these were all toys of the "same" generation. They were all "Boomer" toys.

In a real sense, Boomer toys belong to all of us, whether we were born within the Boomer years or not. Some of the toys that have become icons of the postwar years have enjoyed continued sales: Barbie, Mr. Potato Head, Cootie, Frisbee, Tonka, Silly Putty, Matchbox, Magic "8" Ball and Slinky are among the names that have endured for 30 and 40 years, or more, even though many of the toys themselves changed through the years.

Other Boomer toys have enjoyed periodic revivals, returning to the public eye and to the playroom here and there through the decades. G.I. Joe toys languished and vanished for a time, then became a Generation-X toy in a new, much smaller version, alongside the incredibly popular *Star Wars* figures of the same scale. Such varied playthings as Mr. Machine, Robert the Robot, Monster Magnet, Fort Apache play sets, Dream Pets, Lincoln Logs, miscellaneous tin robots, and even Johnny Lightning cars experienced a nostalgic renaissance in the late 20th and early 21st centuries.

In reshaping the book into its new form, I have kept in mind the discussions I have had with many Boomers—sometimes in correspondence, sometimes in person, sometimes in on-air radio conversations. I have tried to give special consideration to those who are older Boomers than I

am and who enjoyed living through other fads and fashions than I did.

Some of them know better than I do what powerful impact various events had: the advent of TV Westerns, the introduction of the wonderful and wonderfully affordable Marx play sets and doll houses, the invasion of Japanese battery toys, the veritable empire of Howdy-Doody-ism in the early 1950s, the high-heel vinyl doll sensations of the mid-1950s, the vast wave of Davy Crockett wannabe-ism in 1955, the Hula Hoop explosion of 1958, the widespread fascination with missile and satellite toys in 1958 and '59....

At the same time, knowing how younger readers want their goodies right out front, I have left the late 1960s and early '70s emphasis in the list. The older readers, after all, will be patient about such things and will not be jumping ahead into the book to find the ones they regard as favorites.

I must note that the current list is not exhaustive. After all, 101 toys are not enough. Rather than being exhaustive, the following list represents the kinds of playthings that abounded during those strange and wonderful years of the 1950s and '60s, years framed on the one side by an exploding atomic bomb far away across the Pacific, and on the other by the blast of an assassin's gun in Dallas.

One last note about toys. Toys are like sand grains of the past that slip between the floor boards and disappear from view. In that blind period we call our first maturity, or young adulthood, or adolescence —or what have you—we suddenly forget toys. Toys no longer impinge on our sensory universe; in fact, they cease to exist. It is as though toys are made of a strangely changeable substance that, once ignored, renders them invisible. Turn away once, and they vanish forever. Years later, then—yes, *then*— we feel the loss. But sadly, by the time we feel it, it is too late. The basement is cleared, the upper shelf of the closet holds only sweaters and scarves, the random shoe boxes in the back only hold dried-up pens and battered rulers, and a single, lonely sock hides under the bed.

This book, however, will bring back those long-vanished toys. Not all, by any means, not all, but the best because it will bring back memories of your own toys—and naturally the ones you remember are the most important of all.

# CHAPTER 1

# The Triumph of the Style Doll

**W**hen Boomers are asked to name the number one Boomer toy off the top of their head, they respond with various top brand names of the 1950s and '60s, especially Frisbee, Slinky and Hula Hoop.

## BARBIE

Many, however, will name Barbie, the doll manufactured by Mattel, Inc., the Los Angeles toy manufacturing giant. The doll was introduced at the midpoint of the Boomer years and kept in production to the end of those years and beyond. Like those other prominent toys, the Barbie doll has enjoyed longevity. Like Frisbee and Slinky, moreover, it has benefited from powerful merchandising muscle. In the Barbie doll's case, it was the muscle of one of the biggest toy companies in history.

If so many people remember Barbie, it is partly because they are not allowed to forget. That in itself argues for the doll's place at the top, since the story of Baby Boomer toys is the story of merchandising, image-building, TV advertising and product placement.

The Barbie doll was one of the great hits of the 1960s, and perhaps the best known "girl's toy" of that decade. It epitomized the real situation children were facing: that of "growing up too soon." It was one of countless toys that evoked and embodied the culture of the teenager, whose existence was due, at least in part, to society's new addiction to TV entertainment.

On the other hand, if we are looking for a toy to represent an entire generation, then we might look for one that both boys and girls enjoyed. We might look for a toy that was present from the beginning, so that not a single child of the generation would have grown up unaware of it. We might also look for a toy that incorporated many of the toy industry trends of the time. Perhaps, too, we might look for a toy that changed enough after the generation grew up that it could be seen to have not only arrived with the generation but also to have departed.

## MR. POTATO HEAD

The Mr. Potato Head sets introduced in 1952 by Hassenfeld Bros., Inc., of Central Falls, R.I., happen to fit those criteria. The toys were not only in existence by the time the first Boomers were entering kindergarten, but they were prominently in existence, thanks to a national advertising campaign.

That the sets were played with by both girls and boys is evident from talking with members of the Boomer generation. The sets also embraced one of the leading American myths of the Boomer years, that of the happy, "nuclear" family, with father, mother, brother and sister—and pets. It was a family toy.

That Mr. Potato Head embodied a variety of toy trends in the 1950s and '60s will be a subject of discussion below; and that it, unlike the Barbie doll, was irrevocably changed by the enactment of toy-safety laws at the end of the Boomer years is unquestionable.

The Frisbee flying toy might also be a good candidate to represent the entire generation—but while the "Flyin' Saucer" was introduced in the late 1940s and produced by many toy companies in the 1950s, as a plastic toy it was not until after Barbie appeared that the Frisbee achieved prominence.

The Slinky arrived on the scene early, too. Like Silly Putty, however, the Slinky was almost purely a novelty. It stood alone on unique merits, almost without reference to the rest of the toy industry.

Perhaps closest to Mr. Potato Head sets would be the odd little game named Cootie. The aim of the game was to construct a hard plastic insect figure, which—like Mr. Potato Head—has achieved iconic status among nostalgia buffs. Cootie, too, arrived early in the Boomer years, was popular throughout and then was irrevocably changed by toy-safety laws.

I keep remembering, however, a conversation I was privileged to have during a call-in radio show a few years ago, with a gentleman who in the 1950s had owned a variety store in one of our northern states.

"Tell me," I asked him out of true curiosity. "What toy could you not keep on your shelves in the 1950s?"

"Mr. Potato Head," he replied promptly.

# MATTEL'S LEADING LADY
# BARBIE

ACCORDING TO commonly accepted tradition, Ruth Handler was watching her daughter Barbara and Barbara's friends playing with paper dolls. The girls, she observed, had little interest in paper-doll children. Instead, they spent their time with paper-doll adults, putting on and taking off their various outfits and then role-playing with these figures.

Conventional wisdom in the toy industry said that girls played with dolls because they liked to pretend to be mothers. This meant they liked to play with baby dolls or with dolls representing girls close to their own age. Barbara and her friends may well have been pretending to be mothers while playing with their paper dolls. Yet they were using dolls of the mothers, not of the children, to do so.

Would girls react positively to dolls that depicted adults and that embodied adult ideals, instead that those that depicted children and embodied child ideals? Ruth Handler thought so. Since she was running the immensely successful toy company Mattel with her husband Elliott, she was in a position to test her idea.

She ran into resistance first from her husband, then from the industry. At the 1959 New York Toy Fair, where the Barbie doll made her debut, store representatives were also dubious about the doll. Some, however, had enough faith in Mattel's track record to order them for their stores. They learned soon enough they had ordered too few.

It may have been the design of the doll that did it. Ruth Handler had found the physical doll to fit her adult-doll idea in Germany. In 1952, an artist named Reinhard Beuthien created a character named Lilli for a spot cartoon in the daily *Bild-Zeitung*. Since the character proved popular, Beuthien drew more Lilli cartoons. Then he designed a doll.

Lilli was a curvaceous, slender-waisted, blonde beauty with striking eyes and a taste for tight fitting clothing. She was both sexy and savvy. She entered the world of toys and dolls with the aid of Max Weissbrodt, who had created the highly prized Elastolin figures manufactured by O. & M. Hausser. The Lilli doll, with sharp-cornered eyes, arched brows, high forehead, thin neck, high breasts and long, slender legs, made her debut in August, 1955, the midpoint of the decade. During her brief period of popularity, Lilli dolls were shipped around the world.

When sales of the doll declined, Lilli rights were sold to Mattel, which, in 1959, test-marketed and then released a remarkably similar doll with a new name. "Barbie," was, appropriately enough, the nickname of the Handlers' daughter.

Barbie succeeded for many reasons, not least of which was the overt way she embodied sexuality. Never mind her high breasts, which immediately established her maturity to any who saw her and which the male-dominated toy industry thought would doom her in the marketplace. The Barbie doll expressed sexuality above all through conspicuous display, for she was a fashion doll.

The traditional story about the Barbie doll's beginnings, which is the story told above about paper dolls, makes it seem the idea for the plastic fashion doll sprang full-blown on the toy scene without any immediate predecessors. This is to be expected, since a toy company naturally wants toy buyers—not just the buyers for such major outfits as Sears and Wards, but even individual buyers who walk into their local Woolworth's store—to think that what is being offered is strikingly new and different. Mattel's publicity department must have had a powerful hand in the shaping of this doll's tale, for toy collectors 40 years later still give lip service to the tale of paper-doll origins.

No one will probably ever know if the homey incident actually occurred between observant mother and playing daughter. Yet the Barbie doll went beyond the idea stage at Mattel not because of the originality of the notion behind the doll, but because of the way it fit perfectly into the times.

Boomer-era fashion dolls were an outgrowth of trends in the pre-World War II doll industry. These trends are probably best exemplified by New York City's Alexander Doll Co., whose success at turning dolls into respectable recipients of "fashion sense" was unquestioned in the 1950s. Madame Alexander even received the 1951 Gold Medal Award from the Fashion Academy, an organization not known for paying attention to toys.

"By dressing Alexander Dolls in clothes that are lovely in fabric and exquisite in design, you have not only made them enchanting and precious in themselves, but you have helped to stimulate in our younger generation an exciting interest in fashion and a growing awareness of style," the Fashion Academy said in presenting the medal.

What Alexander Doll Co. had done for higher-end display dolls, other companies proved more than willing to do for lower-end and dime store dolls. One such was the Hollywood Doll

Mfg. Co. This Glendale, Calif., company made "dolls of the stars," which were inexpensive toy figures with elaborate and gaudy costumes—and, by the 1950s, with moving eyes. That they embodied the fashion hopes of young girls seems certain, as they sported such names as "The Lucky Star Doll" and "Queen for a Day"—and they were tidily distinguished from the company's more realistic dolls, which Hollywood Dolls grouped in its "Everyday Series."

Events progressed rapidly enough among fashion-doll makers that by around 1956-57, the buzzwords in the doll industry were "high fashion," with "high heel" having almost the same sizzle.

Vinyl fashion dolls seemed to multiply with each passing year in the middle 1950s, with some dolls having some of the adult orientation that the Barbie doll would later fully embody. P&M Doll Co., Inc., of New York City, boasted of "high heeled, high fashion dolls in all sizes." Roberta Doll Co., Inc., also of New York City, was making "Miss Babette," described as "the full-jointed, newly designed High Heel Dolls in four sizes," and as the leader of Roberta's "quality designed line of High Heel Glamour Dolls, consisting of Formal, Brides', and Novelty Dolls."

In mail-order catalogs, a variety of high-heeled dolls were appearing: "Jantzen Girl" and "Sis-Teen" from Valentine Doll Co., of New York City. "Tinyteens" and "Junior Miss" were made by Uneeda Doll Co., Inc., of Brooklyn, and Effanbee Doll Co., Inc., of New York City, respectively. Cosmopolitan Doll & Toy Corp., of Jamaica, N.Y., soon boasted of "high-fashion dolls."

The undergarment element, which some observers thought was so striking with the Barbie doll, was definitely also present in the 1950s. The "Lingerie Lou" dolls of mid-decade were made by Doll Bodies, Inc. of New York City, and promoted as having "removable panties and bra." Doll undies were a standard feature later in the decade.

**The many faces of Barbie.**

# 1

Mattel went ahead with production on its new fashion doll not because no one else had such dolls, but because so many did. Other companies were already doing extremely well with plastic dolls with mature features and with changeable lingerie, swimsuits and debutante wear. Mattel was simply aware of their success and knew there was profit to be had.

## DEBUTANTE

The Toy Fair in 1959 is usually remembered now as the event at which Mattel introduced Barbie to the world.

To the toy industry at the time, however, it positioned itself primarily along the lines of its established strengths. Two years earlier, in 1957, it had summed them up in four words: "mechanical and musical toys." Toy buyers finding their way up to the fifth floor of the Fifth Avenue Building, which was calling itself The Toy Center, could thumb through their fair guides and see what they could expect from the thriving Los Angeles company in 1959: "Musical, Mechanical Mickey Mouse Club Toys, Guns, Pistols and Holsters, Popeye Toys, Educational Toys, Children's Sporting Goods, Dolls, Space Toys, Doll Furniture."

While the word "dolls" is mentioned, toy buyers probably paid it little heed. They knew

the Mattel name for the Mousegetar, among other musical and sound-making toys. If they were looking for dolls, there were dozens of doll companies active within the American toy industry.

That toy buyers initially felt reluctant to invest in the Barbie line hardly seems surprising. If they were looking for something in the fashion-doll line, they had plenty of options. Sears, in its 1959 Christmas catalog, showed some of them. In a section entitled "Grown-up Fashion Dolls Are We," the mail-order company showcased "Miss Revlon," "Happi-Time," and "Bride-doll," followed by a half-page of outfits, from party gowns to lacy underwear, for these dolls.

The difference between the German Lilli doll's design and these "grown-up fashion dolls" was partly in Lilli's lankiness and sexual maturity. Partly, too, it was in her older, thinner face. The grown-up fashion dolls in the Sears catalog had rounder, bigger-eyed faces. If they were teenager dolls, they were in their youngest teens. They also had only light touches of mascara and eye-shadow.

Lilli, naturally, had no such compunctions. Soon, neither did Babette, or a host of other high-heel dolls from the multitude of other companies that accepted the idea that aggressively presented sexuality could sell dolls to children, just as it sold cars, cigarettes and liquor to adults.

## ACCESSORIZE!

Barbie was born into an age of accessories. Accessories made a toy complete. The Sun Rubber Co. of Barberton, Ohio, made squeezable baby dolls in the 1940s and '50s that were only complete if they had diapers,

**Barbie, Roman Holiday, 1959.** *Photo courtesy of Mattel.*

**Made in the shade.** *Barbie relaxes on a covered swing in a 1964 advertisement. Playthings, March 1964.*

exclusive at Sears

**Barbie in Pink.** *Sears Toys, 1966-67.*

water bottles and extra clothes. They were necessary adjuncts to proper play. In the same way, the Nanette Dolls by New York City's Arranbee Doll Co., Inc., were sold with "personal" comb, curlers and two-color instruction sheet during the 1950s. Doing the doll's hair was an important part of play. It was play that required accessories to the main toy.

Barbie's were not just accessories to play with, but also accessories in the sense used by the style industry. They were items serving no intrinsic purpose beyond display. Looking good was enough. In fact, it was more than enough: it was everything.

Barbie appeared at the watershed point, when Baby Boomer toys became something new and distinctive. The rest of the Boomer years might justifiably be called the triumph of the fashion doll. Fashion and style dolls dominated the toy landscape. Even non-doll toys took on the aspect of fashion dolls or appeared in guises that acknowledged their dominance. Accessories for the sake of accessories was the ruling principle.

Just as it had seemed utterly natural in the mid-1950s that a popular toy robot, Robert the Robot, had plastic sides that mimicked austere, undecorated sheets of metal, so it seemed utterly natural, not long after Barbie's appearance, that Yakkity Yob, a popular toy robot of the early 1960s, wore a tie and good-luck ring. Gone was the austerity. Fashion, high society and style-defined personality were "in." Likewise, Dick Tracy in his rough-and-tumble trench coat gave way to James Bond in his immaculate suits.

**FASHION QUEEN BARBIE**

The Fashion Queen Barbie acknowledged her preeminence in the toy world through her name. Issued without the rooted hair of her earlier incarnations, the Fashion Queen could indulge in the '60s passion for wigs. Mattel, 1963.

**Barbie and Ken.** *General Merchandise Catalog, Fall-Winter 1962.*

# 1

**Twist 'N Turn Barbie.** *Mattel, 1966.*

**Bendable Leg Skipper.** *Mattel, 1960s.*

**Barbie and Ken.** *General Merchandise Catalog, Fall-Winter, 1962.*

*"Teen Fashions for Barbie and Her Friends." Mattel, 1969.*

TEEN FASHIONS FOR AND HER FRIENDS

Barbie® P.J. Stacey Christie AND JULIA

By the mid-1960s, children were of the mind that everything needed to be accessorized. Even their schoolbooks and notebooks had to sport every kind of sticker and decal available. Unlike the rub-on and water-applied decorations of wild animals and alphabet letters found inside children's books from the late 1800s, with their muted colors and book-of-nature subjects, the 1960s decorations were garish, conspicuous and boisterously rude. Far from being designed for the quiet enjoyment of the solitary child, they were bright and loud and meant to be noticed by the crowd. They added not to the book or notebook, but to the person. They were the person's "style."

Accessories mattered to even the youngest of both sexes. Barbie caused none of this. The trend was already building in society to value appearance above all else. Neat, indistinguishable lawns enhanced neat, indistinguishable suburban houses, while housewives wearing the current hairstyle sent husbands off to work driving the latest nice car. The way to excel and stand out was through conspicuous excellence of display, perhaps over-conspicuous excellence. Barbie coolly achieved that among dolls and made everyone follow suit.

The fashion dolls of the remainder of the 1960s were legion. Among Barbie look-alikes were generic "Fashion Dolls" sold by Sears, Polly the Livin' Doll model sold through Alden's of Chicago, and Ideal's Mitzi dolls. How many casual rip-off dolls from Hong Kong appeared on dime-store shelves will probably remain forever unknown.

Barbie's own corner of the toy world gradually expanded through the 1960s, with her innocuous boyfriend Ken appearing in 1961, her friend Midge in 1963, her little sister Skipper and Ken's buddy Allan in 1964, Skipper's friends Skooter and Ricky in 1965, and Barbie's Mod cousin Francie in 1966.

Mattel's original story of the Barbie doll, that the idea for it arose out of watching a child play with paper dolls, did have more than a grain of truth in it. Paper dolls of adult figures, with changeable costumes, had an important role in helping American doll manufacturing get started back in the 1800s. Paper dolls were usually handmade affairs in the earlier part of that century. Then the public imagination was seized, in the 1840s and '50s, with an enthusiasm for the European ballerinas and singers touring the States. Their beauty and glamour dazzled children and adults alike. On their heels, imported paper dolls based on Marie Taglioni, Fanny Essler and Jenny Lind flowed into this country from Europe. It was one of America's early toy fads. They were fashion dolls made of paper.

A century later, paper fashion dolls still featured famous entertainment stars. Saalfield Publishing Co., of Akron, Ohio, published cut-out books of paper dolls in the 1950s. Big releases in 1958 that Barbara Handler might have been playing with included Julie Andrews, singing star of the Broadway hit *My Fair Lady* and the spectacularly popular Jenny Lind of her time.

If it is true that the Barbie doll had its origins in a clutter of two-dimensional bodies and costumes, then it is fitting that the vinyl doll came full circle as early as 1962, when Barbie became a paper doll from Whitman Publishing Co., of Racine, Wis. ■

Mattel: Barbie, Fashion Queen doll, 1963, $145
Mattel: Barbie & Francie Case, 1967, $35
Mattel: Barbie Queen of the Prom Game, 1960, $60
Mattel: Christie, talking, 1970, $100
Mattel: Ken doll, flocked hair, 1961, $100
Mattel: Skipper doll, straight leg, 1964, $50
Whitman: Barbie and Ken Paper Dolls, 1970, $35

**Accessories galore.** *Even these small plastic figures were packaged with accessories. Figures, 3-½" high, Multiple Products Corp., New York City, 1960s.*

THE ROAD to the plastic beauty doll was paved, oddly enough, with potatoes. Potatoes turned their eyes in every direction except toward fashion until seven years after World War II. That year, by introducing potatoes to the toy fashion world, one of the smallest companies in the business, Hassenfeld Bros., changed the way children looked at their food almost overnight. Food, in its raw, original form, became a plaything through a box filled with plastic pieces. It was called The Mr. Potato Head Funny-Face Kit.

Hassenfeld Bros. issued plastic bodies, eyes, hats, pipes, noses, mouths, eyebrows, ears, feet and hands, all of them expressly meant to decorate food. The spike-like necks of the hard plastic bodies were stuck upward into the potato, while the hand pieces and feet pieces were inserted into the plastic bodies. The eyes, nose, mouth, pipe, ears and hat had small, pointed spikes that were inserted into the raw vegetable.

Once assembled, the potato adopted a distinguished, yet somewhat ridiculous appearance. He wore a tie and a respectable hat. He had bushy eyebrows of felt, held in place by the eye spikes. Perhaps he had a mustache or some hair, if you chose to be creative and use some scrap felt or garden foliage for that purpose. His nose and ears were oversized and funny-looking. His eyes were round and slightly buggy or oval and comic-bookish. Were kids delighted? Fabulously.

Not long before, Hassenfeld Bros. had been primarily a manufacturer of stationery, pencils and pencil boxes. Then Merril Hassenfeld, a son of one of the original Hassenfeld brothers, started inching the company into the toy business. It started selling junior doctor and nurse kits before World War II, then Junior Air Raid Warden kits during the war, for kids of the coastal cities starting to experience black outs. Under the young Hassenfeld's direction, the company followed with junior sewing, mailman, jewelry and school kits. The company also started dipping a toe into licensing, creating Donald Duck doctor kits and Roy Rogers pistol-shaped pencil cases.

In 1951 a novelty inventor named George Lerner offered the company the set of noses, eyes, ears and other plastic features that would become Mr. Potato

**Food for funny thoughts.** *Hasbro advertised its Mr. Potato Head pieces as usable on apples, bananas, cucumbers, oranges, pears and peppers, too. Hasbro Mr. Potato Head pieces from the 1950s and '60s, in potato, apple and tangerine.*

**The Hassenfeld legacy.** *In its early days, Hassenfeld Bros. specialized in school supplies, especially pencils and pencil boxes. When the toy division made waves with Mr. Potato Head, the school-supplies division cashed in with tie-in pencil boxes. The acceptability of taking toys to the classroom increased during the Boomer years, even becoming routine through "Show and Tell" periods. School Days Potato Head Pencil Case, 11" long, Hasbro, 1950s.*

Head. The toy pieces had been packaged earlier as a cereal premium. Once Hassenfeld Bros. obtained rights, it gave Lerner an advance against royalties—only a small one, since prospects for success seemed small for a toy that everyone else in the business had already turned down. Yet it succeeded far beyond Lerner's or Merril Hassenfeld's imagination.

It succeeded in part because of intrinsic charm. When children saw the toy, they understood how it could always be a different toy from one playtime to the next. It was a plaything that seemed to increase the possibilities of make-believe, rather than decrease them, as many toys managed to do. Yet it succeeded even more because of where children first saw this toy. Parents first saw it in the pages of *Life* magazine, while kids saw it on TV.

After the war, toys in the United States took a few years to become what we know now as Baby Boomer toys. For a time they remained the same as those issued in the war years—and those toys of wartime were not quite the same as the ones that came before. Toy makers were working under severe restrictions because they were cut off from their usual supplies of metals and rubber. They were forced to become adept again at working with wood, paper and cardboard.

Nearly everything could be made of wood, from puzzles, riding toys, alphabet boards, pull toys and alphabet blocks

**Advertised on TV.** *Telling kids that a toy was advertised on television remained important through the late Boomer years. Hasbro Mr. Potato Head logo, 1968.*

(which in the late 1940s still lacked the interlocking ridges to which we later became so accustomed) to toy cars, trucks, ships, trains and airplanes. A few of the more popular construction toys of the prewar years were made of wood anyway, and were largely unaffected by the wartime rationing.

The expertise manufacturers developed during the war no doubt helped them hold on to wood as a toy-making material in the Boomer years—perhaps for longer than might have been the case otherwise.

**In the Parade.** *In the late 1960s, many kits still promoted the use of real fruit and vegetables. This Mr. Potato Head in the Parade kit suggested kids make a lemon majorette, onion clown and cucumber calliope. Hasbro, 1968. Courtesy Becky Stubbe.*

**Space Age!** *By the mid-1960s, many accessory-based toys established some connection with America's push for the moon. Hasbro's decorated potato beat Neil Armstrong by only one year. Mr. Potato Head on the Moon, 1968.*

# 2

Cardboard, which had filled in for other toy-making materials during the war, likewise continued to be important afterwards. Play sets with cardboard farms, tractors, implements, people and animals gave some children their imaginary life in the country. Other sets used masonite, which made sturdy service stations and doll houses.

Toys made of such restricted materials as lead alloy, tin and pressed steel slowly returned to production after the war: toy trucks and cars, windup spinning toys, wheeled toys, toy sewing machines, toy typewriters, construction sets and cap guns. Even toys made of thick, heavy rubber returned, looking largely unchanged from their prewar, Art Deco-inspired predecessors.

Yet change was in the air. Some children were playing with toys their parents never had and never could have had. During the 1930s, the plastics industry had moved decisively beyond celluloid and Bakelite into newly formulated acetates and other plastics. Plastics manufacturers began courting toy makers, whom they thought should be perfect consumers of synthetic materials.

They were right. A few companies had already experimented with new plastics before the war, making toy cars and airplanes. They either kept up production during the early 1940s or resumed shortly afterwards and found themselves joined by other forward-looking manufacturers.

By the second Christmas after World War II, plastic seemed to be headed for a permanent place in the toy industry. The new plastics made ideal material for doll house furniture, for one. It was advertised as "well proportioned, beautifully made. Copied from fine adult furniture in color, finish. Details are expertly reproduced." No toy maker could have made such claims for its toy furniture before the advent of hard plastic, at least not for 98 cents, which bought an entire dining room set, including some pieces with moving parts, or for $1.98, which bought the living room set, including grand piano.

The new plastic also worked extremely well for small vehicle toys, which could be sold for less than $1.50 a dozen, and for tea sets. A tea service for two might cost 95 cents, and a 40-piece set for six, only $2.25. Manufacturers also saw the potential of hard plastic for the very young. Pull toys made of "washable plastic in bright harmless colors" began appearing.

Most of us will look back at these toys of the later 1940s and wonder what was missing. Plastic was part of the picture, certainly. Yet some color or vital spark was absent. Some element of excitement we associate with the toys of our lost Boomer childhood was missing.

**Nationally known funny faces.**
*While Mr. Potato Head is now famous for being the first toy advertised on TV, in the early 1950s far more prestige accrued from another claim: "Advertised in LIFE." Mr. and Mrs. Potato Head Funny Face Ideas instruction pamphlets, Hasbro, 1950s. Behind the pamphlets, a package of metal jacks with the same claim.*

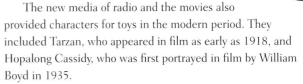

What was that spark? It was akin to the one given off by the Yellow Kid and other early cartoon characters at the end of the 19th century. By the early 20th, cartoon personalities were becoming as well known as real ones—and often better known. Things really started taking off in 1906 to 1907, when *Mr. Mutt*, the first daily comic strip, was making a name for itself, and again in 1933, the year that saw *Funnies on Parade* and its immediate successors, the first comic books in the modern sense of the word.

In the meantime, Winsor McCay's 1911 animated film *Little Nemo* set in motion a series of events that would result in Walt Disney's 1928 film *Steamboat Willie*. That animated short was the first to combine animation with synchronized sound, and it marked the beginning of an animation empire.

The "funnies" gave the toy industry the push it needed to change playthings into something we now recognize as modern. Where would the childhoods of the 1920s, '30s, and '40s have been without Popeye and Olive Oyl, Dick Tracy, Buck Rogers, Flash Gordon, Blondie, Superman, Happy Hooligan, Barney

Google, Little Orphan Annie, Krazy Kat, Felix the Cat, and, of course, Mickey Mouse and the rest of that rubbery and ebullient Disney cast?

The new media of radio and the movies also provided characters for toys in the modern period. They included Tarzan, who appeared in film as early as 1918, and Hopalong Cassidy, who was first portrayed in film by William Boyd in 1935.

The groundwork for the medium that would make the most difference in the Boomer years was laid at the same time. A far-sighted farmer's boy, Philo Farnsworth, dreamed up a practical way to deliver images electronically. WGY in Schenectady, N.Y., made the first scheduled television broadcast in 1928. Within a year, Bell Labs was experimenting with color television. It was an explosion waiting to happen.

As the 1950s began, toy manufacturers were showing signs of a new sophistication. Toys appeared in catalogs and advertisements with the following statement, presented as a worthy and notable credential: "As advertised in *Life*."

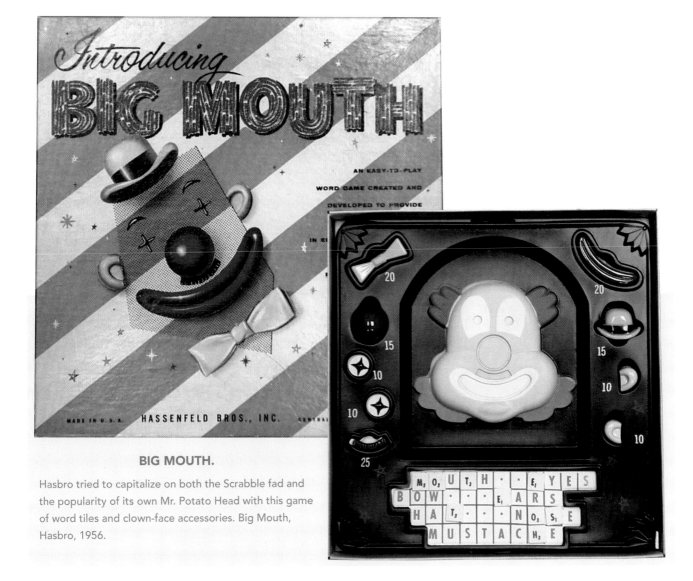

**BIG MOUTH.**

Hasbro tried to capitalize on both the Scrabble fad and the popularity of its own Mr. Potato Head with this game of word tiles and clown-face accessories. Big Mouth, Hasbro, 1956.

**2**

Toy makers including Auburn Rubber, Banner Plastics, Doepke Manufacturing, Electric Game Co., Milton Bradley, Nosco Plastics, Parker Brothers, and Structo Manufacturing Co. were advertising in America's leading popular magazine. From the start, *Life* magazine captivated readers with its large format and remarkable photojournalism.

At the same time, television was making huge strides. While only two broadcasting stations existed in 1941, television's first year as a viable medium, more than 100 were operating by 1948. By the mid-1950s, over 400 stations were broadcasting across the country. For the biggest pool of Boomers in the late 1960s, over 600 stations were telecasting commercial programs. Meanwhile, viewer growth kept pace.

Many people saw their first TV broadcasts related to the New York World's Fair of 1939, where the medium had its public debut. My father remembers being taken by my grandfather, a young pastor at the time, to a DuMont television dealership in New Jersey to see a student choir perform at the fair's opening ceremonies on the dealership's TV screens. As broadcasting stations developed, people congregated at bars to watch wrestling, boxing or the *Author Meets the Critics* show, a popular program of verbal sparring that began as a local New York show. As TV programming increased, TV ownership spread, with the TVs themselves becoming conspicuous symbols of social status.

In 1946, only seven years after the world's fair, 8,000 households owned TVs. The number nearly doubled in a year. Then the explosion occurred. In 1948, nearly 200,000 households had TVs; in 1949, over 900,000. In 1950, the number zoomed upward to nearly 4 million, and to 10 million in 1951. The increasing numbers meant advertisers took greater and greater interest—to the tune of $58 million in 1949, nearly $200 million in 1950 and over $300 million in 1951.

In 1952, when over 15 million households owned television sets, advertisers were spending an amount on TV sponsorships closing in on $600 million. The year marked a watershed, for those advertisers were close to spending as much on upstart TV as they were on well-established radio.

In that year CBS also delivered one of many blows the pioneering network DuMont would suffer, by luring Jackie Gleason away from DuMont's two-year-old hit program, *The Cavalcade of Stars*. Art Carney, the June Taylor Dancers, and the Ray Bloch Orchestra followed Gleason from DuMont to CBS, where increased resources, monetary and otherwise, helped make their new show an even bigger hit.

In that year, too, Hassenfeld's Mr. Potato Head appeared on the burgeoning media scene. For many years it has been claimed that Mr. Potato Head was the first toy to be advertised on TV. As with Barbie's paper-doll origin, it is simply one of those stories its parent company would like to be true. Even so, Mr. Potato Head may have been the first toy advertised on a TV show aimed primarily at adults. It appeared on *The Jackie Gleason Show*.

"Meet Mr. Potato Head—the most wonderful friend a boy or girl could have," said the TV ad. "The most novel toy in years," said the "Hasbro" catalog. "The ideal item for gift, party favor, or the young invalid."

While the promotion was unsophisticated by later standards, the ads did the job. A million Hasbro sets, each containing several dozen accessories, went out to a million buyers. At a time when the Arthur Godfrey Flamingo Ukulele cost $5, an Auburn Rubber farm set cost $3, and American Logs or a Wolverine tin pull train cost $2, the Mr. Potato Head Funny-Face Kit ("Any Fruit or Vegetable Makes a Funny Face Man") sold for only $1. The pieces, while small, promised unlimited fun, for they were endlessly reusable and could be employed in a multitude of ways.

The new Hasbro catalog showed the face pieces inserted into all the standard products from the grocer's produce aisle: not only a potato, but an apple, banana, cucumber, orange, pear and pepper. To keep him from being lonely in his popularity, the

next year Hasbro introduced Mrs. Potato Head, son Spud, and daughter Yam.

The toy remained a steady seller in Hassenfeld's growing toy line through the Boomer years. It went through several changes, most notably in 1964 when the first kits appeared with a hollow plastic potato provided. Once Hasbro crossed that threshold, Mr. Potato Head's universe started expanding, with the other roots, fruits and vegetables turned into new personalities. Dubbed his Tooty Frooty Friends, they included Katie the Carrot, Cooky the Cucumber, Oscar the Orange, and Pete the Pepper. Later in the decade, the Picnic Pals appeared, including Mr. Soda Pop Head and Franky Frank. The end of the decade saw the appearance of the most complex Mr. Potato Head toys, including the whimsical Mr. Potato Head on the Moon play set.

Although in the late 1960s Hassenfeld was again issuing kits to be used on actual fruits and vegetables, new child safety laws soon blunted the piercing ends of the hard-plastic pieces, until they were useful only for poking through pre-poked polyethylene potatoes.

Mr. Potato Head is perhaps the single most characteristic toy of the Boomer years. It appeared early enough and with enough fanfare to be a factor in the childhoods of even the first Boomer children. It established for the first time the connection between everyday toys—as opposed to "premiums"—and television, the then-blossoming medium that would largely define the times. It consisted entirely of the material that would come to dominate toy making by the 1960s: plastic, in both hard and soft forms.

In almost pure form, it encompassed one of the greatest trends seen in toys of the Boomer years, the ascendance of the accessory toy. After all, for its first decade and more, Hassenfeld Bros. was not selling the toy itself, which was the potato out of the vegetable bin. It was simply selling accessories for the toy. A generation eager for accessories of any kind embraced Mr. Potato Head as their own, recognizing kinship.

At the same time, Mr. Potato Head stood for the ever-growing American postwar wealth, which economists were describing as "disposable income." The country was enjoying such economic success that America's children could play with their food with adult sanction.

Moreover, in the change from the emphasis on real fruits and vegetables to artificial ones, Mr. Potato Head represented changes in the toy world that increasingly took children further and further from homemade toy experiences to industry-made ones.

In that and other changes, Mr. Potato Head's development also reflected the changes forced on childhood by government-imposed standards. For all these reasons, Mr. Potato Head ranks as the top toy for many Boomers, especially those millions who never played with—and who may have never even seen—a Barbie doll.

The toy as it was known to Boomers then would give joy and hours of quiet fun to no other generation—not in quite the same form, not in quite the same way. The toy's name would be all that would remain the same. ■

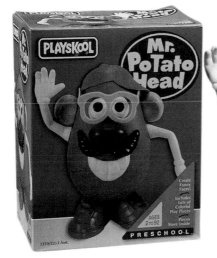

**Modern Potato Head.** *Current Potato Heads are made of plastic with appendages ending in rounded points that insert into ready-made holes in the body. The design change was a result of toy safety laws that prohibited the sharp points needed to attach body parts into real potatoes.*

Hasbro: Jumpin' Mr. Potato Head Set, 1966, $30
Hasbro: Leave It to Beaver Rocket to the Moon Game, 1959, $45
Hasbro: Little Miss No Name, doll, 1965, $75
Hasbro: Mr. & Mrs. Potato Head Set, 1960s, $50
Hasbro: Mr. Potato Head on the Moon, $200
Hasbro: School Days Potato Head Pencil Case, $35
Marx: Jackie Gleason, plastic figure, 60 mm, $50

"A RECENT SURVEY SHOWS THAT, TODAY, MORE PEOPLE WATCH SHOWS ON TELEVISION THAN ON ANY OTHER APPLIANCE. TOASTERS ARE SECOND."

—PAT PAULSEN ON THE SMOTHERS BROTHERS

# ...*And the* Triumph of Television: *Hits of the Sixties*

By the time the 1960s arrived, toy companies had embraced the notion that TV advertising offered the road to success. By all previous standards, advertising budgets were becoming astronomical. For 1961, Mattel was talking about a budget of $2.5 million.

New York City's Ideal Toy Corp., an old hand at the game after having sponsored the Macy's Thanksgiving Day Parade since the mid-1950s, had a $3 million advertising budget in 1961—enough for it to contemplate making the move into color-TV advertising. Ideal, by itself, was spending on TV advertising in 1961 what all the nation's businesses combined spent on TV advertising in 1951.

By the mid-1960s, when over 50 million households in the country had TVs, the connection between television advertising and toy success had become a matter of common sense. Rather than boast of the play potential of their toys and games, toy manufacturers convinced retailers to carry their toys by proudly proclaiming how much they were spending on TV ads.

The example of Topper Toys in 1964 is typical. Topper Toys were made by DeLuxe Reading Corp. of Elizabeth,

T 2804

N.Y. In support of its Johnny Seven military toys and Penny Brite doll line, Topper had a vigorous program for Saturday mornings, with 48 minutes of fall commercials for the *Alvin Show* at 9:00 a.m., 99 minutes for *Tennessee Tuxedo* at 9:30 a.m., 57 minutes for *Quick Draw McGraw* at 10:00 a.m., 30 minutes for *The Jetsons* at 10:30 a.m., 46 minutes for *Roy Rogers* at 11:30 a.m., over an hour for *Bugs Bunny* at noon, and 30 minutes for *The Magic Land of Allakazam* at 1:00 p.m.

Even Louis Marx & Co., which had viewed television advertising with wise-old-owl disdain in the earlier Boomer years, in that same year claimed that "MARX starts with the premise that the Toy Business begins with 'toys' (not TV promises)," but then trumpeted, "We're starting off with the greatest line of TV merchandise in toy history ... All supported by the most powerful wave of NETWORK and LOCAL SPOT TV ever rolled out by MARX— the toy maker who 'pays off' on TV promises!"

Did a toy work in a TV spot? The question was suddenly more pressing than whether it worked on the playroom floor. Fortunately, some toys ended up being pretty good, despite the hoopla.

# SEEING ACTION
# G.I. JOE

ACCORDING to conventional wisdom at mid-century, girls played with baby dolls, child dolls, and teenager dolls, not adult-looking dolls. Conventional wisdom also said boys never played with dolls at all, however cute the dolls were. Never played with them ... unless, that is, someone looked away and the boy-kid nabbed a baby doll and started playing with it.

This actually happened all the time because boys, like girls, grew up in Boomer America knowing exactly what a toy was: anything in reach. The postwar stiffness of gender roles would hit the boy-kid soon enough, but not until he stretched his fingers and made that reach. Then came the slap. "That's for girls, kid," said the gentle guardians of social behavior. Conventional wisdom followed the postulate to its necessary conclusion: boys would never play with adult-looking dolls either.

Child play by its nature is weighted towards make-believe. Make-believe embraces the worlds outside the child's reach. Before World War II, those out-of-reach worlds were presented

**G.I. Joe, the traditional soldier of America's youth.**

to children through storybooks, comic strips, radio serials and the adult lives they saw being played out in the world around them.

Those adult lives were always the most important. The adults lived in a world so full of complexly organized noises, smells, textures, appearances and words that it endlessly fascinated kids. They play-acted being those adults because it was so interesting.

Characteristic of the postwar years would be the increasing intrusion of the toy industry into those make-believe moments. Before the war and immediately afterwards, boys would move directly from having no woodworking tools at all to having actual, working tools. Although the tools were designed for children and made in accommodating sizes, they were real. Even if children started with a building set from Erector, Meccano or Structo, the tools in the sets were real working tools made expressly for the job.

During the subsequent Boomer period, however, children could emulate mother's or father's use of tools at an earlier age,

**G.I. Joe Action Sailor hits the beach on a dangerous mission.**

*Action Sailor, from G.I. Joe, America's Movable Fighting Man, Hasbro, 1965.*

with realistic but not actual tools. For some companies, this was a vital niche in the toy world. Handy Andy made tin boxes with toy tools. Auburn Rubber manufactured vinyl saws and hammers. Adults instinctively approved of these toys and bought them in great numbers.

Toy manufacturers devoted increasing inventory to toys that helped kids project themselves into ever more varieties of adult experience. Kids could spend less time imagining and more time being "just like Mom" and "just like Dad." Not the same as, but just like.

Even so, the toy industry stopped short of giving boys a fashion-doll figure whose clothes could be changed to reflect different careers and different aspirations. Many boys undoubtedly played with Ken dolls or the figures of Dad and Ted from the Ideal's Tammy line, or Dr. John from the Littlechap Family, made by Remco Industries of Newark, N.J., in the early 1960s.

As they did so, however, they probably glanced over their shoulders to see who was looking. These male figural toys came from the doll aisles at department stores and were seen in the doll pages of toy catalogs. This was enough to make boys nervous.

Even though the Boomer generation was America's largest, what was more significant was that they were being raised by the largest pool of war veterans in the country's history. That was what mattered. Long before the war, Americans had coined the word "Sis," for sister or young woman. Its diminutive, "Sissy," took on such derogatory power for Boomer boys that the word by itself could stop almost any behavior, even if it was the normal behavior of a boy imagining being older than he was by means of a doll. Girls casually played being men, and frequently had to because of the nature of "playing house," which boys felt uneasy playing. Even as girls grew older, their engaging in male-stereotype activities led to relatively few social repercussions. Boys were forced to toe closer to the line, and the pressure to do so started early.

The 1960s saw rising social unrest and change, in part as a reaction to the stiff social conventions people pulled up around them like blankets as comfort against the triple threats of war memories, the Bomb and the Communist scare. Since toys often reflected society quickly, toy manufacturers by that decade were veering further from the dictates of tradition than ever before. The fashion doll marketed specifically for boys was bound to arise.

It did so in 1964 from Hassenfeld Bros., now based in Pawtucket, R.I. At the time, the company was struggling to recover from the debacle of its Son of Flubber tie-in toy, a putty that had caused allergic reactions that were followed by lawsuits.

G.I. Joe charges up the hill.

**G.I. Joe as Green Beret.**
*Sears Toys, 1967-68*

**Accessories of war.** *The G.I. Joe line gave boys a chance to participate in the fashion revolution, but within a narrow range. G.I. Joe accessories, Hassenfeld Bros., 1960s.*

*Action Pilot, from G.I. Joe, America's Movable Fighting Man, Hasbro catalog, 1965. Photo courtesy Krause Publications.*

# 3

Not surprisingly, since war toys were in Vietnam-inspired ascendance while Western-style toys declined, the new Hasbro fashion doll for boys was a military figure, with a suite of clothing changes and accessories that were all military in nature.

He was America's Movable Fighting Man, marketed under a severe policy that steered clear of that sissy word, "doll." He was the G.I. Joe Action Soldier, G.I. Joe Action Marine, G.I. Joe Action Sailor and G.I. Joe Action Pilot.

"He's over 11" tall, has 21 movable parts, stands, sits, kneels! Takes combat-action poses. Has equipment authentically scaled from actual G.I. issue. Even has dog tag and training manual." "Joe," Hasbro said, "is ready to carry out your orders!"

Near the same time, the Louis Marx Co. released Stony, a paratrooper who had molded-in fatigues but still plenty of accessories in the form of hats, helmets, packs and weaponry. Even the veterans of battles in Europe and Asia would approve of the purchase of such dolls for their boys. Boys with

such toys, they knew, would all grow up to be men.

The timing turned out to be right. G.I. Joe enjoyed phenomenal sales in his first two years, pulling the Hasbro toy division well out of its losses of 1964, and bringing in a profit of $6 million in 1965.

In some ways, however, the time was also wrong. The true nature of America's involvement in Vietnam was settling into public consciousness. The draft loomed over the older brothers of the boys who received G.I. Joes. Even younger boys felt the knowledge dawning on them: the draft calmly awaited them too. Part of maturing in the 1960s meant coming to realize what a body count was, and that the draft and the body count were rather closely related. The romance of war was wearing thin.

In an effort to prop up G.I. Joe's declining popularity, Hasbro introduced outfits that made him more of a civilian. He was a boater, a scuba diver, a hunter. Yet he never lived down his initial image associated with his name. He was G.I. Joe. He was a grunt. A pawn for others, he fell short of mastering his own

**Johnny West.** *Louis Marx & Co., 1960s.*

**Best fashion dolls of the Old West.** *While the Louis Marx Co. went head-to-head with Hassenfeld Bros.' Stony soldier figure, it enjoyed more lasting success with its Western line called Best of the West. Unlike the Mattel and Hasbro plastic fashion dolls, the slightly larger Johnny and Jane West came with molded-on clothing. Also unlike the Mattel or Hasbro lines, the Best of the West line of cowboys and cowgirls, Indians, cavalry, horses, buffaloes, dogs, buckboards and Fort Apache stockade appealed to both boys and girls of the later 1960s. Accessories came in the form of vinyl guns, canteens, hats, vests and chaps for people, and bridles and saddles for horses. Jane West, the "fully jointed cowgirl," with Thunderbolt and Thundercolt, Sears Toys, 1966-67, and Josie West, Jane's daughter, with Poncho and dog Flack, Sears Toys, 1967-68.*

**Jane West.** *Louis Marx & Co., 1960s.*

fate. What was happening to his ilk overseas, after all? They were being shipped and flown into a slaughterhouse and sent home in body bags.

Hassenfeld Bros. learned one lesson from Mattel without absorbing another. Barbie started without a specific career or calling. She simply depicted success. She had a great sense of style and an obviously ample purse. She could be only one thing: a celebrity. Being a celebrity meant being a television star or member of high society, which was nearly the same, since high society tended to appear on television. Being a celebrity meant having glamour, above all. Glamour in the TV Age mattered immensely. Even boys wanted TV's glamour. They happily played at being Roy Rogers or a Bonanza star, pretending to be fighting rustlers or running a ranch, because doing so meant having glamour. They played Rat Patrol because being on the Rat Patrol jeep had glamour. They played Captain Video and, later, Star Trek because of the glamour of television science-fiction. They played Ben Casey because of the glamour of television hospital work.

Was Barbie a hard worker? Her self-assured, side-glancing eyes made the question superfluous. She had glamour. What

more did she need? Did she ever follow anyone's orders?

"What kind of question is that?" the girls would have wondered.

Boys never had to wonder if G.I. Joe followed anyone's orders. They were told. ■

Aladdin: G.I. Joe lunch box, 1967, $350
Hasbro: G.I. Joe Action Marine, 1964, $125
Hasbro: G.I. Joe Action Pilot, 1964, $130
Hasbro: G.I. Joe Action Soldier, 1964, $100
Hasbro: G.I. Joe Talking Action Marine, 1967, $175
Hasbro: G.I. Nurse, 1967, $1,750
Ideal: Action Box with space suit, 1968, $350
Marx: Chief Cherokee, 1965, $150
Marx: Jane West, 1966, $60
Marx: Johnny West, 1960s-70s, $75
Mego: Spider-Man, 8", 1972, $20

**Meet the boldest, bravest hero!**
**CAPTAIN ACTION with Batman Costume and Quick-change Chamber**

Fully jointed 12-inch figure in uniform, fully armed, ready for adventure. Then presto . . transform him into another popular hero in the quick-change-chamber

Only Sears offers this complete Captain Action Set

$8.29

Uniformed plastic figure with lightning sword, scabbard, action gun, belt, hat . . even removable boots. Batman costume includes plastic cape, helmet-mask, belt, weapons. Colorful, detailed cardboard transformation chamber with swinging door. Sets up quickly. About 18 inches high and 13 inches wide.
79 N 6018C—Shipping weight 3 pounds.......................Set $8.29

**Total makeovers.** *While never as widely popular as G.I. Joe or Best of the West, Ideal's Captain Action was perhaps the ultimate fashion doll. Kids could transform the versatile Captain into their favorite superheroes by changing clothes, weapons and even faces, which were tight-fitting, rubbery, full-head masks that could be pulled over Captain Action's craggy features. By 1967, Action Girl and Action Boy joined the line. Sears Toys, 1966-67.*

**Jane Apollo.** *With the Johnny West and Johnny Apollo series of Marx plastic dolls, children engaged in make-believe fun involving the idea of the frontier, whether the frontier of the mythical Old West or the speculative frontier of Outer Space. Jane Apollo, with her Space Crawler, was one of the best toys to capture the hopeful era of space exploration being launched with the NASA rockets of the 1960s. Louis Marx & Co., late 1960s.*

# JUST PULL THE CHATTY RING
# CHATTY CATHY
## AND HER FRIENDS

MATTEL HOISTED a defiant flag of ownership in Noisy Toyland when the '60s started. This flag was not an ordinary flag. It was a small box that fit inside a toy, to be set into motion by something called the Chatty Ring. You pulled the Chatty Ring, and the toy talked.

Mattel suddenly found itself with a new spokesperson in the form of a 20-inch vinyl doll with sleepy eyes and freckles who could speak Toylandese: "Please change my dress." "I'm so tired." "I love you." "Please brush my hair."

Her name?

"Hi! I'm Chatty Cathy!"

Mattel's new talking doll, which met with enormous success, used an idea that was not exactly new. Advance Doll & Toy Co. of West Haven, Conn., had been making a business of making talking dolls through much of the 1950s. The idea of a talking doll was not even new to that decade—nor even new to the 20th century, for that matter. Dolls capable of a few words could be had cheaply in France even before America's first clockwork-run talking doll of 1890.

Thomas Edison and his constantly inventive workers introduced the Phonographic Doll in that year and geared up for a production capacity of 500 per day. A 30-inch mechanism, the Phonographic Doll could recite nursery rhymes including "Jack and Jill" and "Mary Had a Little Lamb," while the child admired the doll's curling hair, charming face, jointed limbs, frilly dress and fancy socks and shoes.

Chatty Cathy had a repertoire of phrases and a charming vinyl appearance. She had something the Phonographic Doll did not, though, and that was TV, as well as a parent company willing to sink millions into promotions.

TV proved to be the perfect medium for a toy such as this. The promotions were so successful that Mattel, by 1961, was seen as the company that had given the world a talking doll. Even as the Hawthorne, Calif., company was introducing the Ken doll to accompany the Barbie doll, the leading toy-industry magazine, *Playthings*, chose these words for describing Mattel, Inc.: "Toymakers, and creators of Chatty Cathy."

Barbie was undoubtedly the bigger property in the company's own mind, as Mattel acknowledged by giving that small doll eight new costumes in 1961, in contrast to Chatty Cathy's six. Even so, Chatty Cathy talked, and that seemed all she needed to do.

**The Original.** *The first version of Chatty Cathy had a slightly older, more mature child-face than did the later versions. The doll also had better defined hand, and a round, cloth-covered voice box on her chest. Mattel, 1960.*

**Chatty Cathy.** *By 1963, Chatty Cathy had 18 phrases. To go with the doll, Mattel also offered extra outfits and accessories including party clothing, play wear, pajamas, wardrobe and bed. Sears Toy Book, 1963-64.*

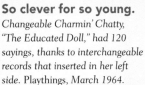

**So clever for so young.** *Changeable Charmin' Chatty, "The Educated Doll," had 120 sayings, thanks to interchangeable records that inserted in her left side. Playthings, March 1964.*

## THE EXPANDED FAMILY

Once the company had a firm grasp on its new toy technology, Mattel started putting it everywhere. "Just pull the Chatty-Ring and they each say many different things," Mattel promised. "You never know what they'll say next!"

"How about some haaay," said Mattel's talking-galloping horse, whose Chatty-Ring was located in its neck, within easy reach of any young cowboy or cowgirl rider. "Whee-ee-ee! My name is Blaze!" Blaze, Mattel promised parents, "gallops, bucks, AND talks! Provides lots of thrills for active youngsters—his legs actually move when they ride him. When they lean in the saddle, he rears or kicks up his heels! Hours of fun!"

Chatty Baby was born in 1961, becoming available in 1962. Like Chatty Cathy, she came with various outfits. Mattel also gave her a cradle, and Cathy a new bed, so kids could have the pleasure of trying to put to sleep little ones who would not hush up.

By 1962 everyone in the Mattel toy cart seemed to talk: Bugs Bunny ("What's Up, Doc?"), Casper the Friendly Ghost ("Let's play ghost!"), Donald Duck ("I live in Disneyland!"), Mickey Mouse ("Pluto is my dog!"), Popeye ("Blow me down!"), Beany ("Help! Save me!") and Cecil ("You called?"). Colonel Claxton and Calvin Burnside appeared, as did Pinocchio and even Matty Mattel, who had to say, "I am Matty Mattel," since kids had no idea who this kid was, with his striped shirt, red hair and crown.

By 1963 and '64, Mattel was using the Chatty Ring in more animals, including the new Animal Yackers series figures Crackers and Larry, the talking plush parrot and lion, and a talking Woody Woodpecker Hand Puppet.

Mattel once again chose dolls to represent the cutting edge of Chatty

technology, especially with "changeable Charmin' Chatty, the educated doll," who was everyone's precocious little talker. Dressed in a sailing outfit and wearing dark-rimmed glasses, Charmin' had 120 sayings at her beck and call, thanks to the five extra records she came with, to be inserted in her left side.

Shrinkin' Violet made her debut in 1964—a cloth doll with fluttering eyebrows and a mouth that moved while she talked. The talker even moved into games: the Animal Talk Game of '64 featured an "Oink-oink! Whinee! Baa-aah! Moo-oo-oo" Chatty-Ring barn.

Traditional "boy toys" were not entirely forgotten. Mattel invested heavily in its V-RROOM! campaign of 1964, which featured the V-RROOM! Real Motor Roar Guide-Whip Racer, Dump Truck and Skiploader. The racer could be guided through obstacle courses or simply raced. To the delight of boys, the faster it went, the louder it got. The Dump Truck idled, roared and revved; the Skiploader, in addition to scooping and dumping loads, featured actions that were guided by control handles and was "big, powerful, loud, and sensational!"

The talking barn of 1964 may have pointed the way to one of Mattel's most significant new early childhood toys introduced the next year: the See 'n Say Educational Toys.

At last even Barbie, long given to lengthy, demure, and yet self-assured silences, gave in. She became yet another chatterbox. She was 9 years old by 1968. Perhaps it was time. ◼

Mattel: Baby Secret, doll, talker, 1965, $45
Mattel: Bugs Bunny, hand puppet, talker, 1960s, $30-$40
Mattel: Chatty Baby, doll, early issue, $85-$95
Mattel: Chatty Cathy, doll, early issues, $125
Mattel: Dr. Dolittle doll, talker, 24", 1969, $130

**Chatty Cathy.** *Mattel's new doll greets the world in the company of a Ruthie doll by Horsman Toys. 1960-61.*

**Minis are smashing!** *In 1968, Barbie seemed to have everything: bending legs, eyelashes—and voices: "I have a date tonight!" "Would you like to go shopping?" "I think minis are smashing!" The Livin' Barbie Dolls were Talking Barbie, Talking Stacey and Talking Christie, costing less than $5 each that Christmas. Alden's Christmas catalog, 1968.*

**"Family Affair."** *"Talking Buffy" appealed to the many fans of the hit TV show Family Affair. Mattel, 1967.*

THE revolution that would forever change American sandbox motoring happened quietly in, of all places, England. There, a young man back from the war had the sensible idea that children would enjoy having toy cars that could be tucked into English-size matchboxes. These then could be slipped into the pocket and carried to school, which is always a good place for showing off toys.

*Matchbox cars, the brainchild of Englishman Jack Odell, were designed to fit inside a box that could be carried in a pocket.*

Jack Odell did more than dream about the idea. He made a small, brass road roller for his daughter, which she did, indeed, immediately slip into a pocket and carry to school, where the novelty of its scale and design created an instant demand for more.

Odell worked in die-casting with Leslie Smith and Rodney Smith, unrelated friends who had joined forces after leaving the Royal Navy to found Lesney Products, basing the name upon their own first names. Among other products, they made miscellaneous die-cast toys, including a large Coronation Coach.

The toy road roller that fit in a matchbox started Lesney Products down an entirely new path. Lesney started its line of Matchbox cars in 1953. Made roughly to the same scale, all were nicely detailed, and all were good fun. Odell and his co-workers based the designs on existing vehicles.

Their master strokes were two: they packaged them in those "matchboxes" and adopted a numbering system from 1 to 75. A numbered series of toys proved to have great appeal for kids, quickly turning them into young collectors.

Many companies followed in the wake of Matchbox. Several other British companies added to the flood of miniature autos being sent to America, under the names of Budgie,

*Matchbox cars were modeled after existing vehicles.*

*Ford G.T., No. 41, 1965.*

*Ford tractor, No. 39, 1967.*

*GMC Tipper Truck, No. 26, 1968.*

Lone Star, and Corgi. Some were almost indistinguishable from early Lesney toys. Japanese company Tomy later produced toys under the name Tomica (literally "Tomy car"), which enjoyed some success in this country.

American companies never quite seemed to get the hang of it, although most tried. The Hubley Mfg. Co. of Lancaster, Pa., a venerable presence in the toy world, turned out a few Matchbox-like vehicles for its Real Cars line. The likewise venerable Dowst Mfg. Co. of Chicago, makers of the less-detailed Tootsietoy toy cars, also launched a short-lived HO-scale series of toy cars, which had much of the appeal of Matchbox toys, but were few in number.

Since the boxes of these British toys proved almost as popular as the cars themselves, for a while even extremely cheap soft-plastic cars made in Hong Kong were issued in Matchbox-style boxes.

Through the 1950s and most of the '60s, nothing else quite caught on, however. Children were perfectly content to play with the toy cars made by other makers, but showed their true allegiance by calling them all by the same name: Matchbox cars.

The floor-level highways, congested as they were with the dozens of attractive models always available, prepared much of the generation for the car-dominated world they were entering. ■

Lesney: Matchbox Alvis Stalwart, #61, 1967, $30
Lesney: Matchbox Bedford Dunlop Van, #25, $50
Lesney: Matchbox Boat and Trailer, #9, 1967, $10
Lesney: Matchbox Hillman Minx, #43, $40
Lesney: Matchbox Leyland Tanker, #32, 1968, $20
Lesney: Matchbox Rolls Royce Silver Cloud, #44, $25
Lesney: Matchbox Safari Land Rover, #12, 1965, $20

**Mobile crane.** *With this crane, a child could spend an entertaining afternoon building a toy service station for a fleet of Matchbox cars.*

**Fifties favorites.** *Matchbox toys from England showed a realism and attention to detail that put Chicago-manufactured Tootsietoys to shame. These three vehicles, the No. 25 Bedford "Dunlop" Van, the No. 43 Millman Minx and the No. 44 Rolls Royce Silver Cloud, were originally issued with metal wheels. These examples have the second wheel type, made of gray plastic. In the 1960s, the wheels were made of black plastic. Lesney Products, late 1950s.*

**Sixties favorites.** *The flow of Matchbox cars from England to America reached flood levels by the late 1960s. Lesney Matchbox cars on a Kenner Bridge & Turnpike road.*

*Eight-Wheel Crane Truck, No. 30, 1965.*

# LIGHT-BULB INSPIRATIONS
# EASY-BAKE OVEN

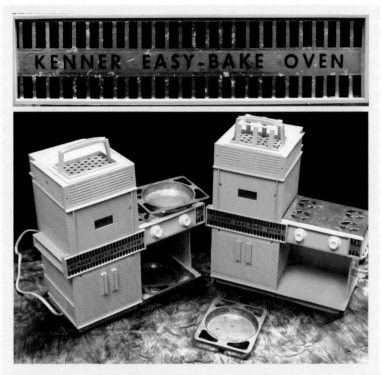

**EVERYTHING MOM HAS, FOR $15.95.**

The early Easy-Bakes came in a distinctive turquoise color. Many earlier toy ovens, working and non-working, had more standard appearances, and came in standard department store colors. The early version had an exposed metal ventilation plate beneath the handle, and cautioned users to use only 100-watt bulbs. The subsequent version added a protective cage at the top, a caution on back about possible burns from the hot surfaces, and a warning against immersion. Kenner, 1964 and later 1960s.

G IRLS had access to play ovens from well before World War II, ranging from cast-iron miniatures made by Arcade Mfg. Co. of Freeport, Ill., to working electric appliances from New York City's electric-train giant, The Lionel Corp. Electric appliances came into their own in the 1950s. Early in the decade, the Metal Ware Corp. of Two Rivers, Wis., offered the Little Lady Electric Range, capable of operating on either A.C. or D.C., with separate elements for burners and oven. The oven even had the feel of the real thing: baked enamel finish and a clear glass oven window. The set came with utensils and a cookbook.

Meanwhile, Aluminum Specialty Co. of Manitowoc, Wis., offered its Alumode Kiddykook cookware, which could be safely used on mother's stove. The percolator was capable of percolating. The teapot, it was promised, would whistle.

The smartest companies capitalized on brand-names mothers already recognized. Model-Craft, Inc., of Chicago advertised on both radio and TV its Kay Stanley's Cake Mix Set, featuring boxes of kid-size Pillsbury cake mixes. Model-Craft also issued the Heinz Kitchen with utensils, chef's hat and six cans of "genuine Heinz products." Within a few years, Ideal Toy Corp. came out with the competing Betty Crocker Junior Baking Kit.

In the mid-'50s, American Metal Specialties Corp., of Hatboro, Pa., expanded its Amsco line to include the Campbell Kids' Chuck Wagon Set, complete with pots, pans, utensils, cans of soup

**Mix batter just like Mom!** *As did all successful toy innovations, the Easy-Bake inspired imitation, most notably Topper Toys' Suzy Homemaker Super Oven of 1966, which made even bigger cakes. Topper issued a full line of kitchen devices, including this battery-operated mixer. Topper Toys Div., Deluxe Reading Corp., 1960s.*

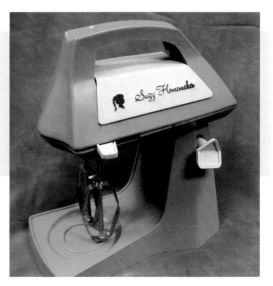

for heating over the campfire, Chuck Wagon Cook Book, two Western-style neckerchiefs and a phonograph record that played a Western tune, setting the proper campfire mood.

These sets enjoyed tremendous success, with catalogs listing kids' baking sets having from 30 to more than 100 pieces by the mid-1960s. Food-related toys were flooding the market by then. Kids could host cookouts with their Electric Hot Dogger Jr., made by Metal Ware. While companies such as Wilson Bros., of Memphis, Tenn., had made popcorn poppers for kids as early as 1950, Metal Ware's Empire Electric See 'Em Pop won over children in unprecedented numbers because of extensive television advertising.

After the hot dogs and popcorn, children could then serve refreshments from their Pepsi-Cola Dispenser, Coca-Cola Dispenser, or Kool-Aid Kooler made by Trim Molded Products Co., of Burlington, Wis. They could even make their own candy, with Metal Ware's Candy-Makette electric sauce-pan set.

In the midst of all this child cookery, a quiet, light bulb-driven revolution took place.

## SAFETY-BAKE

In 1964, Kenner Products Co. of Cincinnati, Ohio, introduced a toy oven made of a distinctive, turquoise-colored plastic. It was plastic—but it worked. And it worked without melting. Designed to be utterly safe and carefree, kids could use it to bake a cake with little or no parental supervision. Using no more heat than could be supplied by two 100-watt light bulbs, it turned specially formulated Betty Crocker cake and cookie mixes into not-quite-steaming-hot goodies—and they were, Kenner promised, "just like Mom's."

The toy Kenner announced to the industry that season was the Safety-Bake Oven. It came with a dozen mixes—devil's food cake, white cake, chocolate icing, brownies, vanilla cookies, biscuits, pie crust, pie filling, pretzels, pizza dough, pizza cheese, and candy in aluminum foil packages.

Although replacement packets of these name-brand items were available, Kenner was large-minded enough to include a recipe book for making Safety Oven baked goods using ingredients available at home—in other words, by a little sneaking-away of mother's supplies.

For accessories, it had a mixing spoon, measuring spoon, spatula, rolling pin, and three metal slide-through baking pans.

The name Safety-Bake Oven was intended to appeal to the safety-conscious parents of the '60s. Broadcasters, however, expressed their concern about Kenner's ability to fully back up the claim implicit in the name. They urged a change. When it appeared on store shelves, the Safety-Bake Oven carried the name that was to be known for many Christmases to come: The Kenner Easy-Bake Oven. ■

**Kenner: Easy-Bake Oven, turquoise, $15-$40**

## FROSTY SNO-MAN SNO-CONE MACHINE

Hassenfeld Bros. enjoyed considerable success in the late Boomer years with its Frosty Sno-Man Sno-Cone Machine. "Your cleverly designed Sno-Cone Machine will shave ordinary ice cubes into snow," said the instructions accompanying the red and white plastic machine in 1967. "Remove snow with shovel and place into cups, top with fruit flavor to make a delicious frozen treat." Children converted one ice cube at a time into shavings, and could use two of 10 flavors at a time.

While children running their pint-sized soda fountains found themselves embarked on a particularly labor-intensive playtime, the sheer pleasure of creating palatable treats overcame all difficulties. For those with friends who could be suckered out of nickels for sno-cones, it was the best of all possible toys. Hassenfeld Bros., late '60s.

# FROM FLYING SAUCER TO
# FRISBEE

FOR some, the greatest phenomenon of the late '40s was the alien-spaceship scare arising from an Air Force pilot's sightings of disc-shaped objects over the Cascades in the Northwest. Newspapers leapt on the story, making the words "flying saucer" the nation's newest, hottest phrase. The Roswell incident in 1947 fanned the flames, with witnesses swearing they saw dead alien beings in the wreckage of an unfamiliar flying craft. Soon editors such as Ray Palmer of *Amazing Stories* and *Fate* magazines were working hard to put a sensational spin on saucer-mania. Other people worked on the toy spin, hoping the mania would translate into a toy fad.

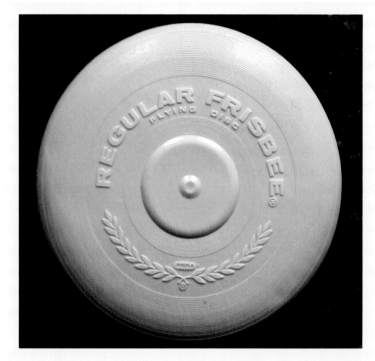

**THE ONE WE ALL THREW.**

Wham-O's regular Frisbee flying disc, "for toy flying saucers, for flying games," dates from 1966. The instructions on the underside make the assumption the would-be player is ignorant of how to use the plaything: "Play catch—invent games—To fly, flip away backhanded. Flat flip flies straight. Tilted flip curves—Experiment!" Wham-O, 1960s.

the country and abroad sought their diversions wherever they could find them. Since lids and coffee can tops could be found anywhere there was a mess hall, the simple recreation probably circled the globe. Kids who entered the armed forces from the East Coast, with their back-and-forth games with cookie-can lids and pie pans, mingled with California kids, who were used to vying against each other to see who could hurl paint can lids farthest across the ocean.

When toy companies were working at developing flying saucer toys in the late 1940s and '50s, the flying-disk seemed a natural. Dozens of companies probably introduced their own

The flying disc has a history much like the yo-yo. The throwing of light flying discs as a casual recreation probably occurred any number of times and places in history. The main record of these instances are related to sports and military functions: discs were used for sport in ancient Greece and disc-like shields served as weapons flung by Roman soldiers.

In America, disk-flinging had a firm place in New England culture even before World War II arrived, with the most well known occurrences involving Yale and the nearby Frisbie Pie Co. The bakery, founded in New Haven in 1871, was famed for its pies and cookies. The pie pans not only flew nicely but hummed, since they had holes arranged around the center. The cookie-tin lids flew nicely too. Just as college students anywhere show little reticence when it comes to throwing things around, Yale students flung various pieces of round tin, yelling "Frisbie!" for the safety of oblivious bystanders, much as golfers yell "Fore!"

Elsewhere around the country, too, materials were at hand for the flying-disc sport: paint can lids, hubcaps, tin plates and pan lids. When World War II arrived, soldiers stationed around

versions without leaving a trace, although some evidence does remain in toy-industry records. The first aerial toy called Flying Saucer may have been the one made by Crandis Associates, of Red Bank, N.J., from around 1950 into the early part of the decade. By 1952, a company named Practi-Cole Products, Inc., based in the saucer hotspot of New Haven, Conn., was making flying saucer aerial toys, which it may have continued making through the decade.

By 1952 the Flying Saucer name had become a popular one to use, with Oak Rubber Co. of Ravenna, Ohio, introducing flying saucer balloons, Sound Spelling Co. of San Antonio, Texas, introducing a flying saucer spelling game and U.S. Plastic Co. of Pasadena, Calif., introducing a flying saucer gun. The number of such playthings increased later in the decade.

Meanwhile, the saucer-shaped flying toys multiplied, too. Crafco Corp., based in Santa Barbara, Calif., issued flying saucers by 1957. Soon, so was a company named Wham-O Mfg. Co., of San Gabriel, Calif. By 1959, it had a full suite of saucers. Wham-O's Pluto Platter discs, Flying Saucer horseshoe game and Sputnik Sailing Satellite had joined a line made famous by the Hula Hoop.

The flying saucer that would, in the end, fly highest in the toy world was the Wham-O aerial toy, which was initially designed by Warren Franscioni, an Air Force major who saw service in the Near and Far East in the war, and Fred Morrison, another Air Force pilot who flew missions over Italy before being shot down and being imprisoned in Germany's notorious Stalag 13.

Plastic and flying discs were natural mates in the minds of Franscioni and Morrison. The two apparently conceived of the notion together. Franscioni created a plastic disc, designing aerodynamic features to make the plastic variety better than any previous metal version. As designer, mold-maker and original partner in the company that probably provided equipment and resources, Franscioni might reasonably be thought the originator of the plastic flying disc, if any one person should be credited.

Working out of Franscioni's basement in the late 1940s, the pair made a prototype out of Tenite, a plastic made by the Tennessee Eastman Co. Tenite, an advanced variety of cellulose acetate, was already a popular plastic for manufacturing, having been used for such items as football helmets, army whistles, tool and utensil handles, and radio housings. It was tough, lustrous and took colors well.

Even Tennessee Eastman itself hinted at a problem, however: "Like most materials, natural and synthetic," the company said, "Tenite is tougher at high than at low temperatures." In flying disc terms, this meant that as night approached and temperatures fell, the toy might start chipping. It might even shatter if the other person failed to catch it.

Franscioni and Morrison's company, Partners in Plastic, or Pipco, contracted with Southern California Plastic Co. of Eagle Rock, Calif., to produce the new disc in a softer plastic at 25 cents per disc. Pipco sold its new Flyin' Saucer for a dollar, the same price Wham-O received for Frisbees 20 years later. The Flyin' Saucer took more salesmanship than the company could muster, however. Franscioni tended to the business end of things in San Luis Obispo, while Morrison went on the road to demonstrate and actively sell the toy.

At a point when the company was still struggling to cover the costs of the original dies, a marketing agreement

with Al Capp, creator of L'il Abner, must have seemed a godsend. The arrangement turned sour, however, when Capp thought Pipco went beyond the agreement and sued for damages. Franscioni borrowed money from his mother and mother-in-law to pay off Capp. Pipco failed, and Franscioni rejoined the Air Force out of necessity.

Southern California Plastic somehow continued making the Flyin' Saucer, however. Morrison continued to sell them while developing a new disc of his own on the side. When Wham-O took an interest in 1955, Morrison signed a deal that eventually earned him millions, but Franscioni not a cent.

The first Wham-O Pluto Platters, which looked more like flying saucers than ever, hit the market at the beginning of 1957. Sales were slow at first. When Wham-O's Richard Knerr belatedly discovered the New Haven "Frisbie" tradition, the company renamed the flying disc. It seemed to add the magic touch. Wham-O registered the Frisbee trademark in 1959. By the early 1960s, America's youth and Frisbees were inseparable. Ironically, 1958, the year Morrison was awarded a flying disc patent, was also the year the Frisbie Pie Factory in New Haven closed its doors.

As the Frisbee, the toy brought joy to millions of children—and teens, and young adults. I know, for I was one of them. Still am, for that matter, on some splendid, calm days of early summer that seem to call for a few flying saucers in the air. ■

Frisbie: Pie tin, $45
Wham-O: Frisbee, 1966, $15
Wham-O: Mars Platter, $50
Wham-O: Mini Frisbee, 4", 1967, $15
Wham-O: Pluto Platter, $225

**Whirly-Whirler.** *This red-plastic whirling toy was one of the many flying-platter toys of the 1950s, and one that enjoyed national distribution on a larger scale than Wham-O's Pluto Platter at the end of the decade. TV advertising helped make it well-known. Touted as "the original plastic juggler's plate," the Whirley Whirley was to be sent spinning atop a stick before it was sent flying or was juggled between players. Whirley Corp., of St. Louis, Mo., late 1950s.*

# THINGMAKERS

**Make 'em Fast & Easy with Gobble-Degoop!** *The trend started by Mr. Potato Head of making toys of food found its ultimate expression in Incredible Edibles from Mattel. "Cook up some fun," the box instructed kids. Parents took heart from the sugarless nature of the Gobble-Degoop and from the Good Housekeeping seal of approval. The set featured the Sooper-Gooper, a covered hotplate in the shape of a buck-toothed, orange-wigged head, with round aluminum molds featuring two or three shapes each. They made Bug Bites, Luscious Lizards, Fancy Flowers, Fabulous Frogs, Gourmet Goldfish, Funny Fruit, Sweet Snakes and Ginger-Men, as well as butterflies, octopi, skull-and-crossbones, cats and a haunted mansion. The flavors? Cinnamon, licorice, cherry, raspberry, root beer, butterscotch, mint and Tutti Fruit. Replacement Gobble-Degoop packets cost $1.25 per pair of flavors. Mattel, 1966.*

**COOK UP SOME FUN! FRIGHTFULLY DELICIOUS! SUGARLESS!**

THINGMAKERS

TOY makers have probably always realized who their biggest competitors are: kids themselves. Kids, after all, take pride and pleasure in making their own toys. It hardly matters what materials are at hand. Toys can be made, one way or another.

Publishers have issued books about making playthings from scratch, from the 1800s to the present day. And while such construction toys as the Meccano and Erector sets of the 1910s provided a means for children to make their own toys, it took until the 1920s and '30s for toy manufacturers to realize they could give children the means to become actual manufacturers of toys—by means of slush-metal casting. They realized that if the toy company supplied the two halves of a casting mold, the child could do the rest.

Soon, kids were buying molds for pouring their own lead soldiers and animals. On kitchen ranges, they melted small ingots of lead, or "slush" metal, for their miniature armies. When they ran out of ingots, they melted whatever they could get their mitts on: toothpaste tubes, Brylcreem tubes and even broken soldiers from the defeated enemy army.

The idea caught on so well that by the mid-1930s the "casting set" had become a major category within the toy industry. The companies issuing them were scattered around the country: Ace Toy Mold Co., in Toledo, Ohio; the A.C. Gilbert Co., in New Haven, Conn.; Home Foundry Mfg. Co., and Rapaport Bros., in Chicago, Ill.; Make-A-Toy Co., in New York City; Henry C. Schiercke, in Ghent, N.Y.; and Williams Kast Art Co., in Stockton, Calif. So useful were the molds being produced by these and other companies that both children and adults set up home businesses producing metal toys, with the result that the official number of "manufacturers" of slush-metal toy soldiers,

animals, autos and airplanes in the 1930s will forever remain unknown.

Some metal-casting sets continued to be issued into the Boomer years, although the companies producing them were less apt to encourage the entrepreneurial spirit in children than they were in the pre-war years. They were also less apt to promote metal-casting.

As the 1950s arrived, four major companies were issuing casting sets. The only New York City firm was Plastine Mfg. Co., which issued plastic two-part molds for animal and human figures, which could be used only with non-metal modeling materials.

Chicago, on the other hand, seemed to be the casting-set capital in those early Boomer years. Rapaport Bros. was still in business, and had been joined by Model-Craft, Inc., and American Toy & Furniture Co. In addition, Bersted's Hobby Craft, Inc., of Monmouth, Ill., issued a wide variety of sets featuring rubber molds for making plaster human figures and dolls, autos and farm animals. As had been true of many metal-casting sets of the 1930s, children could pick and choose the individual molds, or they could buy sets to make arrays of baseball or football players, costume dolls or even a Bozo circus.

## A WHOLE SILLY WORLD

In 1964, however, Mattel put a twist into the old home-casting idea, introducing a low-temperature hot plate that heated the molds themselves instead of the raw material, and a plastic that hardened, rather than softened, with the application of heat.

The plastic was called Plastigoop. The kits were called Thingmakers. Or maybe the children were the Thingmakers.

**Grotesqueries.** *Mattel marketed the Creeple Peeple Thingmaker as an accessory toy: "Make lovable Creeple Peeple! Creeple Peeple pencils you make and take everywhere! Wear 'em! Clip 'em on pockets, notebooks! Write & erase with 'em! Stand them up! GIVE 'EM! WEAR 'EM! TRADE 'EM!" Creeple Peeple molds and figure, Mattel, mid-1960s.*

• **101 GREATEST BABY BOOMER TOYS** • 39

# 8

With their hot plates, molds and goop, they found themselves fantastically empowered. With some kits, they could make superhero figures. With others, they could make toy soldiers, using two-piece molds. They could make flowers with Fun Flowers. They could make Picadoos, which were odds-and-ends for use in arts and crafts projects. The Mini-Dragons kit promised "a whole silly world of crazy mixed-up wigglin' jigglin' creatures."

Children could even make toys they could eat, which was a decisive step up from eating crayons or white paste. Or kids could stick to basics and make the original and most popular things of all: the Creepy Crawlers, which were everything from snakes, lizards and frogs to centipedes, spiders, cockroaches and trilobites.

The Creeple Peeple of 1965 proved especially delightful to kids. The Creeple Peeple molds made various parts—heads, arms, feet—that transformed the contents of the school desk pencil box full of Eberhard Faber #2s into a mysterious population of oddities. As a nod to the Troll fad sweeping the country, garish plumes of hair topped the Creeples. Since the feet were the part stuck onto the sharpened tip of the pencil, they were the part most often lost. They simply fell off. The loss was not a great one, however. If you yourself had no kit for making new feet, by the end of the school day—for you always took your Creeple Person to school—you could walk home, eyes to the sidewalk, and find feet that someone else had dropped.

My particular Thingmaker was a Creepy Crawler set intended for children already equipped with the basic hot plate. Mother let me use the electric range on the kitchen stove. I put the trays in an aluminum pie pan, then tried to bake that yellow or green Plastigoop in the molds. I heavily favored the trilobite mold, since it provided accessories to go with my MPC dinosaurs, even though I knew with boyish erudition that

trilobites and dinosaurs never coexisted. But then, too, I knew most of the dinosaurs never coexisted, either.

Invariably, I undercooked my goop and produced a good many toys with soft, sticky centers, which fortunately—or unfortunately, for the tabletops involved—were on the undersides of the toys. Undercooked toys ... Another '60s innovation from Mattel.

Mattel led the pack with its Thingmakers, yet was not quite alone at the top. Topper Toys was breathing down its neck with a popular kit using Super Plastic. Rings 'n Things, introduced in 1968, enjoyed considerable vogue among the young earring-and-necklace set, who were delighted to be making all the gaudy personal accouterments they always knew they deserved.

Other toy-making kits enjoyed considerable success as well. Mattel issued the Electric Vac-U-Form, with plastic sheets and molds that shaped those sheets into numerous toys and novelty items. Similarly, Topper issued the Johnny Toymaker as a partner to its popular Suzy Homemaker toys.

Surprisingly, the innovations of the Thingmakers line still left room for old-fashioned home casting. Kits, now marketed under such names as the Electric Metal Casting Set and sold through Sears in the mid-'60s, allowed kids to melt ingots of metal and pour them into matched molds.

New York City's Emenee Industries, Inc., released several 1965 kits using the same idea with plastic. Its Formex Casting Sets allowed kids to cast soldiers or monsters using a reusable plastic. It also made a Munsters Casting Set, using Castex 5 Compound, for one-time use in producing Herman and his family.

Kenner Products Co. came up with the most up-to-date version of home casting, however, with its Electric Mold Master. The kit made soldiers, tanks, jeeps, cannons, and even a pistol that could shoot bullets. The kit put plastic injection molding

into the hands of children. At low heat, the Mold Master melted the plastic compounds, which came in four colors. A plunger then forced the material into the molds, making a variety of three-dimensional toys. They were good toys. They just weren't crazy and weird. Mattel almost took out a patent on crazy and weird with its Thingmakers.

I remember no one person in my various classes in elementary school voicing the desire to grow up to be a toy maker. They all already knew better. They knew you didn't have to grow up to be one. ■

Mattel: Creeple Peeple Thingmaker, 1965, $95
Mattel: Thingmaker/Creepy Crawler, 1964, $80
Mattel: Vac-U-Form Casting Set, 162, $65
Topper: Johnny Toymaker, 1968, $50

**This takes the cake.** *Makery Bakery, Mattel, 1967.*

# MOUSE TRAP!

**The sensation of '63.** *After its unprecedented success in 1963, Ideal started advertising it on the Magilla Gorilla Show, which boosted the remarkable game, and Ideal, into a second surprisingly successful spring. Ideal, 1963.*

THE IDEAL TOY CORPORATION of New York City was hitting its stride in the early 1960s. The designs of Marvin Glass were startling and new, and were being greeted with open arms by children and parents. As nice as this was, things were about to get better. In 1963, Ideal suddenly found itself with a mega-hit on its hands.

It was a board game, with plastic parts to be assembled. It was clever and interesting, and it sold phenomenally well—in the spring of '63. Observers in the business shook their heads. When did a board game do well in the spring? By that Christmas, it was a sell-out.

What was so different about it? Marvin Glass had given Ideal a board game whose object was not to earn millions, or even to emerge with the sense of "winning." His new game did involve the travel of playing pieces across the board, as was traditional. But it also involved the construction of a Rube Goldberg device consisting of carefully molded plastic pieces. These resembled ramshackle gutters, stairways, concatenations of pipes, a shoe, a bathtub and an old man in his bathing suit. The real aim? To get everything connected and put together—

then to set the bizarre structure in motion.

Much like Glass's earlier success for Ideal—see No. 28—the Mousetrap board game was a machine. The same delight children had long felt in setting dominoes on end in long rows, just for the pleasure of knocking one over and watching the chain reaction, came into play in Ideal's new board game.

This strange assemblage actually worked. You turned a crank and set in motion a process that produced the feeling of inevitability, the same feeling evoked by those clattering dominoes. It took time for the whole mechanism to finish the process—and it was an utter delight watching it go through the motions. The old boot that kicked, the heavy steel ball rolling back-and-forth down the uneven stairs, the old man who jumped off a springboard (he jumped better if he stood backwards, we discovered in our household) and the precariously perched hard-plastic net that clattered down over the hapless playing piece, which was a stylized, pear-shaped creature with a long, looping tail.

For the first time in decades, Mickey was no longer the Number One Mouse. ■

> Ideal: Crazy Clock, 1964, $80
> Ideal: Mouse Trap, 1963, $30

# mouse trap game

## FOLLOW THE BOUNCING BALL!

The ball rolls down the rickety stairs ...

... the old man jumps for the barrel ...

... and lands (sometimes on his feet!) ...

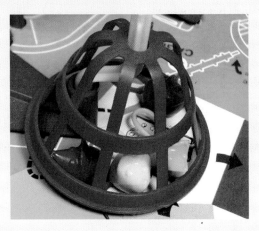

... and the basket descends over the mice.

## THE TYPICAL TEEN
# TAMMY

**The girl next door.** *Tammy gave children the option of playing with a fashion doll who was first and foremost a hometown sweetheart, unlike a certain other citified, European-inspired fashion doll. Ideal, 1960s.*

**"Our Favorite School Girl."** *The Penny Brite dolls of mid-decade, 8-¼" tall, were akin to the dolls of Tammy's younger sister Pepper, 9" tall. Topper Toys Div., Deluxe Reading Corp., Elizabeth, N.J., ca. 1963-66.*

T surely reflects on the American public, or at least on our Boomer generation, that the first doll to come to mind from the Boomer years is Barbie, not Tammy. A late friend of mine, who demonstrated a homespun Kansas wisdom her entire life, had a piece of advice she dispensed to those trembling on the edge of romance, especially dubious romance: "Always choose wholesome," she said.

Although Barbie herself would ultimately transmute into an all-too-wholesome model of teenage perky cheer, in the early 1960s, her leggy seductiveness and predatory glances found their antithesis in Tammy, who represented America's apple-pie Girl Next Door. Tammy was more grown-up than the fashion dolls of the 1950s, but was more akin to them than to Barbie in her open expression and her rounder, younger face. She had the obligatory accessories of the fashion doll: "a pretty two-piece lingerie outfit with strapless top, full skirt, and

Tammy.
*Ideal, 1964.*

**TAMMY'S OUTFITS**

©
Pay Only
2.17

**Leading the cheers.** *Tammy, depicted as an everyday, midde-class girl, could let loose and be herself. In the 1960s, Barbie was still too superbly poised for such antics. Tin plate, Ideal, 1960s.*

matching panties—all lace-trimmed," reported the General Merchandise Company catalog in the year of her introduction. Tammy's clothing was not high-fashion, however. It tended more toward the practical, the everyday and the charming.

Introduced by Ideal Toy Corp. in 1962, she found easy acceptance among children and parents. They liked her. How could they not? She looked like a nice kid.

Hers was an unassuming childhood empire, too, that grew slowly through the mid-decade, helped in part by her parent company's willingness to grant Tammy licenses to other toy companies.

Hassenfeld Bros. made Tammy activity sets and jewelry sets. Whitman Publishing Co. made puzzles and story, coloring, cutout and Sticker Fun books. Metaltex, Inc., a Bayone, N.J., firm specializing in doll combs, brushes and mirrors, made the Tammy Pretty Miss Set. Newark Comfort Co., of Newark, N.J., made Tammy doll bedding and accessories. Winthrop-Atkins Co., Inc., of Middleboro, Mass., made the Tammy Magic Mirror.

Hassenfeld Bros. added Tammy nurse sets later in the '60s, while Mirro Aluminum Co. of Manitowoc, Wis., made Tammy aluminum miniatures, and Colorforms, of Norwood, N.J., issued a Tammy Dress-Up Kit.

**Wholesome fun.** *The cards for the board game reflected Tammy's orientation: happy at home and happy at school. The Tammy Game, Ideal, 1963.*

Ideal Toy Corp. made the rest: Tammy plastic tea sets, Tammy doll furniture, Tammy sports car, Tammy travel cases, and the Tammy game—and Tammy's fellow fashion dolls: Pepper, Pos'n Pete, Pos'n Salty, Dodi, Ted ... and Mom and Dad.

Ideal managed to do with Tammy what Hassenfeld Bros. had done with Mr. Potato Head, but Mattel never did with Barbie: it made a toy that resonated with the American myth of the happy, suburban-dwelling, nuclear family.

Barbie, an expression of the teenager myth of youthful independence, had friends. The catch-line for the doll in the 1963 Sears catalogs gave perfect expression to self-absorbed adolescence: "Barbie and Her Friends, with four pages of wardrobes and accessories." Four pages!

The previous two pages opened with the headline: "Meet Tammy's Delightful Family." Mom and Dad as fashion dolls ... what a notion! Some children probably never recovered. ∎

Ideal: Tammy, $35
Ideal: Tammy's Dad, in original box, $75
Ideal: Tammy's Mom, in original box, $75

**Friendly fashion.** *Unlike Barbie, Betsy McCall actually did have her start as a paper doll, in the pages of McCall Magazine, which had a readership of around 6 million in the middle Boomer years. As a doll, Betsy McCall was manufactured by Ideal Toy Corp., in the mid-1950s; and then by American Character Doll, of Brooklyn, then famous for its Tiny Tears crying doll, in the later '50s. The latter became American Doll & Toy Corp., of New York City, a company that in 1961 turned her into a fully-jointed doll. Sears Toy Book, 1963-64.*

# FROM UNDER THE BRIDGE
# TROLLS

"H OMELY. Look at those ears."

"And those eyes."

"Ugly!"

"Look—naked! Ecch!"

"So cute," said the little one, taking the trolls in arm and walking away.

Trolls hit with such force that comparisons with another overnight sensation, the Hula Hoop, prompted Uneeda Doll Co., Inc., of New York City to crow, in a 1964 ad: "They call it a 'Hula Hoop' ... Its correct name is WISHNIK."

Making troll dolls was a departure for Uneeda. It was known for its dolls with names of sugar-spoon sweetness: Weepsy Wiggles, Dew Drop, Blabby, Yummy Kiss, Needa Toddles, Baby Dollikins, Bundle of Love, Baby Bumpkins and Sweetums.

Sugar-spoon sweet? Uneeda's Wishnik Trolls were not quite that. They were squat-bodied, round-bellied, pointed-eared, snub-nosed, tan-skinned, grinning, sexless vinyl creatures. The little ones wore no clothes for a few years, although in 1967 even the 3-inch trolls learned modesty or else style. They started appearing that year in costumes and outfits that did their best to remain on the far side of the ridiculous. Even then, the very smallest, the size of charms and bubble-gum prizes, that being what they were, came naked into the world and stayed that way.

Trolls were all vinyl except for glassine eyes and plentiful hair. The stuff erupted from above their heavy brow-ridges with an exuberance extinct since the wooly mammoth. It swept up

with a shape like that of an onion, or of the flame on a match ... or it did so, at least at first. In the hands of a child, the hair was apt to spread every which way or to come out altogether.

Soon the various troll manufacturers of the 1960s grew dissatisfied with traditional hair colors and began the great color explosion. Many Wishniks appeared with red, yellow, orange and blue hair—great flowing waves of the stuff. The hair was a huge part of troll appeal. While they had bellies much like the Japanese god Hotei, whose belly is rubbed for good luck, Wishniks came with a a different injunction: "Rub my hair for good luck."

Trolls turned out to be good character players, fitting into all the various niches of everyday life, from graduation to marriage. With equal ease they slipped into some of the best imaginary roles around. The Doll Troll Heroes of 1967 showed that even the most level-headed superheroes took on a troll identity. "Whether fighting crime, winning wars or games, Doll Troll Heroes keep smiling," Sears trumpeted in its Christmas catalogs. The Superman Troll had a great swatch of flowing red hair, matching his red briefs. Batman Troll's yellow hair matched his briefs, too ... as he drove his vacuum-formed Batnik-Mobile out of his vinyl, "complete fake rock laboratory" Bat Cave.

Vinyl troll dolls were the innovation of a Danish baker, Thomas Dam, who started carving wooden troll figures for his children. He put them up for sale to troll-minded sorts when the baking business was going through hard times after the war. The

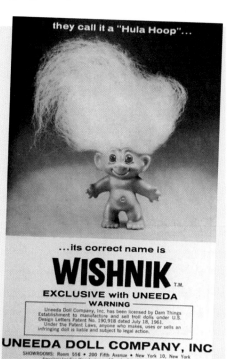

**Saving for a rainy day.** *Larger troll banks such as this slicker-clad example came with clothing permanently attached to the vinyl body. Troll bank, 7" tall, Dam, 1960s.*

**Hula Hoop.** *Uneeda's announcement of its license from Dam used a term for "massive hit" everyone in the toy industry knew. Playthings, March 1964.*

they call it a "Hula Hoop"...

...its correct name is

# WISHNIK T.M.

EXCLUSIVE with UNEEDA

— WARNING —

Uneeda Doll Company, Inc. has been licensed by Dam Things Establishment to manufacture and sell troll dolls under U.S. Design Letters Patent No. 190,918 dated July 18, 1961. Under the Patent Laws, anyone who makes, uses or sells an infringing doll is liable and subject to legal action.

**UNEEDA DOLL COMPANY, INC**

SHOWROOMS: Room 556 • 200 Fifth Avenue • New York 10, New York

America's Leading Manufacturers of Popular Priced Dolls Since 1917

**Graduation party.** *Although wannabe trolls flooded the market in the 1960s, Uneeda obtained a license from Dam to produce vinyl trolls for the American market. Uneeda used both "Wishnik" and "Wish-Nik" trade names for the homely-cute dolls. Uneeda Wishniks, 1960s.*

trolls sold so well he set up a factory in Gjol in 1959, getting a fad rolling that would encourage countless imitators.

In 1964, Dam issued a license to make trolls to Uneeda Doll Co. of Brooklyn, N.Y., a doll-maker since 1917. The license was such news that Uneeda gave it bigger press than its other licensing agreement that year. Through an agreement with *McCall's* magazine, Uneeda was launching a new Betsy McCall doll. Betsy had previously been made by American Character Doll Co. from 1957 to 1963. Any other year, Betsy would have been the top Uneeda news.

In 1966 Dam entered into another agreement with Skandia House, a subsidiary of Royalty House in Florida. While they carefully skirted around the Troll name, other manufacturers did turn out miscellaneous troll-like creatures, with some of the most appealing made as curios out of the material Thomas Dam first used: wood.

One other firm successfully used the Troll name, however. For at least a half-decade, Bunallan, Inc., based in Woodland Hills, Calif., made a specialty of Trogs for Trolls doll clothes to fit the stubby creatures.

Trolls appeared everywhere. On family trips out West when I was a child, I remember it being a highlight to stop at Little America, a tourist trap set up in the middle of nowhere that sold every tourist curio imaginable, including a huge vinyl troll that must have stood taller than at least some of us kids.

By the late '60s the boom was waning. Although trolls were still riding high on a crest of European popularity, the wave was dying back in this country. Although other companies made trollish this-and-thats, Uneeda dropped the Wishnik trade name after 1969. ■

> Uneeda: Wishnik, hula Troll doll, $30
> Uneeda: Wishnik, two-headed Troll, $50
> Uneeda: Wishnik, graduation gown Troll, $20

# GREASED-WHEEL REVOLUTION
# HOT WHEELS

IN the 1960s, the English company Lesney ruled the sidewalk highways. Suburbs were growing at a fantastic pace around every major city, all following the basic suburban model: wide streets, pleasant houses, lawns, trees and sidewalks.

Millions of toy cars poured into this country from England, proving such a phenomenon that Mattel executives decided they needed something like Matchbox cars in their line. Their designers set to work in this direction, but ended up being slightly more influenced by the California ethic: beaches and surfing, crazy cars and Ed Roth.

When the first Hot Wheels appeared on toy stands in 1968, Mattel had a revolution on its hands. For the first time, a manufacturer was selling die-cast car toys based not on model accuracy or roll-on-the-floor fun, but on speedway performance. To be fully appreciated, Hot Wheels cars needed tracks. Why? Because the low-friction wheels made the cars run so fast they could do stunts, including leaping from one ramp to the next, or doing loop-the-loops on special sections of track.

Although they arrived relatively late in the Boomer period, Hot Wheels had enormous influence, changing the toy scene much the way Barbie had a decade before. The new dominance of the performance car, as opposed to the model car, was made startlingly clear by the waves of imitations that attempted to compete with the head of the pack. Topper introduced its sleek Johnny Lightning cars, which some said were faster than the original Hot Wheels. Although well liked by children, the line had a short life due to the bankruptcy of the company for reasons unrelated to the toy car.

The Louis Marx Co., ever eager to follow any toy trail scent, came out with its relatively tame and clunky Mini-Marx Blazers. Being low-budget imitations of Hot Wheels, these toys made little inroad into the toy market and ended up having only a few models in its line. Topper Toys did far better, with its Johnny Lightning cars.

Even Matchbox faced the music. By 1971 most of the Matchbox line had Superfast wheels, which were not quite the fast-spinning Mattel wheels, but still satisfying to kids. I remember having a collection of "regular wheel" Matchboxes, as they are now called, and then becoming the proud owner of one of the new Superfast cars. To me, it was better than the Hot Wheels: it still looked like a real car and had doors that opened and a detailed interior. It fascinated me.

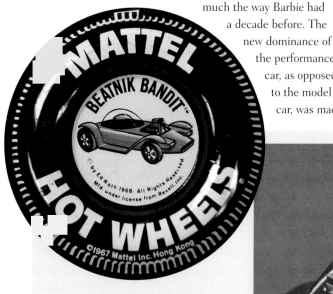

**Performance car accessory.** *The metal tab-buttons packaged with early Hot Wheels toy cars became as much a part of the play scene as the cars themselves. Mattel showed its usual good sense regarding the fashion needs of children with the innovation. Ed Roth Beatnik Bandit and Maserati Mistral buttons, Mattel, 1968 and '69.*

**Custom cool.** *Hot Wheels capitalized on the "custom" craze sweeping an already car-obsessed nation, and issued hot rod versions of popular cars. Custom Volkswagen, Mattel, 1968.*

Yet so did Hot Wheels. I ended up with only one, a Volkswagen bug. I had one Johnny Lightning, the Custom Turbine, with a bubble top that hearkened back to old science fiction pulp covers of spaceships and space cars, or even to Ed Roth's Beatnik Bandit, issued by Hot Wheels in 1968.

Instead of a Hot Wheels set with tracks, I received a then lower-end Marx set. It suited me fine, after the initial qualms I must have felt at not having gotten the TV-endorsed brand name. The set included a couple of primitive-looking die-cast cars, a Chaparral racer and a Jeep, and a track with a device for making a loop.

That loop made the toy. We tried the Matchbox (not bad) and Marx cars (pretty good) and Hot Wheels Volkswagen (it tended to get halfway and not make it all around the loop) and Custom Turbine (oooh). Then we tried marbles and had loads of fun shooting marbles down the track and through the loop-the-loop. Marbles out-raced Hot Wheels or Johnny Lightnings any day. Then, of course, we had to try the huge steel ball-bearing from the Hit the Spot game, and made the whole thing collapse.

Best evidence of the fact that Hot Wheels redefined toy cars at the end of the '60s came from Barclay, a toy-making outfit operating since the mid-1920s that produced what is known as "slush-mold" or "white-metal" cars. The operative word is this: cheap. Cheap, but not unappealing as toys. Many kids appreciated them, just as many collectors highly appreciate them now. They had a simplicity and no-frill approach that left lots of room for the imagination.

The marketing department at Barclay must have had lots of imagination, too, since they started a small set of Barclay racers using normal axles and plastic wheels, with a length of track. This was meant to draw the low-penny crowd, who could not afford the high-penny, fast-wheeled competition. It might have drawn them—but how long would it have held them? Barclay cars could barely roll when pushed along by hand, let alone on gravity power down a track.

Barclay swiftly passed away. Mattel's Hot Wheels thrived and became such a fixture that many Boomers find it hard to believe that it was, among toys, one of the latecomers, touching only the tail end of the generation. ■

Mattel: Hot Wheels Beatnik Bandit, 1968-71, $10-$20
Mattel: Hot Wheels Custom Volkswagen, 1968-71, $10-$15
Mattel: Hot Wheels Deora, 1968-69, $40-$60
Mattel: Hot Wheels Red Baron, 1970-79, $10-$20
Whitman: Hot Wheels sticker book, 1968, $10
Whitman: Hot Wheels T.V. Show, frame tray puzzle, 1970, $10

**Hot on Mattel's wheels.** *Companies including Topper and Marx jumped on the idea of the high-performance toy die-cast car after Mattel's massive success with Hot Wheels. Chaparral, Marx, late 1960s.*

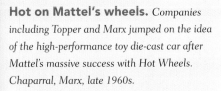

**Big Daddy Roth's bubble top.** *Daring designs such as this Beatnik Bandit stood in contrast to Matchbox cars of the time.*

**Blazing speed.** *The flame logo on Hot Wheels packages became a universally recognized symbol of burning rubber.*

"1,250,000 KIDS (BY LATEST HOOPER RATING) FROM COAST TO COAST SEE THIS UNIQUE DISPLAY OF MECHANICAL TOYS ON TELEVISION VIA THE HOWDY DOODY SHOW. THEY KNOW UNIQUE TOYS AS THEIR PARENTS KNOW THEIR FAVORITE CIGARETTES. THEY KNOW NOT ONLY THE UNIQUE BRAND NAME, BUT ALSO EACH OF THE UNIQUE TOYS BY NAME. IN FACT KIDS VISITING THE SHOW HAVE IDENTIFIED THE VARIOUS UNIQUE TOYS WRAPPED IN PAPER MERELY BY THE SIZE OF THE PACKAGE. ALERT TOY DEALERS THROUGHOUT THE COUNTRY ARE SETTING UP REPLICAS OF THE UNIQUE TELEVISION DISPLAY IN THEIR DEPARTMENTS. THEY REPORT IMMEDIATE RECOGNITION BY CHILDREN AND MOTHERS AND 'NOISY' DEMAND FOR THE WONDERFUL UNIQUE TOYS THAT THE KIDS HAVE SO OFTEN SEEN ON THE HOWDY DOODY SHOW."

—ADVERTISEMENT, UNIQUE ART MFG. CO., INC., NEWARK, N.J., 1949.

# Fads and Faves of the Fifties

In the 1950s, toy manufacturers faced a world of uncertainty. If people felt optimistic one Christmas season, it was nice for that year—but sometimes then the major stores overbought for their toy departments. That meant tightened belts for manufacturers the next season, when those stores still had old stock to sell. The supply of raw materials, seemingly back to normal by the end of the 1940s, experienced unexpected ups and downs again—especially with the return of war in far-away Korea.

In promotions, the radio shows that had generated income for the industry, partly through the manufacture of small-toy premiums, were still attracting audiences. Yet public focus was switching to TV. Licensors feared that the stars of radio, or even of the movies, might not make the leap to the small screen successfully. No one knew who

the new TV stars would really be from season to season, although a handful of shows seemed to be turning into dependable attractions, month after month and sometimes year after year.

In contrast, magazines still offered solid footing for toy companies trying out new products. Some firms relied on women's magazines to reach toy-buying mothers. New York City's American Character Doll Co. was one such, using *Look* magazine ads to make Tiny Tears one of the popular dolls of the early decade. Others used general-readership magazines, as did Wolverine Supply & Mfg. Co. of Pittsburgh, Pa., which advertised its new-in-1950 Wolverine Kitchen Set in *Life*.

Some toy companies, however, felt more adventurous and dipped their toes into the shimmering waters of black-and-white television. As early as 1949, Unique Art Mfg. Co., Inc., of Newark, N.J., and Atlas Toy Mfg. Corp., of

New York City, had placed themselves among the nation's pioneering TV-show advertisers.

A stuffed animal named Butch was among the first toy TV stars. Atlas modeled the toy on a dog featured in TV programs and on magazine covers, as well as in drawings by Butch's cartoonist owner, Al Staehle. Butch made its appearance on DuMont station WABD on March 7, 1949, on the Kathi Norris program, *Your Television Shopper.*

Goodly amounts of early toy advertising on TV came about through local programming produced by department stores. Goldblatt's of Chicago, for instance, ran a daily television show 11 a.m. to noon in the 1950-51 season. Toys were featured alongside the many other products of the day.

Most companies paying attention to television still relied on magazines to get the word out, however. New York City firm E-Z Do, for instance, was one of the early companies jumping on the Howdy Doody bandwagon. When it started promoting its Howdy Doody-decorated wardrobes, chests of drawers, toy chests, play tables, folding screens and wallpaper border—with four rolls of Howdy Doody wallpaper free with every purchase of the entire ensemble—it did so not on TV, but in *Parents and Children's Activities* magazines.

To toymakers, the rapidly increasing use of plastics was probably as exciting and unnerving as the popularity of television. Toy plastic cars and airplanes seemed almost natural: after all, they had already appeared in the late 1930s. A few companies had shown plastics could serve pretty well during wartime, too, making plastic toy soldiers, cowboys and Indians, and animals commonplace playthings.

Plastics kept appearing in ever-new applications, however. Back in the 1930s, a few purists were no doubt disturbed by the idea that some boys and girls were playing with cap guns having holsters made not of real leather, but of leatherette. Imagine, then, the eyebrows being raised among people reading advertisements at the dawn of the 1950s from that stalwart of the toy-gun world, the Kilgore Mfg. Co. of Westerville, Ohio:

*"Kilgore's plastic holster sets offer more for less! Look at these features: molded in one strong piece ... no seams to rip out ... colors won't fade or stain clothing ... unaffected by sun, snow or rain ... can be washed with soap ... beautiful color combinations ... "*

The reaction against plastic was substantial enough that some companies, such as Brooklyn's R. & S. Toy Mfg. Co., Inc., made a good business of emphasizing "genuine leather gun and holster sets" through the 1950s. For many other people, however, a look at Kilgore's $2.50 price tag was all it took.

# DATELINE 1958
# HULA HOOP

EVEN IF hoop toys, hoop-rolling and hoop exercise go back to the ancient Greeks and Egyptians ...

Even if missionaries may have first drawn the connection between hip-whirling Hula dancers in Hawaii and the sport of hoop-twirling in far-away England ...

Even if Australian health-nuts were thinning their waists by whirling wooden hoops just the year before ...

Even if these things were so, the advent of the Hula Hoop in 1958 remains very much a Boomer phenomenon.

These new hoops were different from any that came before. When Wham-O's Richard Knerr and Arthur Melin decided to adopt the Australian fad for the American market, they made their prototypes out of colorful plastic. They tested it with local children and discovered they had a toy on their hands with far greater potential than any other they had thus far introduced.

The pair had started their toy business in 1948 in a garage, making inexpensive slingshots. Ten years later they unleashed the Hula Hoop on a world obviously eagerly ready for it, kicking off a one-season fad that at its crest would see Wham-O producing 20,000 hoops per day. They flew from stores, at $1.98 each. Since Wham-O was unable to patent the toy, competing toy companies jumped in with Spin-A-Hoops and Hoop-D-Doos, among many others.

So popular were the toys that plastics manufacturers had trouble keeping up with the demands of the toy manufacturers—and toy manufacturers found it impossible to keep up with demand.

For one dizzying summer, all of America had a slimmer waistline. Since the hoops provided an outdoorsy recreation, as the weather grew colder sales slumped. Wham-O gamely moved along overseas and made the sensation a world-spanning, if not world-spinning, phenomenon.

It was almost impossible for anyone, young or old, to not give it a try at least once. Coming as it did in 1958, when even the earliest Boomers were old enough to enjoy it—and when they were certainly still interested in showing off to each other—the Hula Hoop is one of those toys that affected the entire generation.

Everyone in the generation has the ignoble memory of feeling the twirling hoop slipping down from not-active-enough hips, to the knees ... and then to the ground. We all had that moment when we realized it was not quite so easy as it looked.

While hoop sales never equaled what they did in their first year, the Hula Hoop did remain a part of playtime through the Boomer years. I remember this well enough, being one of those boys who grew up in the 1960s, well after the fad, with an older sister who did a pretty tidy job with her pink plastic Hula Hoop. I could do it, too—kind of. The fad was over. To the delight of some, and the embarrassed frustration of others, however, the toy remained. ■

**Wham-O: Hula-Hoop, 1950s-60s, $10**

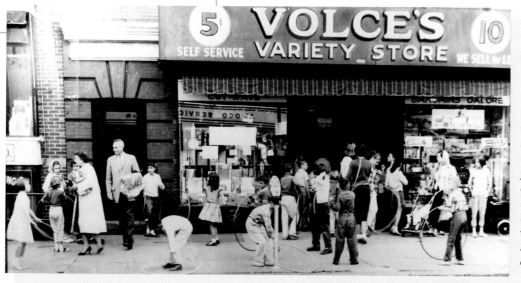

**Waist-high phenomenon.** *The Hula Hoop was far from the first American hoop toy. Even so, its arrival triggered a fad that made scenes such as this commonplace around the country. Here, in front of an Albany, N.Y., five-and-dime store, kids are clustering with their new hoops. One boy was twirling his so successfully the hoop was invisible to the camera. Albany, N.Y., 1958; photo collection of the author.*

**W**ALT DISNEY'S new weekly television series *Disneyland* was barely underway when it started the nation singing about a frontier hero. The original format of *Disneyland*, which started in October 1954, called for a rotation of programs under the banners of *Frontierland, Fantasyland, Tomorrowland and Adventureland.* On Dec. 15, in the Frontierland slot, Disney aired *Davy Crockett, Indian Fighter,* in which the resourceful scout tracks down and confronts Chief Red Stick. It featured the low-key young actor Fess Parker, whose prior claim to fame was a bit part in the science fiction feature *Them.*

Disneyland was already ABC's first hit program. Even

**COONSKIN ICON.**

This vinyl figure, with flintlock rifle, fringed buckskin clothing and coonskin cap, was issued as a generic pioneer figure but was instantly a Davy Crockett figure for millions of children. Auburn Rubber, 1950s.

against that background, *Davy Crockett, Indian Fighter* was one of the biggest overnight successes in TV history, giving rise to an instant coonskin craze and a chart-hogging hit single, "The Ballad of Davy Crockett." The sudden success of the show caught Disney by surprise. By the time the first segment aired, the studio already had the third and final one in production.

In the second segment, *Davy Crockett Goes to Congress,* which first aired on Jan. 26 the next year, the hero successfully runs for office only to be hoodwinked by his former general, President Andrew Jackson. In the last segment, *Davy Crockett at the Alamo,* first aired on Feb. 23, Crockett leads a heroic and hopeless defense of an old fort against the Mexicans and is last seen swinging his rifle as a club.

Even having killed off their hero, Disney was not without resources. Disney cannily had been producing his black-and-white ABC programs in color, which allowed the studio to patch together a feature film for summer release. The notion of live-action features coming from the Walt Disney studio was not entirely new. In July 1950, Disney had released its first entirely live-action feature film, *Treasure Island,* followed by the popular *The Story of Robin Hood* in 1952. The release in 1955 of *Davy Crockett, King of the Wild Frontier,* far from being taken as a rehash of TV material, was greeted with all the enthusiasm of an entirely new production.

**Still wearing coonskin.** *The Daniel Boone TV show inadvertently helped keep the memory of Davy Crockett alive. Daniel Boone, No. 3, K.K. Publications, 1965.*

# 14

The enthusiastic endorsement of *Boy's Life* magazine that summer was typical: "Fess Parker, who plays Davy, is six feet, five inches tall, and a good likeness of the historical hero. 'Fess' is his real name; it means 'proud' in old English, and Parker's proud of it. The movie shows the legendary Crockett as hunter, fighter, frontier statesman, and hero of the Alamo. Best of this month's motion picture releases," the magazine told its more than 1 million readers.

While some American children wanted nothing more than to wear mouse ears later in 1955 due to Disney's next TV hit, *The Mickey Mouse Club*, a far greater percentage yearned to wear a coonskin cap.

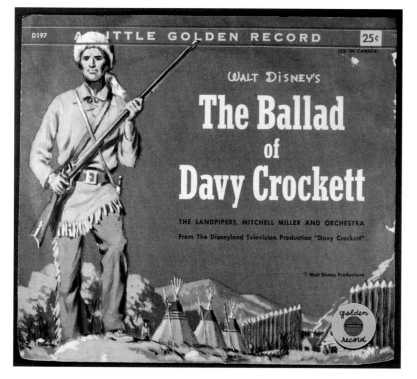

A list of available gifts available through Montgomery Ward's that Christmas gives a good indication of the scope of the fad. They included a Davy Crockett Outfit, Davy Crockett Girl's Outfit, Davy Crockett Hunting Jacket, Davy Crockett Canteen Outfit, Davy Crockett Holster and Knife Set, sparks-shooting "Old Betsy" Shootin' Iron, Davy Crockett Pistol, Davy Crockett Camera Outfit, Davy Crockett Scouting Set, Davy Crockett Flashlight, Davy Crockett Play Tents in two sizes, Davy Crockett Lamp with plastic figure of a horse-riding Davy, Davy Crockett Dish Set, a Davy Crockett Guitar as well as a "Ge-Tar" with a crank handle that played the hit song, Davy Crockett Dancing Doll ("Tall as a child, ideal dancing partner when elastic on his feet and hands are slipped over child's shoes and hands"), album of three Tru-Vue Davy Crockett Film Card Stories, Walt Disney's Davy Crockett on Record, Davy Crockett Phonograph with recording

**Gumball charms.** *Plastic charms became commonplace in the Boomer years. These two celebrated one of America's biggest pop heroes. Davy Crockett charms, 1950s-'60s.*

# 14

of "The Ballad of Davy Crockett," Davy Crockett School Bag, Davy Crockett Lunch Kit, Davy Crockett Binocular Set, Davy Crockett Wallet, Barlow Knife with genuine rabbit's foot key ring charm attached and Davy Crockett Watch.

This wasn't all. Ward's also offered a twill shirt-and-pants set, pajamas, three-piece shirt set, knit shirt, girl's jackets, suede vest, beanie, girl's challis square ("The girls want their hero with them wherever they go!"), Miss Davy's Blouse and Skirt, mittens, steer-hide gauntlet gloves, combed cotton blazer, stretch nylon blazer, dude tie, steer hide belt, plastic wallet, moccasins, slippers, slipper socks, towel set, quilt, pinpoint-chenille and buckskin-tan spread, available for four bed sizes. It also offered Walt Disney's Official Davy Crockett at the Alamo Model Set by Marx, with a small figure of Crockett modeled on Fess Parker.

Strangest of all was the Davy Crockett Bear's Head Trophy, a shield-shaped birch plaque bearing the head of the animal Davy shot when he was only three. "Realistic enough for recreation rooms," Ward's promised. Best of all, Wards offered coonskin caps.

Why the proliferation? Despite the phenomenal drawing power of Fess Parker's character and the Walt Disney name, almost every toy, clothing and novelty company in the business capitalized on the fact that Davy Crockett's name and story were historic in nature.

Only Walt Disney could issue licenses for "Walt Disney's Official Davy Crockett" items—but anyone could issue a plain-old Davy Crockett item. So everyone did, with the result that the quickly created market was equally quickly flooded.

Walt Disney kept Davy Crockett alive as a pop-culture figure during subsequent years. It received a further boost in 1964 when NBC launched the long-lived *Daniel Boone*, also starring Fess Parker. While the TV show focused on another character altogether, the closeness of the two figures' outfits and outlooks, not to mention the identical nature of their screen appearance, made the two melt into one in the minds of children growing up in the 1960s. *Boy's Life* even had a cover devoted to Boone when *Davy Crockett* came out, which might mean some kids were confused right from the start.

I remember having discussions with friends about who we liked better: Davy Crockett or Daniel Boone. The former usually won, probably because of the song. Not that it mattered. All that mattered was having that coonskin cap. ■

---

**Colorforms: Daniel Boone Fess Parker Cartoon Kit, 164, $85**
**Hartland: Davy Crockett plastic figure on horse, $550**
**Marx: Alamo Play Set, #3530, $300**
**Marx: Davy Crockett Frontier Rifle, 32" long, 1950s, $75**
**Marx: plastic figure, Davy Crockett, on stand, 60 mm, $15**
**Parker Bros.: Davy Crockett Frontierland Game, 1955, $40-$50**
**Peter Puppet: Davy Crockett guitar, $175**
**Various Mfrs.: Coonskin cap, 1960s and '70s, $35-$45**

### Riding the crest of the West.
*The prewar fascination with the Old West continued through much of the Boomer period, with Crockett mania bringing it to a peak. Western toys gave many children their first hands-on experience with altering their own identities through accessories. Western costumes, Wards Christmas Book, 1947.*

# IT'S SLINKY!

EARLY BOXES for Slinky, made by James Industries, Inc., of Philadelphia, spelled out the facts of the new toy. "Place Slinky on the top step of your stairs, then lift one end and let go, so that the end falls on the middle of the next lower step. Slinky will then walk down the stairs step by step, or down an inclined surface. ... See how Slinky moves as if he were alive." This soon became common knowledge.

But it took some work to make it so well known. Richard James, inventor of the walking spring, had trouble convincing people his toy would sell. When they looked at it, they saw no more than an unpainted pile of coiled metal wire. Why would people buy it? After considerable effort, James convinced Gimbels Department Store of Philadelphia to let him personally introduce Slinky to its customers.

It was nearing the end of 1946. James had already arranged with a local machine shop to manufacture 400 of the metal coils for him. They measured 2-½ inches tall, and each included 98

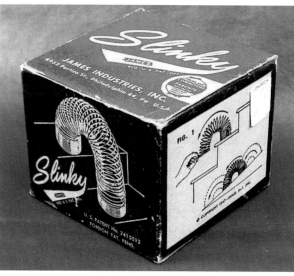

**THE GIMBELS SLINKY.**

The 1947 box for the James Slinky, in brown and white, is almost as simple as the toy within. The price on the side, from Gimbels: $1. Perhaps with tongue in cheek, James promised stores "quick turnover" of the toys. James Industries, 1940s and '50s.

coils of high-grade, blue-black Swedish steel. In addition to the toys, James took with him a small set of stairs for the demonstration. His wife, Betty, and a friend came later, each bringing a dollar so he would have at least two sales.

Customers shopping at Gimbels that day saw something much different than what the skeptical store management had seen earlier. On one level, true enough, they saw nothing more than a metal spring. Yet this spring acted unlike any spring in their experience. Slinky acted strangely lifelike. It walked down stairs. It could be shuffled back and forth between your hands like a supernaturally controlled pile of cards. It made such a pleasing sound, too. How could anyone see it as no more than metal wire? The 400 sold within hours.

The year before, Richard James had become intimate with metal springs of every variety. An engineer, he had been struggling with the challenge of isolating a sensitive marine torsion meter from outside motions caused by heavy weather around the boat or the firing of a shipboard gun. He experimented with spring after spring. At one point, when he

**The '60s Slinky.** *While the earliest Slinkys were coppery in color, the dull silver look became the one most Boomers knew. James Industries, 1960s.*

had springs piled on a table, he happened to knock one over and watched in surprise as it acted unlike any spring he had seen before. He soon discovered it could "walk" down piles of books. The spring's action was no mere fluke, for it performed the same trick over and over again.

Amused, he took it home to his children, who promptly shared it with their friends. That it became a neighborhood phenomenon nudged James down the road to Gimbels.

Near Philadelphia, in Holidaysburg, the new James Industries built a half-dozen machines that could make a Slinky out of 80 feet of wire in less than 12 seconds. The machines lasted through hundreds of millions of Slinkys and served the company through its entire life as a family-owned venture.

Although the original dark steel was replaced with a silvery steel, the toy remained much the same through the Boomer years. Only the addition of crimped ends made the toy different for the last Boomers. Even the price remained roughly the same. It started at a dollar in Philadelphia and never went much higher.

What was true for the toy was not true for the family, where things changed drastically. Betty James, who named her inventor husband's toy, took over control of the company in 1960 after Richard apparently fled the toy-making life, leaving wife, six children and Slinky to pursue their own fortunes. ■

> James Industries: Slinky, early box, $50
> James Industries: Slinky Dog, 1950s, $35

**Soldiers, Seal and Handcar.** *James Industries knew it would take more than just Slinky itself to compete in the 1950s. Offerings included the wacky Slinky Eyes. Life magazine, Nov. 11, 1957.*

**Slinking along.** *Wire-spring connections between body parts gave charming realism to this multiwheeled Mr. Wiggle's Cata-Puller. Wilkening, the manufacturer of Mr. Wiggle toys, was James' main competitor in the 1950s. The company also made Mr. Wiggle's Cowboy and Mr. Wiggle's Leap Frog, among many other toys. Wilkening Mfg. Co., Philadelphia and Toronto, 1950s.*

**Rover or roller?** *The Slinky Dog was one of the most charming of Boomer toys, and, with its wagging, springy tail, probably the friendliest. Pairs of wheels attached to the feet allowed the dog to roll forward. The short Slinky in between the front and back halves helped the latter catch up with the former. Although the company would later claim the dog never had a name, it was called Tommy, the Slinky Pup, in at least one 1955 advertisement. The Slinky worm was named Suzie, and the Slinky train, Loco. James Industries, 1950s.*

# HOWDY DOODY
## PUPPETS

### TV'S HAPPIEST FACE.

Howdy Doody introduced many children to puppet theater, which they could then experiment with themselves with the aid of toys such as this hand puppet from the 1950s. While Howdy Doody marionettes were widely available, most kids in the '50s played with less expensive toys, or simply collected books, comics, or premiums off bread packages. Howdy Doody hand puppet, marked "Bob Smith," 1950s.

Puppet maker Velma Dawson, who had worked for Walt Disney, created the new marionette based on drawings submitted to Smith by Disney artists. The new Howdy was a 10-year-old boy dressed in cowboy hat, boots, flannel shirt, blue jeans and Western neckerchief. Bob Smith changed Howdy's voice slightly to match the new less doltish look, while puppeteer Rhoda Mann brought the figure to kid-mesmerizing life.

THE MOST famous TV marionette star was born on radio, on WEAF's "Triple B Ranch," broadcast from Buffalo, New York. The show featured Big Brother Bob Smith, and a character named Elmer. Elmer was a dunce-hatted hick with a "hyuck-hyuck" laugh, forever fond of saying "Howdy Doody!" Elmer's name proved to be a slippery one. Kids were soon asking who this "Howdy Doody" was.

The name change took place, presaging other changes. The radio star turned into a TV star in 1948, becoming a marionette with an ungainly, doltish appearance. Then the sudden need for a wholly new marionette—brought about by a disagreement over money and ownership—forced the situation. Howdy Doody changed again, becoming the affable, freckle-faced figure that came to be known to millions as Howdy Doody.

Many elements besides Howdy himself contributed to the success of the *Howdy Doody Show*. Tantrum-throwing Clarabell the Clown, played by Bob Keeshan, certainly helped. Fellow puppet characters including Flubadub and Phineas T. Bluster added more than just wooden dimensions. Human characters helped, too, including Bill Lecornec's Chief Thunderthud, who gave the Boomers, not to mention a later generation, the nonsense cry, "Kowabonga!" When Judy Tyler took over the role of Princess Summerfall Winterspring from a puppet predecessor, she added an energy of an entirely different kind. Now even Dad watched.

The main responsibility for the show's success, however, rested with Bob Smith, a musician with a talent not only for voices but for sales, too. He could sell kids on the existence of a

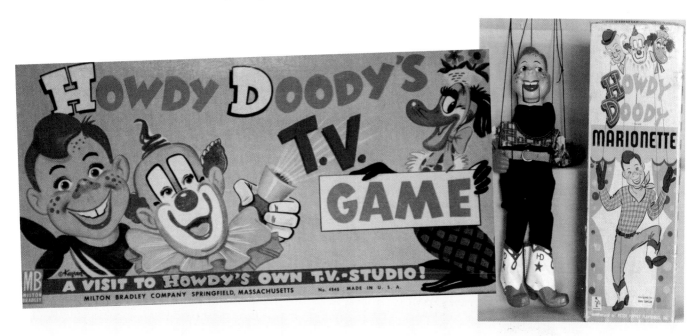

marionette named Howdy. He could sell them on a whole cast of Doodyville regulars, half wooden, half flesh.

He could sell them on anything, in fact, as he learned when the dragon-like hodgepodge named Flubadub made its first appearance and declared its diet to be flowers. It ate nothing else. Upset mothers quickly wrote in. Now their kids were eating flowers. Another change: Flubadub now ate spaghetti and meatballs.

Endorsements from Howdy Doody and Buffalo Bob, as Smith came to be known, could sell anything from toothpaste to shoes to bread. They also sold toys, games, a popular series of Little Golden Books and comic books. Doodyville was a productive little town.

Puppets of various sorts were among the most popular of the toys, for natural reasons, and Peter Puppet Playthings, Inc., was the most successful of the companies making them. Based in Brooklyn, N.Y., the company made the vinyl-headed hand puppets that appeared in mail-order catalogs and five-and-dimes, as well as marionettes, which were more expensive toys for the lucky few. The hand puppets and marionettes were taken over by Pride Products, Inc., of Brooklyn, in

the later 1950s. Tee Vee Toys, Inc., of Leominster, Mass., also considered its Howdy Doody toys to be puppets. Small figures made of hard plastic, they had mouths that could be made to "talk."

The lively and unpredictable show enjoyed enormous success across the country in the early to mid-1950s, then suffered a slow slide from its place at the top of the television pile. Something of the spirit of the show lived on, however, since Howdy Doody puppets, marionettes and painting sets kept appearing on through the next decade, pleasing even the kids born too late to know anything about the puppet. To a lot of us, Howdy Doody was just some smiley, goofy-looking freckled kid. No longer a star on TV, he was still one in the playroom. ■

**Kohner: Howdy Doody Push Puppet, 1950s, wood and plastic, $50**
**Marx: Howdy Doody, play set figure, 60 mm, $35**
**Milton Bradley: Howdy Doody Adventure Game, 1950s, $50**
**Milton Bradley: Howdy Doody's TV Game, 1950s, $50**
**Parker Bros.: Howdy Doody's Own Game, 1949, $45**
**Peter Puppet: Flub-A-Dub, marionette, 1950s, $375**
**Peter Puppet: Howdy Doody, marionette, 1950s, $150**
**Rushton: Zip the Monkey, plush and vinyl, $50**
**Tee-Vee Toys: Howdy Doody figures, 4", $15-$20**

**Zippy, by Rushton.** *The most enduring toy to emerge from Doodyville was based on neither puppet nor human actor, but on Zippy the Chimp. Zippy, a trained chimp originally used in a "blue" act in Louisiana, tended to cause chaos on the Howdy Doody set, thereby becoming greatly beloved by children. Zippy toys were popular from the 1950s well into the 1970s. Rushton specialized in stuffed, plush toys with soft vinyl faces.*

**Push-puppet.** *Howdy Doody puppets took many forms. This Clarabell Clown push-button puppet sways and dances as he plays his xylophone, his motions controlled by the large wooden button beneath the plastic base. Kohner Bros., New York City, middle 1950s.*

**Mr. Bluster and the Princess.** *Miniature marionettes in hard plastic, these toys had one moving part each: the lower jaw, which could be moved by a lever behind the head. The Princess appears here in the puppet form she had before she transformed into a living, breathing person. Tee Vee Toys, Inc., early to mid-1950s.*

# ROBERT THE ROBOT
## THE MECHANICAL MAN

SOMETHING surprisingly different appeared on department store shelves and in store catalog pages in time for Christmas, 1954. His name was Robert.

Robert was 14 inches of gray plastic, with two arms that moved back and forth, flashing eyes and a flashing light at the top of his head. The head was a cube set on squared shoulders, while the body was shaped like an angular bell. Wheels hidden beneath the "skirt" of Robert's body allowed the figure to move when the controls, which looked like a space gun, were used.

He was a robot. Robert knew this about himself, for when the crank turned on his back, his high-pitched voice would say, "I am Robert the Robot, the mechanical man."

Robot toys had been circulating since the late '40s, with the first ones arriving in this country from overseas, especially Japan. Japan was rebuilding its economy in part through the production of inexpensive but attractive tin toys of every variety, much of which sold through American dime stores.

Robert the Robot, however, was made by Ideal Toy Corp., a long-established toy and novelty company with a well-deserved reputation for its dolls. Being made by a major American toy manufacturer meant that Robert benefited from merchandising and sales efforts that foreign-made robot toys never received.

Robert was also made of hard plastic, not metal, even though the surface of his body had bumps, square edges, and seams as though actually made of riveted metal. In the eyes of many, metal, especially tin, was the "old" toy-making material. Plastic was the new one. Not for nothing did Dillon Beck Manufacturing Co. choose plastic for its popular futuristic Coupe in the late '40s, or Mattel for its Modern Dream Car in 1953, or Ideal itself for its own line of small futuristic vehicles.

Plastic was the future. ■

**MECHANICAL MAN OF TOMORROW.**

"This mechanical man of tomorrow moves forward, reverse, left or right, swinging his arms, carrying objects in his hands—all by battery-operated remote control," enthuses one toy catalog over the first toy robot to reach widespread acceptance through department and catalog stores. Ideal, Robert the Robot, 1955 version.

Ideal: Robert the Robot, opening tool box, 1954, $200
Ideal: Robert the Robot, no opening tool box, 1955, $150
Ideal: Robert the Robot, no glassy eyes or antenna, 1956-59, $90
Ideal: King Zor, 1964, $150
Marx: Electric Robot & Son, $500
Marx: Mr. Mercury, $350
Remco: Melvin the Moon Man, 1960s, $75

# BANG, YOU'RE DEAD! ...
# ROY ROGERS CAP GUN

WHEN THE first Boomers started clamoring for toy guns of their very own, they cared exactly nothing that toy cap-firing pistols were an old-fashioned kind of toy. Toys that evoked the Old West had been popular before World War II, with guns of one kind or another always being among the most desirable toys to own.

Even so, the toy cap-gun was entering its glory days when the Boomers arrived on the scene. Those glory days arrived, in part, because of new manufacturing capabilities. High-quality die-casting offered a considerable amount of detail for the metal parts of the gun, making them more attractive than the cast-iron cap-guns common before the war. Nickel and chrome finishes put a new luster on the toys, too. New plastic parts helped their appearance as well, making possible imitation wood, bone or mother-of-pearl grips.

Boomer kids enjoyed any number of distinctive, new toy cap pistols. One of the most successful and most important was the Pony Boy, issued in real-leather holster sets. Esquire Novelty Co., of New York City, began making them just before the end of World War II. It saw enough success that it added Lone Ranger

pistols to its line by 1950 and moved its factory to Jersey City, N.J.

Esquire also emphasized juvenile sports equipment and gradually added to its licensed properties for its toy line: Flash Gordon by 1952; Tonto by 1955; Wyatt Earp, Cheyenne and Rin Tin Tin by 1957; Restless Gun by 1959; and Wells Fargo and Shotgun Slade by 1960.

In the 1960s, the company diversified its toy line and soon was making law-and-order badges, combat toys including toy hand grenades and Daniel Boone accessories including coonskin caps. All the while, however, it held true to the toy it began with. Pony Boy was one of those toys that enjoyed success year after year and which survived well beyond the end of the Boomer years to be a plaything of later generations.

## GOOD-GUY GUNS

Esquire's approach of issuing toy guns named after popular TV Western heroes was shared by the industry as a whole. Bad guys came and went in the TV serials. The good guys, on the other hand, kept coming back week after week, and it was the good guys the new generation of TV-watchers wanted to be. This meant that to succeed in the toy-gun business, the toy maker needed good licenses.

Thus, around 1959-60, Carnell Mfg. Co., Inc., of Brooklyn, N.Y., was making the Bat Masterson cane, gun and holster sets and *Maverick*

**Don't shoot the man, shoot the guns out of his hands!** *Roy Rogers had such aim that he never hurt a soul. A number of die-cast cap-pistol companies made Roy Rogers guns in the 1950s, including Kilgore and Classy Products. This beautiful example was made by George Schmidt around mid-decade. Toy courtesy Ken Boyer.*

**Singing cowboy.** *Roy Rogers was so famous for his singing that guitars bearing his name were still sought by youngsters in the late 1960s. Sears Toys, 1967-68.*

$3.99

Deep . . vibrant tones are created in wood fiber sound chamber

**#18**

pistols. New York City's Academy Die-Casting & Plating Co. was making Buffalo Bill cap pistols, as well as its Big Chief pistols. Daisy Mfg. Co., then of Rogers, Ark., was making the *Cheyenne Singin' Saddle* gun, as well as Walt Disney's *Elfago Baca* holster sets. J. Halpern Co., of Pittsburgh, Pa., made *The Deputy, Gunsmoke, Lawman,* Steve Canyon, *Wells Fargo Pony Express, The Texan* and *Have Gun Will Travel* holsters in its Halco line. R. & S. Toy Mfg. Co., of Brooklyn, N.Y., made Hopalong Cassidy guns and holsters. Leslie-Henry Mfg. Co. made *Maverick, Wagon Train, Texas Ranger, Bonanza* and *Young Buffalo Bill* cap pistol and holster sets. Hubley Mfg. Co., of Lancaster, Pa., made The Rifleman Flip Special repeating cap rifle.

Meanwhile, Withington, a toy company based in West Minot, Maine, was busily issuing Little Beaver archery sets.

It was Classy Products Corp. of Woodside, N.Y., that nabbed the top nice-guy Western hero and heroine pair, for it was making the Roy Rogers and Dale Evans pistol and holster sets.

Unlike most of the other popular Old West figures being celebrated through toy pistols, rifles and holsters, Roy Rogers had a fairly long history in the toy arena. In 1940, just before the war, children could pick up a Roy Rogers cap pistol made by The Kilgore Mfg. Co., of Westerville, Ohio. It took most of a decade for Roy Rogers guns to return to production. By 1950, Classy Products was making Roy Rogers cap pistols. Then, around 1951, Leslie-Henry Co., Inc. was making both Roy Rogers pistols and spur sets. By 1952, it was George Schmidt Mfg. Co. making Roy Rogers guns and spurs, with Classy Products making holsters.

Based in Los Angeles, Calif., Schmidt was one of the growing number of toy companies getting its footing on the West Coast. It established itself around 1950-51 with a line of Buck 'N Bronc guns, holsters and spurs. It also leapt off the starting line with a popular Western name from Paramount Pictures. Alan Ladd and the Circle-A-Bar-L brand from Schmidt appeared on guns, spurs, cuffs and holster sets for those first few years of the '50s.

Roy Rogers toy-gun rights went back to Kilgore, Inc. by 1955, and soon thereafter back to Classy Products, which remained official maker of the Roy Rogers cap pistol through the end of the '50s.

Roy Rogers cap pistols were far more a characteristic of that decade than the one following, although a few did still appear— such as the Roy Rogers Quick Shooter, which Ideal Toy Corp. brought out for the 1961-62 season alongside its Trick Shot Rifle, "the only gun that fires backwards."

The Roy Rogers Quick Shooter was a trick gun, too. All the child had to do was put on his cowboy hat, look toward the villain to be shot and press a button at his side. Out of the crown of the cowboy hat, a derringer popped up and—bang!

## TV FAME

While Roy Rogers' career began in 1938, when Republic Pictures cast him as a last-minute replacement for Gene Autry, Roy and his onscreen family became a part of Boomer history through that generation's usual path to fame: TV.

The man who would become Roy Rogers started a bit earlier—in 1911, in Cincinnati, Ohio, under the name Leonard Franklin Slye. After the family went west to California during the Depression, he started taking music jobs that paid little or nothing. Fame came slowly until his lucky break with Republic.

Movie theater operators ranked Roy Rogers as the top Western box office star from 1943 to 1954. By the end of this unprecedented run, the King of the Cowboys had ridden to the top of Western TV, beginning with *The Roy Rogers Show,* which originally aired 1951 through 1957. He returned for *The Roy Rogers and Dale Evans Show,* originally airing 1962 to 1963. He lent his name to restaurants, issued popular recordings and opened a Roy Rogers museum in Apple Valley, Calif.

Most importantly, he hired a man named Art Rush to be his agent. Rush was the man who made the childhood West what it was for millions of kids. He put together the contract that gave Roy and Dale full rights to their own names, voices and likenesses for all commercial tie-ins.

Did this matter? Did it ever! Companies rushed to produce Roy Rogers, Trigger and Dale Evans neckerchiefs, toy pistols, clothing, jewelry, games, novels and song books. The contract probably made Rogers and Evans a little more willing to go along with it all.

Rogers' picture appeared on 2.5 million Post cereal boxes and on the cover of 25 million comic books per year. Mutual Network's radio broadcasts attracted 20 million listeners a week, while the Roy Rogers comics in newspapers reached more than three times that many fans. One year, Sears advertised more than 400 licensed Roy Rogers items for eager buyers scattered across America.

Rogers ranked second only to Walt Disney for the number of promotional tie-in items produced and sold. How did he do this? Just by playing himself. Playing himself after he became Roy Rogers, that is. He legally changed his name to his screen name in 1942.

The Roy Rogers he played was consistently the easygoing, good-looking, good-singing, good gun-slinging Good Guy. And everyone thought: Good.

The other Good Guy TV cowboy of the times likewise had his start well before the war. Hopalong Cassidy was the invention of Clarence Mulford, who published his first Hopalong story in *Outing* magazine in 1906. Mulford followed it with dozens more stories and then novels about Hoppy (whose limp earned him his name) and Hoppy's Bar 20 Ranch.

Hoppy cussed, smoked, chewed tobacco, drank whiskey and played cards. It might come as small surprise, then, to learn that Mulford cared little for the version that sprang to life on the silver screen. "Ludicrous," he said.

Hollywood remade Hopalong just as it had remade so many other literary creations—with the help of William Boyd, who made a remarkable number of Hopalong Cassidy movies in the 1930s and '40s—66 in all, with the last appearing in 1948.

Boyd's Hopalong became a true Boomer figure the following year when he hit the nation with not only a radio show but an NBC TV show, starting in June of 1949 and continuing through 1954.

The annual *Toy Fair* catalog advertised a great many popular items in 1951, including Monopoly ("Advertised in *Life*"), dish sets by Banner ("Advertised in *Life*"), Doepke's Heiliner Scraper ("Advertised in *Life*") and the Schoenhut Baby Grand Piano ("with 18 true-pitch keys ... As advertised in *Life*.")

Then it announced a set of puzzles. "Hard riding, fast-shootin' Hoppy fans, produce your own color TV show! Assemble these four puzzles and insert them into the realistic television screen. Watch Hoppy and Topper come alive in hard-hittin' action-packed scenes!" They were just puzzles, but they were called "Hopalong Cassidy Television." A television toy meant Hoppy had firmly arrived. ■

**Aladdin:** Hopalong Cassidy lunch box, 1952, $250
**Automatic Toy Co.:** Hopalong Cassidy Automatic Television Set, $100
**Hartland:** Roy Rogers plastic figure, walking, MIB, $250
**Ideal:** Roy Rogers Fix-It Stage Coach, with box, '50s, $125
**Marx:** Roy Rogers Double R Bar Ranch, #3989 play set, $300
**Marx:** play set figure, Bullet, $10
**Marx:** play set figure, Dale Evans, 60 mm, $10
**Schmidt:** Hopalong Cassidy Buck 'N Bronc Cap Gun, $250
**Schmidt:** Roy Rogers Gun & Holster Set, $500
**Whitman:** Gene Autry coloring book, 1950, $65

*Fanner 50, Mattel, 1950s and later.*

**Not too hard, not too easy.** Whitman made puzzles "for boys and girls who want REAL puzzles." Roy Rogers Jr. Jigsaw Puzzle, Whitman, 1950s.

**Two TV faithfuls.** Dale Evans and Bullet, 60 mm cream-colored plastic figures. Marx, 1950s. Courtesy Ken Boyer.

**In the face of overwhelming odds, run!** ABC-TV ran its spoof Western, Maverick, from 1957-62, featuring James Garner and Jack Kelly as Bret and Bart Maverick. The Maverick brothers found tongue-in-cheek trouble in such Old West towns as Apocalypse and Oblivion. Vinyl wallet, 1950s, and Hopalong Cassidy cap gun, 1950s.

# MARX'S MODERN FARM

AFTER WORLD WAR II, Louis Marx & Co., while not quite resting on its laurels, took the stance of the time-tested and firm-footed Old Man of the industry. The toy-making giant went about its business of making toys, eschewing the new ways of massive promotional budgets and kid-oriented television advertising. It had risen to the top of the heap on the strength of its excellent toy making, and it thought it would stay there.

To a degree, Marx was right. It could succeed without advertising—partly because of the excellence of the play sets it issued in the Boomer years. Many were offered through mail-order outfits, whose catalogs gave them all the advertising necessary.

These were wonderful playthings, typically featuring a tin building, a host of figures in various poses, some animals and a miscellany of small objects—such as the hoes, rakes, feed bins and milking stools in the farm sets.

Marx's farm play sets proved reliable sellers for the company and solid sources of entertainment for children through the 1950s, '60s, and early '70s. Sears and Wards catalogs regularly presented full pages showcasing these model farms. They were among the most attractive toys of the time, incorporating enough different elements to keep any child happy and enough detail to stimulate hours of serious daydreaming.

The barns usually had two stories, with the roof cut away to allow play on the second story. The tin walls were lithographed inside and out. Sometimes even the undersides of floors were lithographed, as was the case with the later raised-foundation barns.

These, the largest of Marx's barns, first appeared at the tail end of the 1950s and were offered as part of the Giant Happi-Time Farm Set, among others, through the '60s. The "stone" lower level gave room to house the dairy herd, while the uppermost hayloft could be filled using the block-and-tackle extended from one end of the roof. The silos and chicken coops were also made of tin.

The true fun came from those multitudinous little parts, some of hard plastic, some of soft. The minuscule implements included shovels, hay forks, saws, lanterns and fire extinguishers. Buckets, milk cans, milking stools, feed sacks, troughs and fences added to the realism. Various vehicles came with the sets—sometimes trucks and cars, sometimes grain elevators, but always the farm tractor, with a selection of heavy equipment to haul behind. Farm hands were seen tossing hay, carrying feed sacks or hoeing the garden. One molded-in farmer sat on the tractor, while others could be placed on the trailers to ride along.

**Top breeds only need apply.** *Marx issued a special set of Prized Livestock as farm play-set accessories. Solid plastic and carefully detailed, they rank among the best plastic figures of the 1960s. Clydesdale, 3-½" long, Louis Marx Co., 1960s.*

**The country charm of the farm.** *No doubt far more Boomer kids visited the tiny world of Marx farm play sets than ever set foot on real, working farms. The play sets included plastic farm hands, tractors, feed sacks, milk cans, tools and animals of every domestic variety. Louis Marx Co., 1960s.*

Most importantly, the sets had marvelously modeled, solid-plastic farm animals: roosters, chickens, chicks, pigs, piglets, goats, sheep, cattle, calves, horses, colts and a Lassie-type dog. For those lucky miniature farmers who had parents willing to shell out the extra 98 cents, there was the Prize Livestock assortment. The prized set included 10 solid-plastic, carefully detailed animals based on favored farming breeds, measuring from 1-¾ inches to 3 inches high.

Also offered were a hay wagon pulled by horses, a combine, a milk truck, a crop-duster airplane, even a working irrigation system. At least one set issued in 1973 and played with by late Boomers had not only irrigation but a supply of dried pellets that burst into green, growing crops after a little watering.

Different sets through the years offered different accessories. All, however, offered a breath of the calm, quiet countryside that seemed increasingly distant as Boomer toys moved deeper into the Space Age. ◼

> Marx: Farm Set, No. 3948, 1958, $250
> Marx: Farm Set, No. 3953, 1969, $225
> Marx: Modern Farm Set, 1951, $150
> Marx: Modern Farm Set, 1967, $185

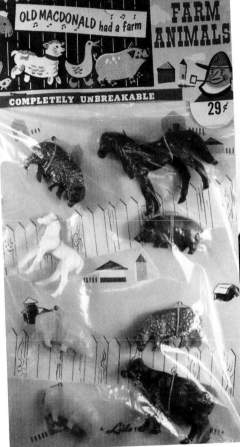

**Plastic tractor.** *Ideal, early 1950s.*

**Farm animals.** *Lido, 1960s.*

# SANDBOX WORKHORSES
# TONKA TRUCKS

**I**N THE YEARS immediately after World War II, countless companies sprang into existence in odd places. Pipco, for instance, started in a house basement. Mattel started in a house garage. Tonka started in a schoolhouse basement in a suburb of Minneapolis with the humblest of names: Mound.

Lynn Baker, Avery Crounse and Alvin Tesch founded Mound Metalcraft Co. to make store display racks and garden furniture. They may have enjoyed some success at this, although evidence suggests otherwise. They happened into toy making by accident in their first year. Among the materials purchased from a competitor, they found tooling to make a toy steam shovel out of metal. That tooling planted the notion in their heads that some tough, true-to-life, but reasonably priced truck and construction toys might have a place in their company.

To their surprise, the results of that notion, the Steam Shovel, modified and improved over the original, was a success. So was the other toy also released in 1947, a working model of a Crane and Clam, which measured about 3 inches longer than the 20-inch Shovel. The toys were sturdy and offered a good deal of play value because they worked more or less the way real shovels and cranes did. It came as a surprise, too, that the toys sold faster than Mound's other offerings.

Mound Metalcraft named the toys Tonkas, in honor of nearby Lake Minnetonka. In the next year, 1948, it expanded its toy offerings to include a Lift Truck and Cart. In 1949, Tonkas became a full-fledged line of toys. New entries included the 22-inch Steam Shovel Deluxe, several versions of a machinery hauler bearing Steam Shovel or Crane loads, the Tonka Toy Transport tractor-trailer, a Loading Tractor, a Wrecker Truck, and finally, and perhaps most importantly, a Dump Truck. Thereafter, a year of Tonkas without a Dump Truck was no year at all.

Tonka remained a relatively low-profile player in the toy world during its early years. It was dwarfed by the pressed-metal powerhouses that had established themselves before the war. Marx, with its abundant catalog-store offerings, was the biggest company operating on the East Coast. The rest, like Mound, were Midwestern.

Structo Mfg. Co., was in Freeport, Ill. All Metal Products Co., whose Wyandotte line was also heavily favored by mail-order stores, was in Wyandotte, Mich. Buddy "L" Toys, was based in East Moline, Ill. Mound also saw competition from another Illinois company that was likewise a newcomer: Ny-Lint Tool & Mfg. Co., of Rockford, Ill.

**3.98**

## WIND-UP
# HI-LIFT DUMP TRUCK

Crank 'er up! This is a Hi-Lift. Six rubber wheels . . . adjustable front wheels. Motor brake. Clock spring motor. The real beauty of all dump trucks. 12½ inches long. By Structo. Ask for 28BR3.

## HEILINER SCRAPER As advertised in LIFE

No. 2011. Attention, junior engineers! Here's a multi-duty earth mover crammed with action. Loads quickly and easily . . . carries huge quantities of material over rough ground . . . dumps with a flick of a finger . . . tows other toys or can be towed. An authentic replica of the famous Heiliner Scraper. Ruggedly constructed of heavy steel with big rubber tires.

**$15.95 EACH**  CHAS. WM. DOEPKE MFG. CO.

**Construction leaders.** *In the early Boomer years, before Tonka rose to the top of the pile, such companies as Doepke Model Toys and Structo had greater fame as manufacturers of sturdy construction toys. Doepke Heiliner, 1951 Toy Fair; Structo Dump Truck, Billy & Ruth, 1952.*

By the 1960s, however, most major toy catalogs reflected the fact that Tonka was *the* company to watch. Unlike the Tonkas of the '50s, which were modeled on Ford trucks, the Tonkas of the '60s were more generic and perhaps more broadly appealing for that fact, or perhaps because they were so recognizably Tonkas.

Several innovations early that decade had other pressed-steel companies scrambling to keep up. One, introduced in 1963, was a new line of trucks about 9 inches long, made of the same durable materials as the larger trucks, down to the double layers of real truck paint. Tonka dubbed them Mini-Tonkas, in a playful return to the original inspiration for the line's name, Lake Minnetonka. The fleet of trucks may have been small, but it sold well: Pickup, Stake Truck, Dump Truck, Wrecker and Camper. The next year Tonka added a Grader, Cement Mixer and three semi-trailers featuring a new futuristic cab in the same scale.

In 1964 Structo followed suit, issuing its Kom-Pak trucks—seven trucks based on a generic cab much like the original Mini-Tonkas. Structo's toys might actually have had more immediate play value, since they included a Vista Dome Kennel Truck with plastic dogs, a Vista Dome Livestock Truck and a Fire Rescue Truck with ladders.

Tonka's other challenge to the toy-making world took the form, once again, of a dump truck—an oversize one this time. It was the Mighty Tonka Dump Truck of 1964, with its small, square cab, huge tires and oversize load capacity. Tonka advertised it as usable as a riding toy. It hauled, dumped and carried kids down driveways through the rest of the Boomer years and far beyond. ◼

**Tonka: Carnation Milk Van, 1965, $200**
**Tonka: Dump Truck #180, 12", 1949, $150-$200**
**Tonka: Dump Truck #6, 1960, $85-$90**
**Tonka: Mini-Tonka Cement Mixer, 1964, $45**
**Tonka: Minute Maid Orange Juice truck, 1955, $300**

**Rugged style.** *Dump trucks became the signature vehicle for the toy maker after their introduction in 1949. Service dump truck, 13", Mound Metalcraft, late 1950s.*

THE WALT DISNEY film crews must have welcomed the end of World War II. Finally they could stop producing such wonderful titles as *Weather at War* for the U.S. Navy, or *Ward Care of Psychotic Patients* and *Operation and Maintenance of the Electronic Turbo Supercharger* for the U.S. Army.

To be sure, Disney had kept up production of animated shorts through the war, and immediately afterwards released major films, including *Bambi* in 1946, *Cinderella* and Disney's first live-action feature *Treasure Island* in 1950, *Alice in Wonderland* in 1951, the live-action *The Story of Robin Hood* in 1952 and *Peter Pan* in 1953.

Disney also moved into the new medium of TV. In December 1950, the Coca-Cola Co. sponsored *One Hour in Wonderland* on NBC. The next year, *The Walt Disney Christmas Show* aired on CBS, sponsored by Johnson and Johnson Co. That year, Walt Disney also established Disneyland, Inc., and then, in 1952, Walt Disney, Inc., to develop ideas for a family entertainment park. Things moved quickly enough that ground was broken two years later for the Magic Kingdom of Disneyland.

Even the ground breaking had its TV connections. The ABC TV network had invested considerably and had guaranteed an even larger loan to help build Disneyland. In return, ABC received a share of Disneyland and a commitment for a weekly Walt Disney TV show. The first one-hour weekly, *Disneyland*, made its debut on ABC only months after the ground breaking in October 1954. That show, under various names, went on to become the longest-lived prime-time series in network history.

Disneyland itself opened in July of 1955, with more than 28,000 people attending. The next month, in Fantasyland, the Mickey Mouse Club Theater opened, followed in October by Disney's second ABC TV show, *The Mickey Mouse Club*.

In addition to bringing children the cartoons of their parents' childhoods, the daily show featured such live-action serials as *The Adventures of Spin and Marty* and *Annette*—and, best of all, the talents of the Mouseketeers, a group of ebullient, always-cheerful, always-on-the-go adolescents who made all of us look bad and feel good about it.

The show, as it happened, permanently changed the world of toys. Mattel, only 10 years old in 1955, made the unprecedented move of committing itself to a full year's worth of advertising on the new *Mickey Mouse Club* TV show. Never before had toys been advertised on a year-round basis.

Mattel had made its name with various noise-making and musical toys, including the Uke-A-Doodle, which was a child-size ukulele, and hand-cranked music boxes. In 1955 the company had a major hit with its Burp Gun, a kind of automatic cap gun. With its new sponsorship of the Disney daily show, it

**The three-fingered hand.** *Mickey Mouse hand puppet, 1960s.*

introduced a new musical toy which was in no way revolutionary in its underlying nature, but which still became a hit for the company: the Official Mousegetar, bright red and featuring Mickey's smiling face.

"Just like Jimmy Dodd's," Mattel promised the young members of America's largest kid's club. "Plays real music—Big Mouse size ... Jimmy Dodd's musical instructions enable youngsters to actually learn to play!" Learn to play what? *Mickey Mouse Club* songs, naturally.

The Mousegetar Jr. followed soon thereafter. Mattel and other companies released a variety of *Mickey Mouse Club* toys in the following years, the most notable of them film-related toys, many of them made by Stephens Products, Inc., of Middletown, Conn., including the *Mickey Mouse Club* Projector and Theater

with 12 films, and the *Mickey Mouse Club* News-reel, which added sound.

Other toys in the last few years of the 1950s included the Mickey Mouse Club Magic Arithmetic Series, which were electronic quiz games by Jacmar Mfg. Co., Inc., of New York City, and the Hasbro Pencil Craft Set, a colored pencil set with six cards with "pre-sketched pictures of *Mickey Mouse Club* Walt Disney characters."

There were abundant ways of role-playing Mouseketeers, too. Besides the hand puppets and marionettes from Pride Products, there were *Mickey Mouse Club* Mousketeer play suits from Herman Iskin & Co., Inc., of Telford, Pa. There were masquerade costumes and masks from Ben Cooper, Inc., of Brooklyn. There were Mickey Mouse and Donald Duck hats

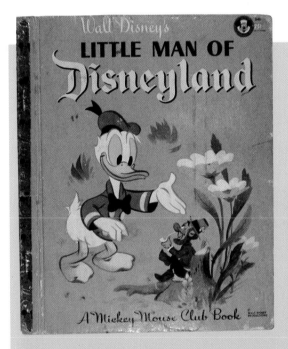

**Official Mickey Mouse Club Book.** *Golden Books and their imitators provided much of the earliest reading for the Boomer generation. Walt Disney's Little Man of Disneyland showed the Disney animated gang hard at work building the theme park. In this book, the last Leprechaun in California, on whose land the park is being built, doesn't recognize the Disney characters and asks who they are. "Who are we?" replies the astonished Donald Duck. "Don't you go to the movies? Don't you watch TV?" Simon and Schuster, 1955.*

**On the verge of TV stardom.** *The Disney cast of animated characters, enormously popular before the war, reached ever more audiences in the postwar years through TV. The medium introduced a new generation to prewar Disney animated films. Well into the early Boomer years new Disney toys closely resembled their prewar predecessors. Walt Disney tray, J. Chein & Co., 1950s.*

**Mouseketeers.** *Mickey Mouse's constant presence on TV made it seem the famous animated character had not retired from films. Mickey Mouse Club costume, nylon, 1950s.*

# 21

from Benay-Albee Novelty Co., of Maspeth, N.Y. And there were, of course, Mousketeer hats, from New York City's Welded Plastics Corp., also makers of Disneyland construction sets and a *Mickey Mouse Club* clubhouse.

One of the most appropriate items to appear was a piece of juvenile furniture manufactured by Himalayan Pak Co., of Los Angeles: The *Mickey Mouse TV Chair*. While the Mickey Mouse phenomenon had been a movie theater experience in the 1930s and '40s, in the 1950s it was all about TV.

After the cancellation of the show in 1959, Disney toys were more likely to promote the Disneyland name over the *"Mickey Mouse Club"* name, or to promote the characters who were stars of the current Disney shorts—Pluto, Goofy and especially Donald Duck. Even so, later Boomers saw the endless reruns in syndication, so that the early 1960s Boomers grew up feeling they knew, in a somehow intimate way, the club members: Jimmy Dodd, Roy Williams, and the Mouseketeers Annette Funicello, Darlene Gillespie, Cubby O'Brien, Karen Pendleton, Bobby Burgess, Doreen Tracy, Sharon Baird and Cheryl Holdridge.

And what of Mickey himself? Mickey Mouse had made his last new film appearance of the Boomer years in 1953, in *The Simple Things*. Reruns of older films on TV, and perhaps the re-releases of *Fantasia* in 1956 and 1963, made it seem the Mouse had not so thoroughly changed from Disney Studios film star to Disneyland Spokesmouse.

Yet he had. If he was a force in the lives of Boomers, it was not in the same way as he was in the lives of their parents. He left the center stage for others: Donald, Alice, Robin Hood, Annette, Peter Pan, Davy Crockett, Old Yeller, Mary Poppins …. It took a great many to fill his place. But there were a lot of them, and they did. ◼

**Aladdin: Disney School Bus Dome, 1968, $70**
**Aladdin: Disneyland Monorail lunch box, 1968, $250**
**Aladdin: Mickey Mouse Club lunch box, 1963, $150**
**Connecticut Leather: Mouseketeer Handbag, $50**
**Hasbro: Mickey Mouse Club pencil case, 1950s, $35**
**Jaymar: Mickey Mouse Lotto Game, 1950s, $15**
**Marx: Walt Disney's Television Car, tin-litho, $450**
**Mattel: Mousegetar Jr., 1950s, $125**
**Parker Bros. : Disney Mouseketeer Game, 1964, $50-$60**
**Parker Bros. : Mary Poppins Carousel Game, 1964, $30**
**Transogram : Disneyland Game, 1965, $25**

**Never say "Grow Up."** *Many toys played off the popularity of postwar Disney movies, including the Walt Disney's Peter Pan game. Transogram, 1952.*

# THE GAME OF
# COOTIE

**M**ANY WHO rattle off a list of their favorite toys start with games. For perfectly good reasons, too. Especially in the TV age, kids tended to spend a lot of time fussing over how they wanted a toy, how they *needed* it, how they *had* to have it because, look, it is so much fun there in the TV ad on my favorite show that I really really *got* to have it please, please, *please*, Mom! Then they had it in their hands, found it not much fun and went back to another game of Monopoly.

Children may have loved their nongame toys more than their game toys and may have invested more imagination time in them. Even so, they usually spent more hours of play time at games with friends or family and sometimes even alone.

Cootie was one such game. It appeared at the same time as the Boomers, having its first commercial appearance in 1949, and lasted through the Boomer years in essentially unchanged form.

As a game, Cootie was simplicity itself: you tossed the die, hoping to be the first to piece together your Cootie bug. The bug itself was a thing of beauty to many kids and probably to many adults, too. Made of shiny hard plastic, it consisted of a beehive-like body, six bent legs, antennae, eyes and, best of all, a coiled proboscis.

The plastic insect would later become an icon. For some, the leggy thing became a symbol for the Boomer generation.

Herb Schaper, Cootie's inventor, ran a shop selling wood toys he carved himself. He also fished, as to be expected of an Upper Midwesterner. One day in 1948, he realized that a fishing lure he was carving had turned into an attractive bug. Within a year his Minnesota company, which he named after himself, became a contender in the national toy stakes.

I have friends who contend that Cootie was one of those games you never actually played. You simply put together the pieces and played with the toy. Yet I find foggy memories emerging, as I think of the game ... memories of worrying over the results of the die.

I have no memories of triumphantly completing my Cootie bug first and winning the game. But I do remember the dire frustration I felt watching brother, sister or parent finishing theirs first. And *I* was the one into bugs. ■

> Schaper: Cootie, single Cootie on box, $15-$25
> Schaper: Don't Spill the Beans, 1967, $15

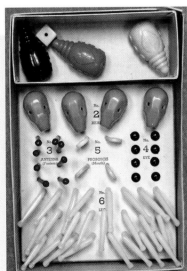

**The best of all possible bugs.** *The early box, with its remarkably homely example of 1940s-'50s graphics, was used for more years than it probably should have been. The Cootie itself remained much the same for most of the Boomer years: buggy, in the extreme. In the late '60s, Sears offered an exclusive Cootie House, featuring a vinyl mat and enough parts for eight Cooties. W.H. Schaper Mfg. Co., Inc., Minneapolis, Minn., 1950s.*

**The Cootie assembly plant.** *Interior of a box, with the Cootie parts in their early arrangement. Schaper, 1950s.*

**Oddball game empire.** *Schaper's many game creations through the Boomer years included Ants in the Pants, Don't Spill the Beans, Don't Break the Ice, and the popular Ticklebee. Skunk, Schaper, 1950s-'60s.*

"ALUMINUM CHRISTMAS TREE SALES WILL CONTINUE TO INCREASE IN 1961, ACCORDING TO NEARLY 80 PERCENT OF THE RETAIL STORE BUYERS INTERVIEWED .... OF THOSE SAMPLED, REPRESENTING STORES IN BOTH URBAN AND SUBURBAN COMMUNITIES, 96.7 PER CENT SOLD ALUMINUM CHRISTMAS TREES IN 1960. OF THAT GROUP, 85.5 PERCENT SAID THEIR SALES WERE GREATER IN 1960 THAN IN 1959."

—*PLAYTHINGS MAGAZINE*, REPORTING IN 1961 ON AN ESTIMATE THAT KAISER ALUMINUM EXPECTED SALES OF 3.5 MILLION ALUMINUM CHRISTMAS TREES THAT YEAR.

# Flip Your Wig! More Fab Sixties Hits

The 1960s promised to be a decade of new toys and new materials. The plastics used by the toy industry at the beginning of the Boomer years had proved good, but not good enough. Too many toys made of those plastics warped when left next to a heating register ... or they faded in the sun ... or they cracked and shattered—even the "unbreakable" ones. Toy manufacturers kept forging ahead.

Christmas itself had been given a brilliant new look in the late '50s, with the advent of aluminum Christmas trees. And the plastic called polyethylene promised to be everything toy makers needed: it was softer and more durable than the old plastic and strong enough to be used in larger toys.

As the 1950s changed over to the '60s, Eldon Industries changed the look of the sandbox play area with its large plastic trucks, beginning the long, slow downslide of the traditional metal toy truck. Companies that made spring horses and shooflies, such as Tremax Industries, of New York City, were converting to polyethylene in droves. Tremax remade its entire line in "poly" by 1961. The new Tremax Palominos could withstand the force of a sledgehammer blow and would not be damaged during shipment. Makers of children's furniture were making the same changeover. Hard plastic toy cars gave way to soft plastic ones. And the rubber toy seemed almost a thing of the past, given the enthusiasm the toy industry was demonstrating for vinyl.

"Tuff to break," as Mattel said of its plastic-head dolls ... the 1960s equivalent of the "Can't Break 'Em" claim for the Sol D. Hoffman dolls of extra-hard composition made in America in the 1890s. The American toy industry had been searching for the perfect toy-making material for most of a century. In polyethylene, it thought it had found it—again.

# THE BEATLES
# FLIP YOUR WIG GAME

I N 1964, Milton Bradley Co., of Springfield, Mass., stood firmly on a foundation of basic playthings: finger paints, puzzles, crayons and pre-school and teaching-aid toys. It also remained true to its original emphasis on games, but with a new twist.

It was now banking heavily on TV-related games. It had a new game based on *The Beverly Hillbillies*, competing against a game based on the same TV show from Standard Toykraft, Inc., in Brooklyn, N.Y. Bradley also had games based on other popular shows: *Password*, *Get the Message*, *The Price Is Right*, *Let's Make a Deal*, *You Don't Say!* and *The Match Game*. For those who failed to get the message, Bradley released a game with the wonderfully fitting name of Boob Tube Race.

Bradley also took the step that was looking increasingly sensible to toy companies. It fully underwrote a new game show making its debut on ABC Network TV in September 1964. The show was *Shenanigans*, with movie and Broadway star Stubby Kaye as M.C. So a leading item for that season was, naturally, the Shenanigans Game.

Part of the reason the company was doing so well in the 1960s was its shrewd use of TV airtime—and TV personalities. Hugh Downs and Steve Allen were on-air personalities whose voices were trusted in American households when they appeared in static-lined, mesmerizing black-and-white ...

And when Downs and Allen talked up Milton Bradley games during televised advertising spots, the country truly seemed to listen. The company's standard line did exceedingly well: Uncle Wiggly, Park and Shop, The Game of Life, Go to the Head of the Class, Easy Money, Video Village, Candy Land, Strategy, The Happy Little Train Game, Racko, and Chutes and Ladders, among others.

Milton Bradley also released its main entry in the race to make the loudest, bang-powiest game in a competitive scene full of loud, bang-pow games: "tic ... tic ... TIME BOMB!" And for those who didn't get *this* message, Bradley had POW, the Cannon Game and WOW Pillow Fight Game.

A time bomb was set to go off in real life, too, in 1964, and it did so, with explosive brilliance, on the live-broadcast TV stage

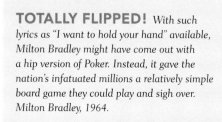

**TOTALLY FLIPPED!** *With such lyrics as "I want to hold your hand" available, Milton Bradley might have come out with a hip version of Poker. Instead, it gave the nation's infatuated millions a relatively simple board game they could play and sigh over. Milton Bradley, 1964.*

so admirably and genially hosted by Ed Sullivan. It was the year the first Fab Four song entered the U.S. singles charts at number 35, just 10 days after its release.

"I Want To Hold Your Hand" was the fastest-breaking, fastest-selling record in the history of Capitol Records. The Beatles immediately became a major force in making kids throw aside their childhood games and toys, in a rash rush to grow up—in a Mod way. Toy companies did try to hold onto these grown-up yearning kids, though. Beatles toys took a place of importance in their lists through the remainder of the '60s.

The first wave was a wonderfully varied one. As to be expected, there were suddenly Beatles guitars, bongos and drums. They were made by Mastro Industries, Inc., a musical-toy specialist based in the Bronx. There were Beatles skateboards for the country's rock-and-roll-loving hotdoggers and gremmies, from Surf Skater Co., Inc., of Del Mar, Calif. There were Beatles bags and wallets from Standard Plastic Products, Inc., of South Plainfield, N.J. There were Beatles balloons from United Industries, Inc., of Philadelphia. There were Beatles coloring books from The Saalfield Publishing Co., of Akron, Ohio. There were Beatles costumes from Ben Cooper, Inc., of Brooklyn; Beatles dolls from Remco Industries, Inc., of Harrison, N.J.; and Beatles model kits from Revell, Inc., of Venice, Calif.

From New York to California ... it was as though the whole country had joined in celebrating the mop-topped, fab foursome. Milton Bradley lost no time in working up its own entry, The Beatles Flip Your Wig Game, in 1964. "Lots of swingin' action as you gain, lose, trade cards," said one advertisement. "For two to four players, 7-14 years, who like the 'yeah, yeah' fun of the Beatles."

Despite the hype, the game was a typical, fairly sedate board game. The pieces went around in a circle. The cards in the center determined the progress of each player. The magic was in the set of game pieces, which were nothing more—and needed be no more—than color photographs of the young Beatles themselves, mounted on cardboard and held up by little holders of the sort found in the games Go to the Head of the Class, Alfred Hitchcock Why, and Cheyenne.

There was magic, too, in the role-playing to be found in the game. Each player could choose a piece that represented an individual player: John, Paul, George or Ringo. Each player had to accumulate the cards that matched the character: a portrait, a signature, a hit record and a musical instrument. Of course, only four could play. Four kids hanging out together, with no one else allowed? It sounded like a clique ... or like The Beatles. ■

Beatles record-shaped gumball charms, set of four, $30
Milton Bradley: Beatles Flip Your Wig Game, $125
Remco: Beatles dolls, each, $150

## ELVIS PRESLEY

The Beatles were not the only musical phenomenon to rise into the toy empyrean. Early Boomers were thrilled by the ukulele-playing of Arthur Godfrey, and many rushed to buy their Arthur Godfrey Uke Players, made by New York City's musical toy company Emenee Industries, Inc.

The popularity of Elvis Presley, too, was felt in the toy world. Rushed to market in early 1957 was an authorized Elvis Presley doll made by Acme Merchandise Co., Inc. Alongside Acme was another New York City company, Magnet Hat & Cap Corp., which made Elvis Presley numbers to hang beside its Mickey Mouse hats.

**Meanies Invade Pepperland.** *Only a few years after their bright-eyed, youthful beginnings, the Beatles introduced the world to psychedelia. The Beatles Yellow Submarine Picture Puzzle, Jaymar Specialty Co., New York City, 1968.*

# INTO THE BAT SUIT
# BATMAN!

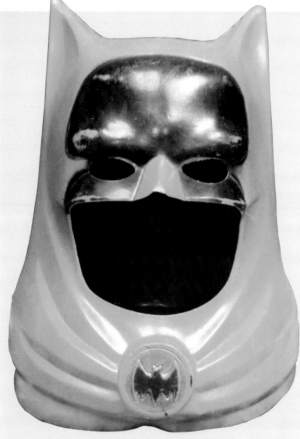

## HOLY HELMET, BATMAN!

With the ultimate costume for 1966, kids turned instantly into caped crusaders. Unlike most costumes, the plastic helmet saw use beyond Halloween. Although Batman started in detective comics, he became an increasingly action-oriented hero in the 1960s. Kids play-acted the action hero more than they did the isolated, ratiocinative genius. Ideal Toy Corp., 1966.

**Masked heroes.** *Masked crime-fighters were popular choices for boys at Halloween throughout the Boomer period. Batman and Zorro, Sears Toys, 1967-68.*

Batman had lingered around the edges of America's popular consciousness since his introduction in *Detective Comics* a few years before the war. He started appearing in a comic book series of his own and on the *Superman* radio series—and even in 1940s movie serials.

While he remained a popular figure among young comic book readers, his character excited relatively few toy manufacturers into producing Batman toys. In 1965, for instance, no one had taken out a license for any high-profile Batman toys.

Then something happened to bring him front and center in 1966. In other words: "Holy hit TV show, Batman!" Suddenly kids—probably mostly boys, although I have no hard and fast data to this effect—were whipping around in bed-sheet capes and dreaming about having on their heads that Batman hood with those perky bat ears.

From its first airing on January 12, 1966, *Batman* created a sensation. It starred Adam West as Bruce Wayne, who secretly was The Caped Crusader, and Burt Ward as Wayne's ward Dick Grayson, The Boy Wonder. The two were tended by loyal family butler Alfred Pennyworth, played by Alan Napier, and Aunt Harriet Cooper, played by Madge Blake. For comic foils, Batman had Police Commissioner Gordon and Chief O'Hara, played by Neil Hamilton and Stafford Repp. In its second and last year, the Dynamic Duo were joined by Batgirl, played by Yvonne Craig.

The show's success was short-lived but intense. The campy action, plots and dialogue were neatly balanced by straight-faced portrayals by the actors. At the same time, in direct reference to Batman's comic book origins, vibrant graphics of BIFF!, BAM!, and POW! filled the full frame of the television screen, giving the show visual novelty.

The villains added another magic touch. Extravagant and well over the top, Gotham City's foes enthralled even the youngest set, who had no idea what acting talents hid behind the masks and face paint. Burgess Meredith played the deviously dapper Penguin, Cesar Romero the singularly sinister Joker, and Frank Gorshin and later John Astin, the twisted Riddler. Vincent Price was the memorably egg-xactly right Egghead, and Victor Buono, the majesterial King Tut.

Best of all, the trio of Julie Newmar, Lee Ann Meriwether and Eartha Kitt at various times played the Catwoman, the ultimate femme fatale for a million breathless boys.

The toys, practically nonexistent in 1965, poured out of the major toy companies in 1966. Ben Cooper, Inc., made playsuits, and Hassenfeld Bros., Inc., issued games. Aurora Plastics put out a Batman model. Miscellaneous playthings issued from other major players: Milton Bradley, Marx and Mattel were among them. So were Multiple Products, Inc., of Bronx, N.Y.; New York City's Pressman Toy Corp. and Transogram Co., Inc.; Standard Plastic Products, Inc., of South Plainfield, N.J., and Whitman Publishing Co., of Racine, Wis.

By 1967, the array of toys was astonishing. While the full range may never be documented, they included everything from the expected activity and coloring books, card games and puzzles, issued by Whitman, to such wonders as the Batscope dart launcher from Sidney A. Tarrson Co., Inc., of Chicago.

Worcester Toy Co. of Worcester, Mass., issued Batman action toys. Transogram created a Batman bank, a Batman flying toy and, best of all, the Batmobile riding toy. Multiple toymakers issued an inflatable Batman bop bag. Chicago's Brunswick Sports Co. manufactured Batman roller skates. And Standard Plastic Products created Batman school bags and Batman wallets so kids would feel Gotham City's protective presence even at school.

The list of companies jumping on the Batman bandwagon was surprising, for it quickly grew to twice the number of companies holding licenses for other high-profile characters that same year. Only half as many companies were making Superman, Winnie-the-Pooh or The Lone Ranger toys. In other words ... "Dada-dada-dada-dada, dada-dada-dada-dada, *Batman!*" ■

**Ben Cooper: Batman Halloween Costume, 1965, $25**
**Hasbro: Batman and Robin Game, 1965, $50**
**Ideal: Batman hand puppet, $45**
**Ideal: Batman Helmet and Cape Set, 1966, $150**

**Finger-controlled crime fighter.** *In addition to head-sized cowls, Ideal made hand-sized ones, too. Hand puppet heads were easily and cheaply made with one of the favorite materials of postwar toy manufacturers, the rubber-like vinyl. Ideal sold these 11"-tall hand puppets in sets with one Batman and one Superman, and also as part of a "Batman Puppet Theater." Ideal Toy Corp., 1966.*

**Dropping from the Batplane.**

**I**T WAS inevitable. Since TV thrived on extravaganza, action, and conflict, the sports that involved the most physical contest thrived in that medium, especially wrestling and boxing. Famed conductor Arturo Toscanini was reportedly a great fan of televised wrestling, which he would watch after dinner on his early, small-screen TV.

And since Boomer toy makers responded to the prompting of television, and since they also vied with one another in making the most outrageous games and toys possible, toy versions of violent sports seemed only natural.

The perfect boxing toy for young Boomers arrived in the mid-1960s from Marx, which had finally overcome its nose-in-the-air attitude concerning TV. If any toy was ever made for the medium, it was Rock 'em Sock 'em Robots.

I must have watched less TV than most kids of my generation—in fact, I am fairly certain of the fact—so I don't have the Mr. Machine song running through my mind at odd moments, or any other toy advertising jingle, for that matter. Yet I clearly remember the jousting robots on TV ads, powered by two young "managers." The expected

denouement occurs, and the voice-over announces: "He *knocked* his *block* off!"

It may not have happened exactly that way. Those may not be the exact words. Whatever they were, the Rock 'em Sock 'ems packed a heady punch on black-and-white and color sets everywhere.

Were they as fun to play with as to *imagine* playing with? I suppose it depended on the kid. The controls gave limited control over the robots, who could move back and forth over only a small area. The battling fists were great fun, however. And the left punch that made the opponent's head spring up, with a nice ratchety sound, was strangely satisfying.

When Marx introduced the toy in 1964, it predicted the "world's only boxing robots" would be one of the most talked-about toys of the year. Since it was busily trying to catch up with other TV-advertising toy companies, Marx spent heavily on TV spots that year. That made it something of a self-fulfilled prophecy. Millions of kids had it ringing in their heads: "He *knocked* his *block* off!" ■

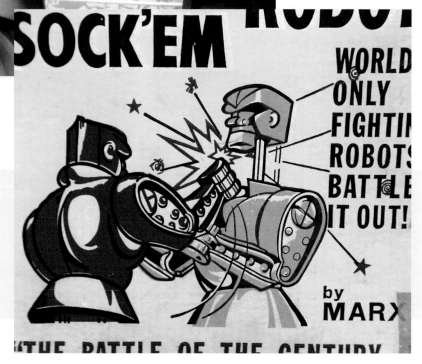

> **Marx: Rock 'em Sock 'em Robots, in good box, $125**

### Rocker Vs. Bomber

*The "rollicking Red Rocker" prize-fighting robot from Soltarus II, fights in the Championship of the Universe against the "beautiful Blue Bomber, pride of Umgluck." The star-traveling robots, according to the box, weighed in at 375 and 382 pounds, respectively. Louis Marx & Co., mid to late 1960s.*

# TWISTER

THE SEDATE and serene Milton Bradley Co., which had started in the 1800s with lithographed building blocks and such card games as Curious Bible Questions, found itself with a second Beatles-era Mod phenomenon on its hands in 1966.

The year before, a man named Reyn Guyer came up with a new party game. Guyer's business was sales promotions, including the development of packaging and store displays. His game had to do with the placement of hands and feet on a large floor mat spotted with different colors.

His name for it? Pretzel. When Milton Bradley bought the game, they renamed it, apparently contrary to Guyer's wishes. Yet the new name Twister was perfect for the Twist-and-Shout times. Milton Bradley advertised it as "the game that ties you up in knots," and "a stockin' feet game." Instead of the usual picture of kids playing, the box featured happy, laughing adults racing to place hands and feet on the colored circles indicated by the spinner, handled by the referee.

At first, it appeared to be yet another ill-fated novelty item of a novelty-filled decade—until the right TV connection was made. Unlike most TV connections for toys and games, however, this one was at a time when kids were either in bed or expected to be there fast asleep.

Johnny Carson introduced the game on *The Tonight Show*. He used it as a prop, bringing it out during the appearance of a sexy Hollywood star on that night's program. Millions of viewers, especially male ones, went to bed that night with the idea dancing through their heads of twisting and contorting ... with Eva Gabor.

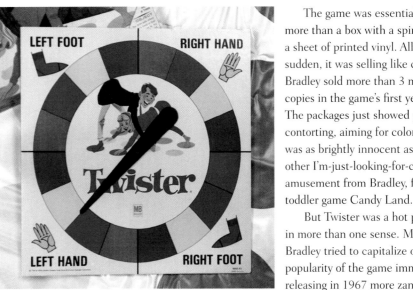

The game was essentially no more than a box with a spinner and a sheet of printed vinyl. All of the sudden, it was selling like crazy. Bradley sold more than 3 million copies in the game's first year. The packages just showed people contorting, aiming for colors. It was as brightly innocent as that other I'm-just-looking-for-colors amusement from Bradley, famous toddler game Candy Land.

But Twister was a hot property in more than one sense. Milton Bradley tried to capitalize on the popularity of the game immediately, releasing in 1967 more zany, touchy party games including Feeley Meeley, in which the players, portrayed on the box as young adults, feel inside the box for winning objects, and Slap Stick, "the WILD and WACKY game that makes everyone slap happy." Again, the aim was the young adult: "Indoor and outdoor fun for everyone—a great party 'warmer-upper,'" the company promised. Another new game, Animal Twister, on the other hand, Milton Bradley billed as "just for kids."

"NOTE," say the instructions of the original Twister: "If a player feels that a new position is impossible or it would cause him to fall, he may concede the game." Concede? Did anyone concede? Overreaching, tangling, stretching to get that blue spot. Then collapsing! That was half the fun ... at least for those too young to understand why the game really sold so well. ■

Milton Bradley: Twister, 1960s, $15-$20

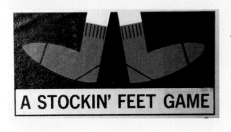

**Twister.** *The instructions give the "Strategy for Winning at Twister: Good strategy is to advance toward an opponent in an attempt to keep him in his end of the vinyl sheet. This will give him a smaller area of circles on which to gain each position, without going under or over the advancing player." Remarkably, chess held its own against this colorful game of strategy. Milton Bradley Co., 1966.*

# THE BEANY-COPTER

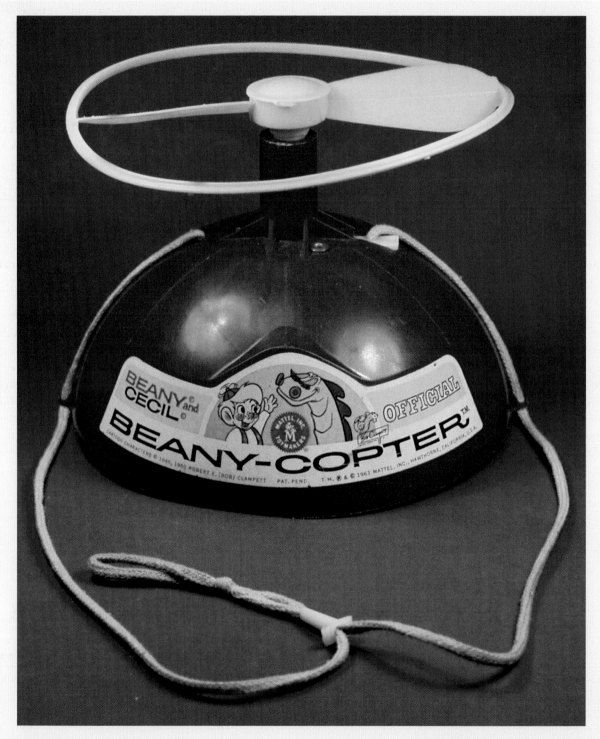

**Whirling thinking-cap.**

*The propeller on the top could be rotated to wind it up. The child wearing it could then just give a tug to the cord hanging by his or her left ear—and sproing, the propeller would go flying! The top of the propeller could be opened to hide a secret message inside. Beany and Cecil Official Beany-Copter, Mattel, 1961.*

FLYING PROPELLERS made of thin sheet-metal were not uncommon toys in the years before World War II. Afterwards, they became decidedly commonplace, especially by the middle 1950s, when such plastic toys as the Flying Saucer Gun had become popular. Propeller-launching ray-guns were cheap tickets to outer space in the hands of the right kids.

No toy selection in the 1950s was truly complete without aerial toys of the helicopter-rotor sort. Montgomery Wards, for instance, offered a Flying Props hand-held launcher in 1955, as well as the Solar Rocket, which launched propellers off its back. In the Captain Space Solar Part play set from Marx that year, the launch platform for flying saucers was an important action feature, just as it had been for all such Marx play sets since the Tom Corbett 25th Century Space Academy play set three years earlier.

At the same time, beany caps with propellers atop them—nonfunctional propellers, that is, capable of spinning freely but having no wind-up mechanisms connected to them—were entering popular culture from the crowded hallways of 1950s science fiction conventions. Introduced as goofball headgear to suggest the high-flying nature of the spaceman, on as low a budget as possible, the helicopter beany became one of the ways the science-fiction fan community, often called "fandom," engaged in gentle self-mockery. In amateur-press magazines, beany-props gave cartoonists the means for depicting a member of fandom, who was usually a person of the brainy, nerdy sort. Propeller beanies gradually came to symbolize nerdy, brainy types to society in general, not just within SF fandom.

As a symbol, the propeller beany soon changed, thanks to the advent of the live-TV hand puppet show *Beanie and Cecil,*

*the Seasick Sea Serpent,* and its 1960s animated successor, *The Beany and Cecil Show.* The propeller beany became one of accepted pieces of childhood headgear, along with the coonskin cap, the space helmet, the Indian headdress and the cowboy hat.

It appeared in its ultimate toy form in the Mattel Beany and Cecil Official Beany-Copter, which had a launchworthy propeller atop a red polyethylene beany.

Beany and Cecil toys proliferated in the early '60s. Mattel's other toys included a large Talking Beany Boy, in its Chatty Cathy-inaugurated line, and a Dishonest John hand puppet. Irwin Corp., of New York City, issued Leakin' Lena, a plastic sailboat toy. Colorforms, of Norwood, N.J., made Beany and Cecil stick-ons. Bantam-Lite, Inc., of New York City, made Beany and Cecil flashlights. In Brooklyn, Ben Cooper made costumes.

Historians of science fiction fandom attribute the invention of the propeller beany to cartoonist and novelist Ray Nelson, who improvised the first one in Cadillac, Mich., in 1947. A friend wore it to an SF convention in Toronto the next year, starting it on its unlikely road into the mainstream public's eye.

Nelson himself drew some of the cartoons that spread the image of the propeller beany around fandom as a whole. Apparently he also drew the image of a boy wearing one, which he submitted to a contest in California. Nelson's drawing turned some heads. He must have won something because his Beany-Boy became a TV star. What he lost, however, was rights. ■

> Irwin: Leakin' Lena Boat, 1962, $50
> Mattel: Beany Talking Doll, 1950s, $90
> Mattel: Cecil in the Music Box, 1961, $80

**Flying Saucer.** *Both U.S. Plastic Co., of Pasadena, Calif., and Park Plastics Co., of Linden, N.J., were making a Flying Saucer Gun by the mid-1950s. Propeller-launching "ray guns" were popular toys from around 1953 to the end of the decade, as were propeller-launching toys of any sort. Changing to match the times, many such toys were "satellite launchers" by 1959. Propeller ammunition for Park Plastics gun, 1950s.*

# MR. MACHINE

**THE SMILING ROBOT**

Mr. Machine had enough personality to become the spokesrobot for Ideal Toy Corp. in its television ads. The large 1970s version, shown here, could not be taken apart, as could the original. Ideal, 1977.

Ideal: Mr. Machine, 1961, $125
Ideal: Mr. Machine, 1970s, $30

**M**ANY TOYS existed in the minds of children even when they were not lucky enough to own them. Parents could afford only so many toys, after all. Not all girls had Barbies. Certainly not all boys had G.I. Joes. In fact, in my circle of friends as a child, I remember only one who had a G.I. Joe. Perhaps because of the kind of children we were, Joe wasn't an object of envy, unlike other, simpler and often cheaper toys.

Yet we all knew about such toys in the mid-1960s. They were part of the mental landscape of childhood, put there by the relentless forces of the Mattel and Hasbro marketing departments.

In the same way, around the beginning of the decade, kids knew about Mr. Machine. Even if we never had one or even saw one in person, Mr. Machine had an incredibly strong television presence. It was distinctive enough to catch the attention and trigger the imaginations of children. It had less a feeling of being a "boy's toy" than previous robots, moreover. His bolt-nosed head had a friendly expression that seemed a world away from Robert the Robot's mechanically austere face.

The toy industry itself may have been unaware of the fact. When this toy was put into the hands of children in 1960 and '61, they had no idea it arrived from the inventor's shop of Marvin Glass, via the manufacturing facilities of Ideal Toy Corp. of New York City.

Marvin Glass was responsible for many of the most prominent toys of the 1960s. His goofy and frog-like Odd Ogg and the aggressive dragon-robot King Zor were big hits. By themselves, they would have been enough to put Glass among the notables of 1960s toy innovators. Yet he produced others: Smarty Bird, Gaylord, and the huge hit of 1963, Mousetrap, for Ideal. He designed Dandy the Lion for Irwin, and Yakkity Yob for Eldon. He designed Golferino for Hubley and the Rock 'em Sock 'em Robots for Marx.

The original 18-inch Mr. Machine came with a wrench. Glass fully intended that children use that tool, as the grinning plastic robot could be dismantled and reassembled endlessly. After the Take-Apart and Fix-It toys of the 1950s, a take-apart toy robot made plenty of sense.

Ideal spent millions on advertising its wide range of playthings during the 1960-61 season. One result of the effort were healthy sales figures for Mr. Machine. Five-hundred thousand robots went out to homes around the country. All of them must have been taken apart, at least once. How many of those 500,000 got put back together? No one will ever know.

After such success, the company pushed forward with increasingly large TV advertising budgets. After Mr. Machine came another Marvin Glass plastic robot: Robot Commando, a battery-operated, one-robot army that responded to voice commands and then lobbed missiles and rockets every which way, to the utter joy of the child. Another great toy ... or, at least, another toy that looked fabulous on the Tube. ∎

# SPIROGRAPH

S OME TOYS looked keen as all get-out on TV, then turned out to be duds on the playroom floor. Others, however, had a way of staying interesting long after the gift wrap was thrown away.

Belonging to the latter group was Spirograph, one of the characteristic toys of the late Boomer years. Unlike painting kits or even coloring books, Spirograph required little in the way of intrinsic artistic talent. Instead, it required physical coordination, a little mechanical talent and patience.

Invented by British mechanical engineer Dennis Fischer, the toy involved a system of clear plastic pieces with toothed edges like gears. Some pieces the child had to fix firmly to the page, usually by tacks that went through holes into the drawing board beneath the paper. Other pieces remained free. These had off-center holes in them large enough for the tip of a ballpoint pen.

The child had to learn to keep an even drawing pressure, not only downward through the moving gear onto the paper, but also sideways, so the gear wouldn't slip out of its track. I remember many a masterpiece flawed by a slip of the pen.

Spirograph was a surprise best seller in its introductory years of 1966 and '67. It sat firmly at the top of toy sales charts both years. They must have been quieter years than any before.

Five-and-a-half million souls bent over kitchen and den tables, trying to execute the perfect geometric designs made possible by this exasperating and inspiring toy. Utter quiet ... and then: "Oh! Darn!" ■

**Perfect for a rainy afternoon.** As a drawing toy, Spirograph had democratic appeal: "Anyone can draw beautiful patterns immediately!" The kits contained 22 clear plastic wheels, rings and "racks," as well as ballpoint pens in four colors. Kenner, 1967.

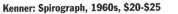

**Kenner: Spirograph, 1960s, $20-$25**

**Magic Designer.** In contrast to Spirograph, its predecessor drawing toy "Magic Designer," provided a geared, metal platform with a drawing area that held a round piece of paper. When cranked, the toy produced the drawing mechanically. It was originally called "Hoot-Nanny" in the 1940s and '50s. In the late 1960s, the toy was still being made, but now by Lakeside Industries. A similar drawing toy, "Dizzy Doodler," was introduced in 1949 by Carter Craft of Dallas, Texas. Magic Designer, Northern Signal Co., Inc., Saukville, Wis., 1960s.

"— ONE OF THE MOST FASCINATING OF ALL TOYS"

the MAGIC designer
formerly called Hoot-Nanny
CREATIVE FUN FOR BOYS AND GIRLS

**Dangling dolls.** *Many Kiddles were small enough to be sold in plastic lockets. Unlike earlier dolls, the Kiddles were themselves fashion accessories. Mattel, 1960s.*

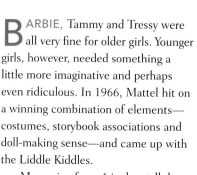

**B**ARBIE, Tammy and Tressy were all very fine for older girls. Younger girls, however, needed something a little more imaginative and perhaps even ridiculous. In 1966, Mattel hit on a winning combination of elements—costumes, storybook associations and doll-making sense—and came up with the Liddle Kiddles.

Measuring from 4-inches tall down to less than 1 inch, these miniatures had oversized, rouge-cheeked faces with *I Dream of Jeannie* eyes. They had long, rooted hair, often in attractively unrealistic colors. And they had vanishingly small bodies.

The names, though ... It must have been the names as much as anything that created the magic aura around these dolls: Bunson Burnie (a Liddle Kiddle fireman); Anabelle Autodiddle; Howard Biff Boodle; Florence Niddle; Suki Skediddler; Sleeping Biddle; Sheila Skediddle.

The very smallest were sold imprisoned within plastic heart necklaces and brooches, lockets and

**Small fires only, please.** *The intrepid firefighter of Kiddlesville measures almost 3-½" tall—if wearing his hat. Small as he was, he towered over the Kiddles sold in lockets. Bunson Bernie, with fire engine, Mattel, 1960s.*

**Too Cute To Be Trolls.**
*New York's Uneeda Doll Co., enjoying considerable success with its Wishnik Trolls, took the logical next step. Knowing the childlike proportions of Trolls struck a chord with children, Uneeda used a similar body for a new, similarly sized doll line called Pee Wees. Pee Wees are marked with their name on one foot and the year 1965 on the other. The Pee Wee Tote, combination tote and dollhouse, were made by Ideal for Uneeda.*

perfume bottles. They were dolls that *were* accessories.

Many children found their favorites among the Storybook Kiddles, based on figures already familiar through traditional fairy tales and children's books. The sprite-like Peter Paniddle, who had red hair to offset his green outfit and cap, came with Tinkerbell, who was no less than a minuscule Barbie doll, and a soft-plastic green reptile, the Crocodiddle. Sleeping Biddle drowsed through the ages on a purple claw-foot bed. Cinderiddle was dressed in rags and toted a broom, but also had a fancy gown and glass slippers—which girls immediately lost, of course, since it was part of the story. Liddle Middle Muffet sat on her tuffet with bowl and spoon, with an octopus-looking spider beside her. Liddle Biddle Peep had sheep and staff, while Alice in Wonderliddle was accompanied by the White Rabbit, with his constantly consulted watch.

These all mildly encouraged literacy, coming as they did with their own storybooks. Except perhaps one Kiddle, who was utterly true to the times: Telly Viddle. ▪

Ideal: Flatsy doll, Baby, $10
Mattel: Little Kiddle, Bunson Burnie,
 with firetruck, $40
Mattel: Little Kiddle, Calamity Jiddle, $60
Mattel: Little Kiddle, Peter Paniddle doll, $25
Uneeda: Pee Wee, doll, $5
Uneeda: Pee Wee Doll Box, paper dolls,
 Whitman/Uneeda, 1966, $10
Uneeda: Pee Wee Tote, Ideal/Uneeda, $10

**Flower child.** *When she appeared, Flatsy seemed a symbolic return to the origins of the style doll. Although not as thin as a paper doll, she was a flat figure for dressing and undressing. Her costumes often played off styles of the time, as did this 5-inch Flatsy flower child. Ideal, 1969.*

## FLATSY

Girls of the 1960s had a wealth of fashion dolls that were small and easy to lose, from the Kiddles and Hasbro Storykins to the Trolls and Pee Wees.

When Ideal applied the bendy concept to the idea of the miniature fashion doll, the results were the Flatsys. Unlike the space bendy toys of the more boy-oriented Major Matt Mason line, Flatsys took the Gumby approach. Looking as though Ideal had used cookie-cutters on vinyl slabs to make them, the dolls were like thick paper dolls.

With changeable clothes, plastic vehicles and the seemingly obligatory vinyl townhouse, the dolls appeared in 2-inch, 5-inch and 8-inch sizes. Definitely children of their time, their hair was long and their outfits hip and trendy.

Ideal issued the Flatsys in 1968-1970 for the last children of the Boomer years.

**Walking Goofy.** *In the later 1960s Mattel issued Disney toys akin to the Kiddles in spirit. This Goofy measures 4-½" tall, with a body disproportionately small. They also showed kinship in their name: the Skediddlers. A rod in the back of the small doll made its arms and legs move, making it seem to walk. Mattel, 1967-68.*

# AURORA MONSTER KITS

**M**ODEL BUILDING went through a boom in the 1950s and '60s, thanks to modern plastics—and thanks, too, to Friday late night and Saturday afternoon TV.

Monster movies, as old as movie-making itself, proliferated in postwar years, spurred by 1950s mass fears about the Bomb, atomic radiation and Communist infiltration. By the 1960s, the same low-budget parade of the bizarre and ugly helped fill the gray air times around Friday midnight and the sleepy downslide from Saturday noon. Kids must have sensed that these monsters and fright films reflected something important about the world in which they were growing up. They attached themselves to the monsters as they would to friends. They wanted them in their lives, in their houses, in their rooms.

Model companies did the best job of responding to that desire, especially Aurora Plastics, of West Hempstead, N.Y., an enterprising and adventurous company that not only gave kids models of TV figures from *The Man from U.N.C.L.E.*, *Lost in Space* and *Star Trek*, and such superheroes as Batman, Superman and Spider-Man, but hordes of horrors: the Forgotten Prisoner, the Bride of Frankenstein, the Hunchback of Notre Dame, Dr. Jekyll as Mr. Hyde, Godzilla, Salem Witch, the Mummy, the Frankenstein Monster, Wolf Man, the Creature from the Black Lagoon, Dracula, Rodan and the Phantom of the Opera.

Millions of kids grew up spending hours with Aurora's Fireproof Styrene Plastic Cement, One Hour Humbrol Plastic Enamel and the Monster Paint Package ("Look for the package with the Haunted House!"). Model-building also created a social

**LORD OF SKULL ISLAND.**

King Kong found renewed popularity in the 1960s, helped in no small part by a dynamic model kit. Aurora, 1967.

**Scientific marriage.** *One of Aurora's more complex monster model kits, The Bride of Frankenstein included such rewarding details for the modeler as "discarded body parts," "severed hand," the bandaged bride herself, and even a plastic "electric bolt." Aurora Plastics Corp., 1965.*

**Monster rods.** *Monsters and hot rods went hand-in-hand in the 1960s, with everyone from Rat Fink to Godzilla burning rubber in model kit form. Some of the weirdest were Aurora's Mummy Chariot, Dracula's Dragster, and Godzilla's Go-Cart. Aurora Plastics Corp., 1966.*

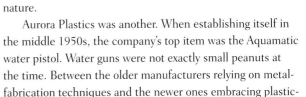

division among kids: those who sniffed airplane glue and those who said they never did.

## THE WATER-PISTOL CONNECTION

As new companies sprang up during the 1950s and tried to find their places in the increasingly competitive world of toy manufacturing, many started with a single toy idea they thought might do well. Usually it would serve just well enough to let the new company find its footing.

In trying to capture and hold toy-buyers' attention for more than a year or two, however, many of these new firms abandoned their initial plans, trying new ideas until something caught on. Mattel was perhaps the most extreme example of this. While it enjoyed considerable early success with its line of musical toys, by the end of the Boomer years it was famous for toys of quite a different nature.

Aurora Plastics was another. When establishing itself in the middle 1950s, the company's top item was the Aquamatic water pistol. Water guns were not exactly small peanuts at the time. Between the older manufacturers relying on metal-fabrication techniques and the newer ones embracing plastic-extrusion technology, more than a dozen companies relied on the toys for a significant portion of their products. They were among the most prominent companies on the scene: All Metal Products Co., Irwin, Buddy "L" Toys, and Daisy Mfg. Co., of Plymouth, Mich., were among them. There were also Empire Plastic Corp., of Pelham Manor, N.Y.; Knickerbocker Plastic Co., of North Hollywood, Calif.; Palmer Plastics, Inc., of Brooklyn, N.Y.; Park Plastics Co., of Linden N.J.; and Renwal Mfg. Co., of Mineola, N.Y., as well as a host of smaller companies.

Cheap, abundant water guns made water pistol fights widespread and commonplace in the 1950s and '60s. While production of these toys had begun in earnest in the 1930s, it was only in the 1950s that, as playthings, the water gun was made a routine and

**Glows in the Dark!** *Creature All Plastic Assembly Kit, Aurora Products Corp., 1972.*

**Monster madness.** *Monsters of every kind were in vogue during the 1960s. Makers of low-end toys made sure the supply never stopped. Monsters, Palmer Plastics, 1960s.*

**#31**

regular item in toy-aisle assortments. Plastics manufacturing especially helped their spread.

Despite such heavy competition, around 1953-54, the Aquamatic probably appeared to offer more promise for Aurora's future over the long term than other products Aurora Plastics was pursuing: bow and arrow sets, archery sets and plastic models.

Aurora was offering all-plastic, scale-model "assembly kits" of airplanes and ships. If anything, the competition was heavier in that arena. Model aircraft had been such an important part of the 1940s toy scene and had proved so vital to the industry's health during the difficult war years that both established and new companies saw it as a natural field of endeavor. It could be a profitable field, too. In the first half of the '50s, more than 30 companies were making a success of it.

Scale-model realism proved the direction Aurora was to take, however. Even though the Aquamatic name was the most important single name for the company in 1955, by 1957 it had been left behind. The company was now resolutely focusing on plastic plane, ship and truck model kits. By 1959, it had

diversified, while holding to its central emphasis. Its plastic model kits now embraced airplanes, missiles, helicopters, bombers, ships, military vehicles, warships, historic ships and warriors, especially knights. The company was also producing figurines, HO accessories, plastic gliders and the vital model-making supplies of cement and paint. In trying to capture the imagination of the countless Boomer kids who seemed eager to work with their hands, Aurora Plastics also offered Totem Craft, Copper Craft, and electronic and radio kits.

Great changes were in store for the 1960s. While Aurora's now-traditional areas of success in scale-model kits and modeling supplies continued, new areas were taking off. Aurora's HO motoring and racing sets were becoming the hands-down favorites of kids living in homes with slightly greater disposable income.

Monster kits were not far behind. Figures of the grotesque and horrible were probably favorite playthings for far more children than were the bigger-dollar items of slot-car race sets. More children of all economic levels had them. Something about monsters seemed to stir their tiny hearts. ■

**Aladdin: King Kong lunch box, 1977, $95**
**Aurora: Frankenstein, built-up kit, 1961, $30**
**Aurora: King Kong, built-up kit, 1964, $75**
**Aurora: King Kong, Glow Kit, built-up, $75**
**Aurora: Odd Job, built-up kit, $200**
**Ideal: Mystic Skull game, 1965, $60**
**Marx: Frankenstein, tin-litho, $900**
**Transogram: Green Ghost Game, 1965, $75**

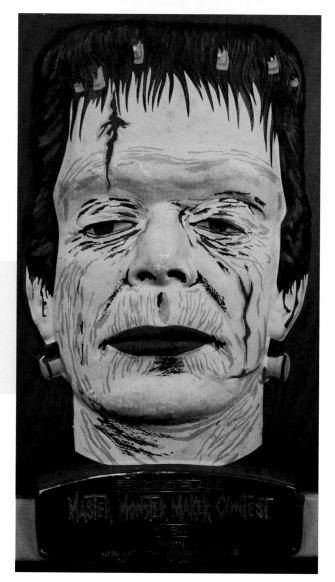

**The Face of a Winner.** *Model companies encouraged kids to build new kits by sponsoring contests. This second-place award, a plaque made of vacuum-formed plastic, was sponsored by Aurora Plastics Corp, Universal Pictures Co., Inc. and Famous Monsters of Filmland magazine. Aurora, 1964.*

# 31

**Stanley Steamer.** *Revell Action Toys Miniature, 1950s.*

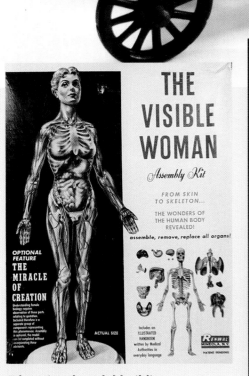

**Educational model-building.**
Some Boomers less into monsters or latest-model cars were fascinated by the educational kits issued by Renwal in the 1960s, including Visible Man and Visible Woman. Renwal, 1960s.

**Santa Maria.** *Countless kids sailed with Columbus with model kits that produced small, 5" ships. Pyro Plastics Corp., Union, N.J., 1950s-60s.*

# GIVE-A-SHOW

KENNER PRODUCT CO. was lucky enough to enjoy several hits in the early 1960s, including a somewhat strange hit that was selling out of stock everywhere in 1963: Flintstones Building Boulders, which looked much like Block City or LEGO pieces at a considerably larger scale and made of lightweight styrofoam. The sheer size of the package beneath—or, rather, beside—the Christmas tree must have made these among the most memorable of Kenner toys for those lucky kids.

Besides the Girder & Panel sets, Kenner devoted much of its TV advertising budget to a toy that proved to be a steady source of enjoyment for kids through the decade: the Give-A-Show Projector.

**Kenner: Give-A-Show Projector Set, 112 slides, 1963, $100**
**Kenner: Roy Rogers Give-A-Show Projector, with slides, 1960s, $50**
**Stori-Views: Cinderella Pixie Viewer, 1950s, $20**

While Kenner would later have a more innovative idea of what to do with light bulbs, with Give-A-Show it found a fairly traditional but still solid way of working wonders in the playroom. The projector was a sturdy plastic affair. It was battery-powered to avoid the hazards of electrical cords. The films it showed were simple too: the short sets of cels, with written narration, were set in strips of cardboard which easily slipped in and out of the projector.

Projectors typically came with a dozen or so strips, each one featuring a different cartoon star. The first version, in 1960, was called the Show Time Projector and was issued with 16 Famous Character Shows.

Kenner stayed away from nature and live-action film strips, which hardly limited its choice of subjects during the TV-cartoon heyday of the early '60s. If children tired of the ones that came with the projector, they could always buy more.

While battery-operated projectors for children had appeared before—for instance the Zoom-Lite of the late 1950s and early '60s, made by Thompson Co. of Binghamton, N.Y.—Give-A-Show's high profile on TV made it the favorite of millions. ∎

**Projecting childhood dreams.**

*Bedrooms became movie houses at the flick of a switch. Kenner sold film strips with the battery-operated projectors and offered more in separate boxes. Almost any animated character might appear on bedroom walls: Dick Tracy, Space Ghost, The Flintstones, Deputy Dawg ... Give-A-Show Projector and slide strips, Kenner, 1960s.*

# ETCH A SKETCH

# #33

**O**F ALL the companies that attempted a toy that looked like a TV, none succeeded the way Ohio Art Co. did with its Magic Etch A Sketch Screen.

"Hours of fascinating fun for the entire family—Doodle Dialing—unlimited design possibilities!" the Bryan, Ohio, company raved on its toy packaging.

Paul Chasse, a garage mechanic and general tinkerer who lived near Paris, invented L'Ecran Magique, or Magic Screen, in 1958. It used a mixture of aluminum powder and plastic beads with a metal stylus guided by twin knobs. Since it was clever, needed no batteries and had no loose parts to be lost, he figured it might be worth a tidy sum.

Most toy companies thought otherwise—including Ohio Art—the first time around. When successive levels of Ohio Art executives were later won over by a prototype, they took it to the boss, not realizing the boss had already turned down Chasse. This time, though, he said yes. Ohio Art described the toy as being "As New as 1960." It seemed new for years to come. ■

> Ohio Art: Etch A Sketch, 1960s, $10-$20

**Everything but dot the i.** *When Ohio Art released its "family-tested toy," it promised that "Etch A Sketch does everything but dot the i," an acknowledgment that everything drawn on the toy had to be connected by a single, roving line. A properly dotted "i" was an impossibility. Ohio Art, 1960s.*

"WE ARE FACED WITH THE ATOMIC THREAT, BUT IT IS NO MORE STARTLING THAN WAS THE DISCOVERY OF GUNPOWDER, AND NO MORE LOADED WITH THE STUFF OF GOOD AND EVIL THAN THE INVENTION OF THE PRINTING PRESS OR THE DISCOVERY OF ELECTRICITY."

—*BUSINESS AS UN-USUAL,* PAMPHLET PUBLISHED BY DUN & BRADSTREET, INC., 1950.

# Winky Dink and You

Despite all the uncertainties, many signs pointed toward a bright future in the 1950s. Employment figures looked rosy, with 61 million people on the work rolls at the start of the decade, for an average weekly wage of almost $60. More goods and services were being produced than ever before, with nearly 4 million businesses in operation across the country.

For toy manufacturers, the number of "consumers" looked greatly promising, for there were 49 million families in 1950, with three times that number of total people.

Both the fears and hopes of the decade were expressed through its toys. Such traditional products as doll carriages, cap guns, paint sets and toy trucks remained important parts of toy-store selections. Alongside them were toys that seemed quite new, even though they had their beginnings in the 1930s: plastic toy cars, robots, spacemen, rockets, gas-powered racers and toy versions of the TV set.

That futuristic toys and space toys became so important a part of the toy scene during the 1950s was fitting. With millions of young souls being ushered into the world, how could parents not worry about the future?

# INTERACTIVE TV
# WINKY DINK
## MAGIC TELEVISION KIT

ONE OF the earliest attempts at interactive television, *Winky Dink and You*, effected the transformation that was bound to come: It turned the television set itself into a toy. *Winky Dink and You* aired on CBS TV from Oct. 10, 1953, through April 27, 1957, hosted by Jack Barry, who had already hosted early TV game shows, including *Juvenile Jury*.

Winky Dink was an animated character with a star-like head and slender, pixy-like body. His voice was provided by Mae Questal, also the voice of Olive Oyl. The cast was completed by Dayton Allen, who played the incompetent Mr. Bungle, and who also provided the voice of Winky Dink's dog, Woofer. The show, concept and Winky Dink animated character were created by Harry W. Pritchett Sr., and Edwin Brit Wyckoff.

**DETAIL OF THE WINKY DINK PUZZLE FROM THE 1955 GAME KIT.**

In fall 1953, advertisements invited kids to write in for their *Winky Dink and You!* Super Magic TV Kit, which included Magic Screen, Winky Dink crayons and Magic Erasing Cloth. The kits then arrived at homes around the country: "Here it is! Your own Winky Dink Magic Television Kit! ...a Barry, Enright & Friendly Production." The thrill must have been unbearable. Here was a magic kit, sanctioned by none other than CBS TV itself and presumably the parent who surrendered the 50 cents needed.

What was the magic? The child was allowed to draw directly on the TV. During the show, Winky Dink would get into an intolerable difficulty. What to do but turn to the audience for a solution? Barry entreated the watching kids to get out their plastic Magic Screen, which could be pressed onto the TV screen. Then Barry instructed the kids

**Interactive TV play set.** *The paper envelope of the original Winky Dink Magic Television Kit contained Winky Dink Magic Crayons, erasing cloth and the Magic Window, which was tinted green. "You may find that you will want to leave the Magic Window up at all times while you are watching your other programs." Its makers assure parents, "You will find that the tint is restful to your eyes." Standard Toykraft Products, 1950s.*

You Got:
8 Magic Crayons • Official Magic Window • DeLuxe Erasing Mitt • Winky Puzzle • 40 Plastic Winky Doodles • Magic TV Game Book

OFFICIAL SUPER
W*inky D*ink
TELEVISION GAME
K*it

winky puzzle

CBS
TELEVISION

**Game Kit.** *More elaborate than the mail-in kit, the Winky Dink Television Game Kit contained not only the usual items— screen, crayons and erasing mitt—but also a die-cut puzzle, 40 plastic "doodles" in assorted colors and game book … not to mention some of the most charming graphics of the 1950s. Standard Toykraft Products, 1955.*

in drawing Winky Dink out of his predicament, using one of the five crayons in the kit.

Crockett Johnson's still-popular children's book *Harold and the Purple Crayon*, in which the title character draws himself out of predicaments by means of a crayon, came out in 1955, at the midpoint of the Winky Dink years.

*Winky Dink and You* also involved kids with secret messages. On the screen, parts of the letters making up the messages appeared, which the children had to trace onto their Magic Screen. Those parts would then disappear, so that when the rest of the parts of the letters then appeared on the screen, only kids with Magic Screens were able to read the secret.

The Magic Screen served much as the Radio Orphan Annie and Captain Midnight decoder rings had for the previous generation, updated for the new medium of television.

Standard Toykraft attempted a revival of *Winky Dink and You* in 1969, only to be stymied by the concern for safety that was then quashing other toys and children's activity games. In this case, Boomer parents were worried about the radiation emitted by television sets and the fact that Winky Dink required that children stand right up against the screen, drawing parts of letters and escape hatches for the beleaguered hero. Television sets did become radiation-free at the beginning of the '70s, another sign of the ending of an era. By then, however, Winky Dink was gone. ∎

**Tiddly Winky Dinks.** *Tying in with the Tiddly Winks fad of the 1950s, Barry & Enright Productions produced Tiddly Winky Dinks. The game "board" is a cardboard cube 9" to a side. Tryne, 1950s.*

Lowe: Jack Barry's Twenty One, 1956, $30
Pressman: Winky Dink Paint Set, 1950s, $75
Super Winky Dink TV Game, Kit #250, 1954, $60
Toykraft: Winky Dink Magic TV Kit, $85

# DICK TRACY
## SQUAD CAR

### TWILIGHT OF THE TIN TOY.

Tin toys, especially domestically manufactured ones, were on their way out in the 1950s, although they never disappeared entirely from the Boomer toy scene. The Squad Car was part of the last wave of high-profile tin toys. Three versions of the Dick Tracy Squad Car No. 1, Marx, 1949 to early '50s.

THE LOUIS MARX CO. in the late 1940s and early '50s was still a happening company in the toy biz. It still knew how to bring out toys that were cheap, appealing and appropriate to the times. A good example of this is Marx's tin-litho Dick Tracy Squad Car, first issued in the late 1940s.

Marx mined this toy concept deeply, issuing a small version called the Dick Tracy Squad Car No. 1, measuring about 7" long, a medium-sized car also called Dick Tracy Squad Car No. 1, a little more than 11" in length and finally a large convertible called simply the Dick Tracy Squad Car, over 20" long with no number.

The first two squad cars stuck to a basic pattern, with the smallest being the most simple of construction. It had three parts. The chassis was a bent piece of tin that held the axles and rear friction motor. This was held to the main body by a means not unusual in these postwar years: the body's lower edge folded out, then back in, making a lip into which the thin edges of the chassis slipped.

The body was a rounded, domed rectangle, shaped just enough to suggest the lines of the hood. It had an oval opening on top, where the roof fitted on. These toys had nothing fancy about them, just some metal with wheels—and nice lithography. The base color was green in both sizes of Squad Car No. 1. The smaller version had the words "Dick Tracy Friction Drive" on the hood and "Squad Car No. 1," "Police Dept." and a yellow shield design with Tracy's profile on the sides. The trunk displayed a "305" license plate just below the round Marx logo.

The main attractions were the cartoon characters themselves, seen "through" the windows with the same flatness of the original comic strips: Tracy and Pat Patton in the front, while Tracy's ever-smoking sidekick Sam Catchem and yellow-haired Junior had the back. From the sides, you saw the sides of their faces. From the front, the fronts. From the back, the backs.

Simple toy? The experienced Marx workers threw these off at night while they were asleep. The toy market was entering a period of extremely intense competition, however. Even with Marx's long-standing prominence in the industry, the company had to make at least half an effort to do more than be bright and colorful.

Consequently, the larger version boasted a few more pieces: a separate grille, a rolled piece meant to represent a machine gun rising from the passenger side and a plastic, nonfunctional spotlight on the roof. Tracy was still driving, while Sam now rode shotgun. Pat and another policeman occupied the back. More

## Argo Action Cars

While shiploads of tin-plate toy cars flowed into this country from Japan in the 1950s, a few American companies made similar products. The only fleet of small, tin-litho cars to be played with by a large segment of the Boomer generation, in fact, was made by Argo Industries Corp., of Woodside, Long Island, N.Y. Sold through catalog stores and known as the "Action Cars" or "Action Fleet," Argo's 4-inch cars had simple but clever mechanisms that were set in motion by rolling them across the floor.

The Fire Chief car featured a tin profile of a bell protruding from the hood, swinging back and forth as the car rolled, with a real bell ringing inside. Passenger cars had tin windows that raised and lowered or windshield wipers that moved back and forth. The Taxi kept a rolling tally of the fare. The detective car's machine gun went in and out, rattling.

The Action Cars remained available from the early to mid-1950s. By around 1956, the combination of cheap imports from abroad and changing toy-market conditions at home brought about their demise.

### Simple toy, simple appeal.
*Small tin toy cars, some with free-running wheels and others with friction motors, were commonplace. Most were imported from Japan. In the early Boomer years, the American-made Action Cars were among the few that had a brand identity. Argo, 1950s.*

**#35**

importantly, the friction motor was moved to sit beneath the hood. A slot in the tin beneath the gun emitted sparks generated by the friction motor and a piece of flint. The original instructions were this simple: "1. Hold car firmly, push along floor and release. 2. Momentum set up in motor will propel it."

Did it work? Beautifully. Sparks spilled out abundantly over the hood, while the friction motor gave a satisfying grinding sound.

With all the distractions now available in catalog stores and dime stores, however, Marx had to keep improving the product. By 1951, the car was advertised as the Dick Tracy Siren Car, for less than $2. "Siren wails, gun sparks, friction motor—Action-Noise Galore!" It now also came with an on-off switch on the

back, since the rooftop searchlight now worked by battery power.

Two years later, Marx, perhaps thinking the Dick Tracy car had run its course, introduced the G-Man Car. This had the features of Tracy's car—sirens, lights and sparks—with the added attraction of a clockwork motor and the option of going either in circles or straight ahead.

G-Man gave the car back to Tracy in 1954 when the Siren Squad Car returned a last time with the clockwork mechanism and the circle/straight option.

The mid-'50s saw many changes in the toy world. The passing of the simple tin Squad Car reflects the fact that it was part of the first wave of postwar toy innovation, and not one that would survive to rise with the next wave. ■

Argo: Action Cars, loose, each, $10-$15

Marx: Deluxe Delivery Truck, 13-¼", 1948, $100

Marx: Sportster convertible, 20", 1950s, $70

Marx: Squad Car No. 1, windup, 11", $150

**Action Cars.** *Unlike most small tin toys, the Argo line appeared in store catalogs through the early to middle 1950s. Toy Fair, 1951.*

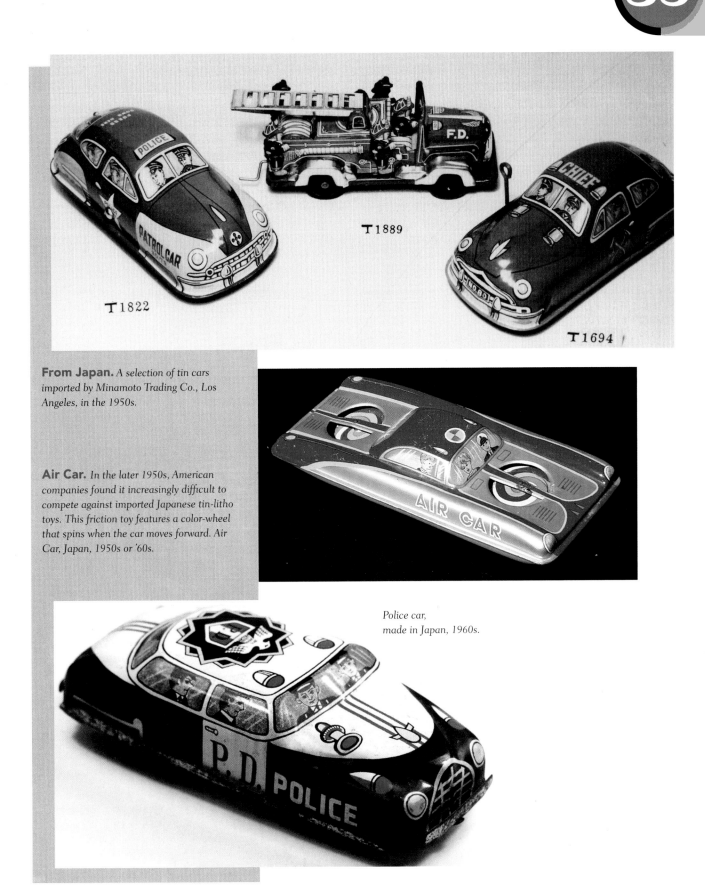

T1889

T1822

T1694

**From Japan.** *A selection of tin cars imported by Minamoto Trading Co., Los Angeles, in the 1950s.*

**Air Car.** *In the later 1950s, American companies found it increasingly difficult to compete against imported Japanese tin-litho toys. This friction toy features a color-wheel that spins when the car moves forward. Air Car, Japan, 1950s or '60s.*

*Police car, made in Japan, 1960s.*

# THE BUBBLE-TOPPED
# COUPE

STEEL, lead and rubber were not the only toy-making materials being rationed and restricted during the war. Plastic was too. As a result, despite the plastic industry's attempts to promote new formulas to the toy industry before and during the war, few manufacturers were poised at war's end to introduce bright new plastic playthings for Christmas.

One of the few was Dillon-Beck Mfg. Co. of Hillside, N.J., which, under its Wannatoys banner, introduced its 25-cent coupe. The Wannatoy Coupe was not an ordinary coupe. It sported a bubble top of transparent acetate, through which a simplified steering wheel and seats were visible. The bubble sat squarely on a streamlined body, vaguely reminiscent of a rowboat set keel-side-up.

Children, or at least their buying parents, reacted with enthusiasm to its Art Deco-inspired futuristic design. In the new Atomic Age, it expressed the hope people felt about times to come. A million units moved off shelves in the 1946 Christmas season. The Coupe sold well into the next decade, at the lower price of a dime per car. With plastic toys being promoted as safe, tough to break, free of sharp edges and hygienically washable, even toddlers must have had their first lessons in Art Deco styling from this wheeled, bubbled bauble, a dime-store best seller at the dawn of the Baby Boomer years. ■

## POSTWAR CHRISTMAS BEST-SELLER.

This futuristic coupe stirred the imagination of millions of children and helped kick-start postwar production of plastic toys. Dillon Beck, 1946-1952.

Dillon Beck: "Wannatoy" Coupe, $25-$30

**WANNATOY**
*Plastic Streamlined Toys*

CARS · TRAINS
BOATS, ETC.

Send for
Catalog
Sheets

We also offer
highly specialized
skills in custom
molded plastic toys

**DILLON-BECK MFG. CO.**
IRVINGTON, N. J.

# SPACE PEOPLE

IN THE EARLY DAYS of plastic, several surprise best sellers were hidden among the dime-store aisles. When Archer Plastics released its colorful, 4-inch Space People in the early 1950s, they were an instant hit, at least in part because of the saucer craze, space-adventure movies and the growing popularity of pulp science fiction magazines.

The Space People were stylized people in angular space suits and clear plastic dome helmets. With wide faces and Modigliani features, the Space People held heroic positions reminiscent of social-realist sculptures of Eastern Bloc statuary.

Why such triumphant postures? America had just emerged victorious from a war won, to a large degree, through technological innovations. Even if Germany had developed rockets to send over London and had initially beaten the Allies senseless with its advanced armored tanks, America's victory was thanks to the quick growth of a military industry at home.

The dream of space was steadily gaining in popularity, and if people were ever to go to space, Americans knew it would have to be, as many writers of the time put it, a "conquest" of space. In those years just after the war, conquest was something Americans thought they knew something about. ∎

Archer: Robot, $20-$25
Archer: Space man, $8-$10
Archer: Space woman, $45-$50

## TRIUMPHANT SCIENCE!

Space would be conquered, many Americans believed in the early 1950s, despite dismissive noises often made in many governmental and scientific circles. These dime-store best-sellers helped bring the future thrillingly near for countless children. Space People and vehicle, Archer Plastics, early 1950s.

**Zooming off.** *Hard plastic space ship, Premier Products Co., 1950s.*

# GUMBY

**W**HO OR WHAT is Gumby? Gumby is a green clay boy with a loyal, earth-toned clay horse pal named Pokey, a lemon-colored clay dinosaur friend named Prickle, and a blue clay mermaid chum named Goo. In the Gumby television series, Gumby is the son of clay people Gumbo and Gumba.

Gumby might be said, just as truthfully, to be the child of the 1953 art film *Gumbasia*, by Art Clokey. For this film, Clokey animated clay forms as an experiment in movement. A showing for movie producer Sam Engel led to the development of a modeling-clay character for television.

The claymation animator created a flat, easily produced figure with a "bump of wisdom," which recalled for Clokey a picture of his father as a young man with a huge cowlick rising like a bump from his head.

The figure's name came from Michigan farm slang— "gumbo"—his father's word for the sticky and slippery mud in the roads after a summer rain.

NBC liked Clokey's pilot show and signed him for a series of *The Adventures of Gumby*. Roger Muir, the producer of the *Howdy Doody Show*,

*Three-inch Gumby, Lakeside Industries, 1960s.*

agreed to introduce Gumby on that already popular program.

The clay boy first hit television in 1955, with Pokey making his debut the following year. These television appearances gave Gumby the springboard he needed to leap into his own NBC program, *The Gumby Show*, in 1957, with Pinky Lee as emcee. Scotty McKee, portraying Clarabell the Clown, gave a sense of continuity from the *Howdy Doody Show*.

New shows were produced in 1966, which enjoyed enough success to stimulate a new Gumby series for 1967, introducing Prickle, Goo and Nopey, the dog who only said, "No." Dr. Zveegee, the fun-ruining mad scientist, also made his first appearance.

Whether young watchers perceived the fact, Gumby was always a philosophic figure, unfailingly smiling, resilient and flexible. Even his friends had philosophic natures. According to Clokey, Alan Watts once told him there were two kinds of people in the world: the prickly and the gooey. Prickle and Goo appeared soon thereafter.

Lakeside Industries of Minneapolis, Minn., having the first license to produce Gumby toys, made available to kids small figures of Gumby and his friends, and accessories to turn Gumby into such grownup characters as Fire Man, Astronaut and Cowboy. Fortunately for his watchers, Gumby's growing up was make-believe. ■

> Lakeside: Gumby figure, 1965, $10-$15
> Lakeside: Pokey, $10-$15
> Whitman: Gumby & Pokey sticker book, 1968, $25

**Sheriff Gumby.** *Sets such as this gave children the chance to change Gumby's identity the way it changed on TV. This Western set included 10-gallon hat, guns, coiled lasso and badge. The guns and badge had small spikes in the back, to be pressed directly into Gumby's plastic. Lakeside Industries, 1965*

**The rubbery Old West.** *Gumby and Pokey, sold with numerous accessories, were the top bendy toys of the 1960s. Others followed, including Mattel's Major Matt Mason of the last few years of the '60s and the Colorform Aliens of around 1969. Gumby and Pokey, Lakeside Industries, 1960s, with American Logs.*

# OTHER BENDIES

**Dare-devil motorcyclist.**

Bendy toys were representing more realistic figures by the late 1960s and early '70s. Hero to many later Boomers, Evel Knievel jumped his ever more elaborate motorcycles to glory. Seven-inch bendy, Ideal, 1972.

**Rocky and Boris.**

The combination of rubber or soft vinyl with internal wires led to countless effective playthings through the end of the Boomer era. The arrangement worked especially well for cartoon characters, such as these characters Rocky, the flying squirrel, and Boris Badenov, from Jay Ward's *Rocky and His Friends*, which first aired in 1959. Wham-O Co., 1972.

# ZAP, YOU'RE DISINTEGRATED
# SPACE PATROL
# RAY GUN

AS WITH so many other kinds of toys, the toy ray gun had its beginnings among the playthings of the previous generation. Spurred by the popularity of Buck Rogers comic strips, Daisy Mfg. Co. of Plymouth, Mich., had introduced the Buck Rogers Disintegrator pistol in the 1930s. An ornate and elaborate metal toy, it ushered in the first generation of space toys in those years after the Great Depression—and then did the same for a second generation, since it was one of the toys quickly brought out again by Daisy in the wake of World War II.

The characteristic ray guns of the Boomer years, however, proved to be plastic toys. While some were drawn from the inspiration of cartoon-page figures like Buck, the majority either stood on their own simply as space toys or drew their inspiration from the TV programs that were fantastically exciting to their young public.

The sleek-looking Space Patrol Rocket Gun was introduced around 1952 by a new Pasadena, Calif., company called

**Superior.** *This imaginatively designed spaceship gun was sold with a tin-litho target board, to which suction-cup tipped darts could stick. The Space Target game was something of a departure for its manufacturer, T. Cohn, Inc., of Brooklyn, N.Y., which, under the "Superior" name, specialized in lithographed metal toys such as sand sets, noise makers, garden sets, toy gas stations and doll houses. This plastic Superior Rocket Gun could fire all three of its darts at once, or one dart at a time. T. Cohn, ca. 1952-54. Toy courtesy Martha Borchardt.*

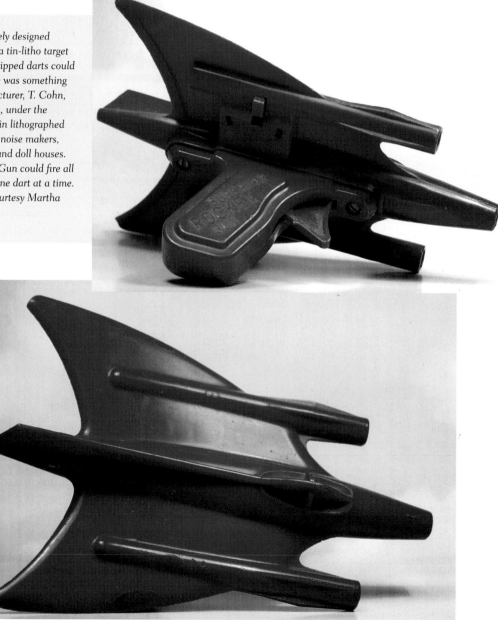

**Rubber-band shooting.**
*Toy ray gun, unknown manufacturer,
1950s. Toy courtesy Martha
Borchardt.*

**Saucer-launcher.** *Sky-Gun,
Mercury Plastics, Des Moines, Iowa,
1950s.*

# 39

U.S. Plastic Co. Large by the standards of plastic ray guns, at 9-½ inches, the gun fired plastic darts tipped with suction cups.

U.S. Plastic had other toys in production, including two that may have been propeller-launching toys: a Flying Saucer Gun and the Heli-Top-Ter. It also branched out in other directions with its California Repeater Top, and Frisky Freddy, a toy frog made to hop by putting pressure on a rubber air bladder.

The Space Patrol toy proved popular enough to last at least to 1955. U.S. Plastic continued expanding its line, until it was making a full range of toys: guns, pull toys, riding toys, tops, banks and toy trucks. The Flying Saucer Gun was still part of its line, too, at the end of the 1950s. Staying in tune with the post-Sputnik times, it also sold the toy as the Satellite Gun. ■

**Marx:** Space Patrol Atomic Pistol, $95
**Park Plastics:** Squirt Ray Water Gun, $25
**Ranger Steel:** Space Patrol Cosmic Ray Gun, 1954, $75
**Remco:** Jupiter 4-Color Signal Gun, 1950s, $90

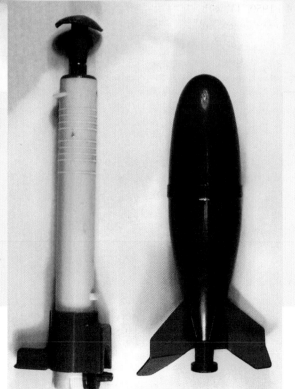

**Space Patrol.** *One of California's new toy companies got off to a start with this popular space toy. U.S. Plastic Co., ca. 1952-55. Toy courtesy Martha Borchardt.*

**Water rockets.** *While some space guns were water pistols, some space rockets were, too, after a manner. Water rockets such as this became common during the 1950s, with the idea applied to increasingly more complex toys that involved launch pads and more realistic rockets. Most kids played with versions such as this one. Park Plastics, 1950s-60s.*

# "WHAT'S MY LINE?"

**B**Y THE middle 1950s, game manufacturers were beginning to see how useful it could be to draw directly on popular TV programs for board-game inspiration. A new board-game company founded at mid-decade, Lowell Toy Mfg. Corp. of Long Island City, got off to an early start in the just-like-TV department with the What's My Line? game, based on the immensely popular CBS panel show.

In the What's My Line? game, as in the TV show, the "panelists" vie in identifying the "guest." The wonderfully attractive aspect of the Lowell game is that these guests appear within a "television screen," which is a sheet of clear plastic pressed into the shape of the front of a 1950s TV, with knobs and buttons below and What's My Line? above. The parts that represent the TV cabinet are painted, in black and yellow, while the central "screen" remains clear. Large cardboard cards bearing the faces of the celebrities can be inserted from above by the "host," who has the benefit of a clue-line on the back of the photograph.

Lowell was unusual in banking so heavily on television. Its line, which became known as Lowell T.V. Games, also included $64,000 Question, Beat the Clock, and I've Got a Secret.

Other makers of games only gradually followed Lowell's lead into the just-like-TV field. Lisbeth Whiting Co., Inc. of Brooklyn, positioned itself strongly in that area, with Adventures of Lassie and Adventures of Sir Lancelot games and TV Magic Casting Sets. Hassenfeld Bros. was also among the first wave,

**What's My Line?** TV was so good in the 1950s it had to be relived on the playroom floor. Lowell Toy Mfg. Corp., ca. 1955-57.

releasing Mickey Mouse Club and Captain Kangaroo activity sets by 1956 and a series of *Leave It to Beaver* games for the 1960-61 season.

Most board-game makers of the middle 1950s were relying on their perennial sellers and traditional approaches to sustain them, rather than banking on new ideas. Milton Bradley Co., for instance, was actively promoting its Uncle Wiggly games as "year in, year out, a proven profit-maker. An unfailing star in our fast-selling line of games, puzzles, color materials, magnetic and paper dolls, activity items and pre-school toys." Its other lead items, such as Game of the States, Chutes and Ladders, Go to the Head of the Class and Candy Land, were also proven, traditional board games.

If games companies were looking at an example to emulate in 1955, it was not Lowell's venture into TV-land. Their attention was riveted—with, no doubt, not a little envy—by the new success of Selchow & Righter Co. The Brooklyn games company that had thrived for nearly a century on the appeal of the incredibly popular Parcheesi now suddenly had another giant hit with Scrabble, a word game that involved wooden, letter-bearing tiles and a board covered with small squares.

It was a measure of Scrabble's success that another company devised an accessory primarily for Scrabble players. Carrom Industries, Inc., of Ludington, Mich., was enjoying success of its own with its table-top Carrom Boards, among other large activity-oriented games, when it introduced the M-K Turn-Table, "for Scrabble and other word games."

**40**

One of the weaknesses of the Scrabble board was that it had a definite orientation. Even though players would set the board in the middle of a table and sit all around it, there was a "top" and a "bottom" to the board itself. In other words, some players had to look at the board sideways and upside-down. Carrom Industries' M-K Turn-Table improved the situation for many of Scrabble's millions of devoted players.

When, in 1957, Selchow & Righter celebrated its centenary, it proudly paraded Parcheesi and Scrabble alongside one another as "America's favorite games." An exaggeration? If so, it wasn't much of one. ∎

Lowell: Groucho's You Bet Your Life, 1955, $75
Lowell: What's My Line? Game, $45
Pressman: Groucho's TV Quiz Game, 1954, $45

START
PROF.
PLUM

**Mr. Green, with the wrench?** *The playing pieces of the 1950s and '60s hit game "Clue," representing Professor Plum, Colonel Mustard, Mrs. Peacock and their friends and enemies, were simple wooden markers. The die-cast weapons, on the other hand, were morbidly realistic. While board-game makers were beginning to draw heavily on TV for inspiration, some of the most popular board games of the '50s remained the ones that were intrinsically fun. Parker Brothers, 1960.*

# TOM CORBETT

PERHAPS IT was because science fiction was seen as visionary literature that so many Tom Corbett toys of the 1950s—or rather, excuse me, the 25th century—had to do with vision, sight and seeing beyond.

One of the first such toys was the Tom Corbett Space Cadet hat, manufactured by Miller Brothers Hat Co., a New York City firm that was also making the official Gene Autrey hat in 1952. Space Cadets could put on the hat, lower the shades beneath the visor—no doubt they protected young eyes from cosmic rays—and then get to business with their Marx play sets full of spacemen, aliens, rockets and saucers.

Those shades anticipated the toy soon brought out by Herold Products Co., Inc., of Chicago. This new company specialized in field glasses and cameras, using the "Hy-Power" name, and issuing Hopalong Cassidy field glasses in addition to the Space Cadet versions. These were sturdily made toys, with cast-metal bodies and hard-plastic eyepieces. The lenses on both sides are tinted yellow, which undoubtedly helped make Earth look a little like a far-away planet.

Space Cadets could also gaze into the impenetrable darkness of interstellar space with the Space Cadet Signal Siren Flashlight made by U.S. Electric Mfg. Corp., a New York City outfit that also made Roy Rogers and Lone Ranger Signal Siren Flashlights. Also on its product list were the Usalite Space Cadet Pin-On Rocket-Lite and the Whistle-Lite, enabling one to sound and blink an alarm at the same time.

These visionary toys proved popular—enough so that the binocular and the signal-siren were still in production in 1957, after most other Tom Corbett toys had fallen by the wayside. While the binoculars then dropped out of sight, the Space Cadet Signal-Siren Flashlight kept on going and was still illuminating the mysteries of outer space when the 1960s rolled in. ■

**Headgear for a Cadet.** *Tom Corbett Space Cadet hat, Miller Bros., ca. 1952.*

**Shedding light on the future.** *This flashlight toy outlasted all the other Tom Corbett toys, perhaps surviving the arrival of Space Age reality because of its utility. U.S. Electric Mfg. Corp., middle to late '50s.*

**Far-seeing.** *Binocular toys were popular accessories for kids wanting to be like their favorite TV heroes. Yellow lenses in this pair gave the necessary off-planet look to everything seen through them. Herold Products Co., mid-1950s.*

Lee: **Tom Corbett Space Hat, $50**
Marx: **Polaris Rocket Ship, $300**
Marx: **Rex Mars Space Tank, tin-litho, $250**
Saalfield: **Tom Corbett Space Cadet coloring book, 1952, $75**
Saalfield: **Tom Corbett Space Cadet punch-out book, 1952, $95**
**Space Cadet Field Glasses, $60**
**Space Cadet Flashlight, $90**
Transogram: **Countdown Space Game, 1959, $50**

DUMONT, the company that offered the world its first all-electronic television receiver, operated a pioneer broadcasting network in the late 1940s and early '50s. The flagship of the network's programming was aptly named *Captain Video and His Video Rangers*, which started off as a daily, radio-style children's program. Greatly popular among children for its futuristic adventures and props, and among parents for the Captain's regular Ranger-to-Ranger talks to his viewers, *Captain Video* inspired the other space-opera TV serials of the '50s, *Space Patrol* and *Tom Corbett*.

The Captain was played by Richard Coogan in the show's first year, 1949-50, and thereafter by Al Hodge, who had reached radio fame before the war as the Green Hornet. Teen actor Don Hastings, 15 years old when the series started, played the onscreen Ranger and was, if not *the* first, at least one of the first, TV-created teen idols of the Boomer generation.

DuMont, always in financial difficulties, operated on a $25 per week budget for the daily series. Captain Video, who was broadcasting from a secret mountain fortress at some time far in the future, used super-advanced space gadgets constructed from Wanamaker's items, since DuMont was renting from the department store at the time. The controls of the good ship *Galaxy* were painted on cardboard. Especially in the early years, producer James Caddigan filled out the program with breaks to view the Rangers themselves in action. Viewed via "Remote Carrier Beam," they were often cowboys in clips from old Westerns.

The show soon turned into a full-fledged science-fiction TV serial, however. The Captain set out to save the universe from such adversaries as Dr. Clysmok, Heng Foo Seeng, Kul of Eos, Mook the Moon Man, Nargola and the beautiful Atar and her unstoppable mechanical robot slave, Tobor.

Captain Video invented a long run of wonderful gadgets, including the Opticon Scillometer, which could see through anything; the Atomic Rifle; the TV-like portable viewer called the Discatron; the palm-held Radio Scillograph for communications;

**Faces of the future.** *Perhaps because the world was growing ever smaller through air travel, television, newsreel and photo magazines, children had to turn to outer space for utterly strange beings. Aliens, Tom Corbett Play Set, Marx, 1950s.*

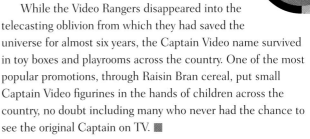

and the Cosmic Ray Vibrator, which made villains vibrate and shake into surrender.

Evil scientist Dr. Pauli, played by Hal Conklin for most of the show's run, fought against the Video Rangers with his Astroidal Society, wielding his Barrier of Silence and Cloak of Invisibility.

DuMont was not fated to survive as a network. The intransigence of Paramount Studios, which had bought a controlling interest and was doing its best to keep down the threatening monster of TV, and the barrier of FCC regulations played into the network's end. DuMont's leadership team was comprised of innovators brilliant at devising new technology for a new medium, but poorly prepared for leading a major corporation in the mid-20th century.

Competition from companies better poised in the industry, even if they were less innovative than DuMont, certainly played its role, too. Who was Dr. Pauli, really? Was he RCA? Was he NBC, or CBS, or the Paramount Theaters/ABC nexus that formed in 1953? Whoever Dr. Pauli was, he won in the end.

DuMont's doors closed in 1955. The Captain's show, now known as *The Secret Files of Captain Video*, last aired April 1, 1955.

While the Video Rangers disappeared into the telecasting oblivion from which they had saved the universe for almost six years, the Captain Video name survived in toy boxes and playrooms across the country. One of the most popular promotions, through Raisin Bran cereal, put small Captain Video figurines in the hands of children across the country, no doubt including many who never had the chance to see the original Captain on TV. ■

**Lido: Captain Video figure, alien or robot, plastic, 2", $15-$20**
**Marx: Play set figure, space alien or robot, 45 mm, $8**
**Milton Bradley: Captain Video Game, 1952, $80**

**They came from out of the Raisin Bran.** *In the 1950s, Raisin Bran cereal issued Captain Video Space Men premiums. T. Cohn made the 2" aliens, robots and space people from a shiny hard plastic. Superior also packaged the figures in small play sets, together with small space vehicles. In the 1960s, they reappeared as premiums in dull, gray-black colored soft plastic. Another plastics company, Lido, made larger Captain Video figures in the 1950s. T. Cohn, 1950s.*

## PAINT BY NUMBER
# RIN TIN TIN

### ENDLESS HOURS OF FUN (OR FRUSTRATION) FOR $1.99.

Painting by number sets kept kids busy producing masterpieces through much of the '50s and '60s. This large Rin Tin Tin set, just over 16" by 13", included eight tubes of paint and nine "easy to color" pictures. Transogram, 1950s.

### BY THE NUMBERS

While New York City's Transogram Co., Inc., would not be heavily pushing its Paint By Numbers Mosaic Art Pictures line until late in the 1950s, the number of companies already issuing paint-by-number kits was impressively large, reflecting the fad-like character of the hobby activity in the middle to late '50s.

As early as 1957, in fact, the term "paint by number" was already a well-enough accepted idea that everyone used the phrase, and no one had made it a trade name for their particular line.

The companies included Peerless Playthings Co., Inc., of Ridgefield Park, N.J.; Avalon Mfg. Corp., of Brooklyn; Palmer Pann Corp. of Toledo, Ohio; Arthur Brown & Bro., Inc., of New York City; The Craftint Mfg. Co. of Cleveland; and The Art Award Co., Inc., of Brooklyn.

EVERYONE, no matter if kid or adult, feels a touch of the miraculous when watching an animal show. The trained animals of showbiz, featured on the magic silver screen or rabbit-eared box, accomplished wonders. They saved people from fires, fetched the rescuing cavalry or jumped on the Bad Man with the gun, diverting the bullet and making everything safe for the Good Guys again. They were champions of sweetness and light.

TV early embraced intelligent animal performers, from Zip the Monkey on the *Howdy Doody Show* to Trigger on *Roy Rogers*. The later Boomers enjoyed a show about a trained porpoise named Flipper.

None could rival the dog heroes, however. Rin Tin Tin, a German shepherd, was the greatly beloved leader of the pack, having started as a movie star in the 1920s. Although that Rinty died in 1932, his descendants included two of the dogs who played the role in the TV series *The Adventures of Rin Tin Tin*, a Western that first aired in October 1954 and continued for nearly five years.

*The Adventures of Rin Tin Tin* was set in the Old West. An orphaned boy named Rusty and his loyal, heroic dog managed to get themselves adopted by a cavalry unit at Fort Apache, Ariz. In a violent world marked by gunfights and warfare against Indians, Rusty and Rin Tin Tin did their best to aid the cavalry and townsfolk of Mesa Grande.

Greatly beloved as a TV star, Rinty appeared on a variety of books, comic books and activity toys. It was inevitable the animal star would be immortalized in art at last—art of the paint-by-number variety, of course. Paint-by-number sets sold in huge numbers through the Boomer years.

While many now will deny having ever painted within the lines, these sets gave many youngsters hours of satisfying entertainment.

By the 1960s, many inexpensive paint-by-number sets gave budding artists the chance to work in more easily controlled acrylics. In the 1950s, however, youths attempting such kits as the Rin Tin Tin Paint By Number had to cope with more temperamental watercolor and tempera paints. ■

> Breyer: Lassie plastic figure, 1958-65, $40
> Transogram: Rin Tin Tin Game, 1950s, $50
> Transogram: Rin Tin Tin Paint By Number, $75
> Whitman: Rin Tin Tin, jigsaw, 1950s, $20

**Bullet.** *Dog toys came in all forms, including small plastic figures to go along with their plastic-cowboy counterparts. Stuart Mfg. Co. of Cincinnati, Ohio, issued this Bullet to accompany its Roy Rogers figures. Here, Bullet strides across a Rin Tin Tin book published by Whitman. Stuart, 1950s.*

**The other dog star.** *Later Boomers grew up knowing Lassie the way early Boomers knew Rin Tin Tin. Lassie coloring sets and other playthings started becoming popular around 1956-57. Frame tray puzzle, Whitman Publishing Co., 1960s.*

# FRAME-TRAY INLAY
# FURY

**FURY.**

Television's Black Stallion, starring figure of a late-1950s TV show, inspired story books, comic books and toys such as this puzzle, which proved a good seller for the company when released in the 1950s. Fury was the second media horse to bear the name. The golden palomino of radio's 1948-51 *Straight Arrow* series was given the same name by children, who selected it through a mail-in promotion sponsored by Nabisco Shredded Wheats. Fury tray puzzle, Whitman Publishing Co., 1950s.

HORSES MOVED from "also-starring" to featured roles as TV matured as a medium. Such popular series as *The Adventures of Champion* in 1955-56, *My Friend Flicka* in 1956-58 and *National Velvet* in 1960-62 moved hooved heroes and heroines closer to the limelight.

None proved as popular or long-lived as *Fury*, aired Saturday mornings from 1955 through 1960. The only show to center primarily on the horse, it featured a Missouri stallion originally named Highland Dale. Ralph McCutcheon, famous at the time for training animal movie stars, discovered Highland Dale at 18 months and moved him to Hollywood, where he appeared in not only his own TV series but also in movies including *Black Beauty*, *Gypsy Colt*, *Wild Is the Wind* and *Giant*, the last one costarring Elizabeth Taylor. Through her hundreds of appearances on film, Fury earned a reputation as the smartest horse in Hollywood.

In the TV show on Saturday mornings, renamed *Brave Stallion* when syndicated from 1960-66, Fury's costars were Peter Graves as Jim, Bobby Diamond as Joey and William Fawcette as Pete.

Horse toys had long proved popular with children, with wheeled riding toys, cast-iron horse-drawn vehicle toys and small lead horses popular early in the 1900s. In the Boomer era, Marx, Stuart, MPC, Ajax, Archer, Tim-Mee and Lido, among other plastics manufacturers, turned out a wide variety of toy horses to fill Western play sets and plastic "header bags" for dime stores. Many of these inexpensive toys were detailed and attractive, often having cast-in saddles and reins and sometimes coming with loose accessories.

Besides the Wonder Products Co., of Collierville, Tenn., which produced countless spring-suspended riding horses for tots, several other toy companies rose in the Boomer years to cater to children with equine infatuations.

Hartland Plastics had its origins outside of the toy industry before the war, producing miscellaneous acetate items for domestic and wartime use. The company, founded by Ed and Iola Walters in Hartland, Wis., in 1941, began

as the Electro Forming Co. After the war, as Hartland Plastics, it started producing a variety of horses and Western and historical figures familiar to children. They included Annie Oakley, Jim Bowie, George Washington and Robert E. Lee. They were joined by characters more abundantly represented in toy form at the time—the Lone Ranger and Tonto, Matt Dillon, Roy Rogers and Dale Evans.

In contrast, Breyer Molding Co., founded in Chicago in the early 1950s, emphasized stallions, mares, mules, ponies and colts to exemplify different breeds, largely passing over their riders. For TV's most popular horse, Breyer produced both Fury and Black Stallion figures. Oddly enough, although Breyer became famous for its realistically modeled horse and dog toys, its first toys, around 1950-52, were Money Manager banks.

The Aurora Plastics Corp. created a Black Fury for model builders and reissued it in the late Boomer years. Kenner Products Co. produced Give-A-Show reels, and publishers including Grosset & Dunlap, Dell, and Whitman made sure Fury's hooves sounded as loudly during reading time as during TV time.

But almost everyone started with Frame-Tray Inlay Puzzles made by Whitman Publishing. The puzzles provided most Boomers with their earliest problem-solving exercises, while also giving them an outlet for their earliest hero worship. They could assemble, disassemble and reassemble Fury and Rin Tin Tin hour after hour.

I had no idea how deeply embedded these puzzles are in our minds until I was talking with a friend who remembered more clearly than I do those hours bent over the Frame-Tray Inlay. But once he started describing how many pieces of these puzzles were different shapes—bells, ships, people, planes—it all came back to me with the vividness of having just put down the puzzle after a play time. ■

---

**Breyer: Fighting Stallion, 1961-71, $150**
**Breyer: Running Foal, glossy gray, 1963-73, $45**
**Jaymar: Bullwinkle & Rocky, frame tray puzzle, 1960s, $30**
**Jaymar: Red Ryder, frame tray puzzle, 1951, $10**
**Jaymar: Winky Dink, frame tray puzzle, 1950s, $40**
**Whitman: Fury, frame tray puzzle, 1950s, $20**
**Whitman: Jetsons, frame tray puzzle, 1962, $30**
**Whitman: Lassie, frame tray puzzle, 1957, $20**
**Whitman: Little Lulu, frame tray puzzle, 1959, $25**
**Whitman: Ruff & Reddy, frame tray puzzle, 1950s, $25**
**Whitman: Zorro, frame tray puzzle, 1950s-60s, $20**

**Grazing beauty.** *Even though cowboys rode horses, too, horse toys were often seen as girl toys in many households. Glossy hard plastic proved to be the material of choice for many horse toy manufacturers. Hartland, 1960s.*

# ATOMIC
# MOBILE UNIT

**K**IDS OF the Boomer years grew up under a shadow new to history. The shadow grew from the fission of atoms, considered the building blocks of the universe. Atom bombs flashed over New Mexico, then over Hiroshima and Nagasaki, ending the war in the Pacific and beginning a generation whose name, "Boomers," had an ironic reverberation to it.

The fission bomb that brought an already crippled Japan to raise the flag of surrender grew into a more powerful fusion bomb. At the same time, the ultimate weapon, as it was then seen, grew from being the proud result of American ingenuity, sweat and willpower, into a global fact of life, as the Soviet Union soon tested a copycat device, only it was not a copycat. It was the real thing.

As the cold war settled over the world, kept cold by the sun-hot temperatures the Bomb threatened, Americans found themselves faced with the prospect of global conflict, one that might come to their very doorsteps. Wendell Willkie promoted the idea of a small world, one in which people could travel from country to country in hours, and in which everyone's concerns were as one neighbor for another. Yet that same nearness and smallness could apply to war, for a bomber could just as easily drop an atomic bomb in the middle of the Great Plains as above a museum dome in Hiroshima.

Adults learned about making their own bomb shelters through the pages of *Popular Mechanics* and other handicraft magazines, while children in schools went through regular

"IT'S A WOW! IT'S A NATURAL!
IT'S THE NEW ATOMIC
SKETCHPAD THAT GLOWS IN
THE DARK! FOR BOYS AND
GIRLS OF ALL AGES!"

—advertisement for the Atomic
Sketchpad, Apco Mossberg Co. of
Attleboro, Mass., 1949.

drills to prepare for nuclear attack. "Duck and cover!" Those two commands seemed sufficient for a time. Black-and-white newsreels distributed through the school systems demonstrated the approach. All the children needed to do was get beneath their wood and steel school desks with their heads beneath their hands.

How strange, then, that children thrilled to the word "atomic." It may have been that the best therapy for children was facing the threat directly. They could drive their Atomic Mobile Unit into the war zone, raise the rocket sights, set the trigger and then launch the atomic missiles, striking decisive blows for Right and for Good and for the American Way.

Children knew these concepts. They were featured in newsreels, in news programs, in their children's television programs and in their classroom history lessons. Best of all, they were featured in their toys. "Best of all?" So it seemed at the time.

In the mid-1950s, Ideal was releasing a number of elaborate larger vehicle toys, with one of the best being its Atomic Mobile Unit, or Rocket Launching Truck, as it is called on its box. Measuring almost a foot long, the hard-plastic truck features a spring-loaded launcher that can be raised with a crank, red polyethylene rockets and an ammo box beneath the nifty control panel at the rocket's side. Why an ammo box? To store powder caps that could be inserted into the "atomic" missiles, which then exploded when they struck their target.

## TAKE-APART TOYS

The Atomic Mobile Unit was one of a series of larger hard-plastic trucks being made by Ideal during the early and middle 1950s. Many of the others emphasized an idea expressed by Ideal's "Fix-It" name: they were toys that could be taken apart and put back together. Such toys typically had a few parts that came off easily and some miniature tools in a tool chest.

Ideal's Fix-It toys were matched by Louis Marx & Co.'s Take-Apart toys of the same time period. The idea of the tool chest even reappeared in nonvehicle toys, with Robert the Robot having a secret tool chamber in his first incarnation.

The idea of the take-apart toy probably found its ultimate expression in another toy by Ideal Corp., Mr. Machine, the best-known plastic robot of the next decade. Yet the idea also found expression in a different sort of toy, which, like Mr. Machine, made a big splash in 1960: Crashmobile, made by Tri-Play Toys Co., Inc., of Chicago, whose products were being promoted on TV by Art Linkletter.

There is an irony here, for toy companies successfully sold these toys to the same kids who spent their playtimes assembling Erector sets and American Bricks buildings, and who hated to take their creations apart at clean-up time. ■

Ideal: Atomic Rocket Launching Truck, with fair box, $75
Marx: Fix-All Wrecker Truck, with tools and box, $100

**First-strike capability.** *Nothing less than atomic weapons empowered postwar children, who were born into a world capable, for the first time, of instant mass-destruction. The toy was renamed the ICBM Launching Truck in 1958. Ideal, mid-1950s.*

# SPUTNIK
## THE MAGNETIC SATELLITE

NOT EVERY TOY that made a hit during the Boomer years received huge promotions in *Life* magazine or on TV. Some simply appeared, were accepted, did their job—which was to entertain someone for a while—and then disappeared.

Maggie Magnetic, Inc., of Paterson, New Jersey, produced one such toy that turned into a minor hit of the late 1950s: the Maggie Whee-Lo, consisting of a thick wire track, a plastic wheel, and a heavily magnetized spoke that ran through the wheel and connected it to the contorted track.

It amused people, watching the wheel roll rapidly up and down. The wheel turned and rolled along the top of the track, looped over the bend, even if it was upside-down, and then passed around to the other side. It went back and forth, and up and down, for as long as the person cared to stand playing with the toy. The wheel hummed as it went more quickly. In seeming to defy gravity, it easily absorbed a child long enough for a storekeeper to make the sale.

Maggie Magnetic issued a more complex version of the toy to capitalize on American furor over Russia's having been the first to launch an artificial satellite into Earth orbit. With

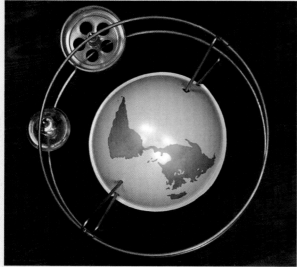

**The space race brought home.** America's astonishment at Russia's satellite program, which included the launch of a living passenger into orbit around Earth, found its way down to child level with this toy. Sputnik, Maggie Magnetic, Inc., late 1950s.

the MAGNETIC WALKING WHEEL

its Sputnik, the Magnetic Satellite, the company turned the hand-held track into a circle on the outer side of which the magnetized wheel, representing an American satellite, could run. On the inside of the track, Maggie Magnetic placed a hollow plastic ball, representing Russia's satellite. Inside was a flat plastic dog, one of Russia's animal cosmonauts.

The child's hand fit over the handle in the center of the circle, where it was hidden by a plastic hemisphere painted to look like the Earth. The Americas were showing, of course.

"Run your own exciting Space Race! Watch our Satellite chase the little traveller 'round and 'round the Outer Space Orbit!" Maggie Magnetic knew exactly what nerve it was striking with those words: America's rawest one.

Whee-Lo turned out to be one of the perennial novelty toys that would keep appearing from different manufacturers through the Boomer years. While Maggie Magnetic, Inc., was the innovator, the tradition was carried on in the 1970s by The Tarrson Co. of Chicago. ■

Dell: Satellite Rocket Launcher punch-out book, 1959, $40
Maggie Magnetic: Sputnik, $75-$100
Maggie Magnetic: The Twister, $45
Maggie Magnetic: Whee-Lo, with box, $15

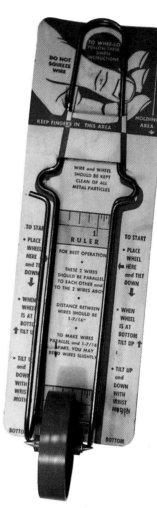

**It goes ... and goes ... and goes.** *The Whee-Lo seemed to defy gravity as it rolled over the top of track and then over the underside. The powerful magnet serving as the axle kept the wheel firmly attached, no matter the orientation. Maggie Magnetic, Inc., 1950s.*

**The first Twister.** *This exceptionally enjoyable spinning toy incorporated, for no doubt the first time in toy history, the Moebius strip. The "spinning mystery wheel" whirls first inside the track, then outside. Maggie Magnetic, Inc., 1958. Photo by Martha Borchardt.*

# PREHISTORIC
## TIMES

READILY ADMIT my biases. One is for dinosaurs. In this bias, I was far from alone in the Boomer years. Trips to the Denver Museum of Natural History were a source of great excitement. There I could see massive skeletons from the Age of Mammals and the Age of Reptiles, and could ponder the plaster casts of Protoceratops eggs from the Roy Chapman Andrews expeditions, and ogle, through the counter glass in the museum shop, the cast-metal dinosaurs for sale there.

I was a kid. How could I buy things like that? They cost something like $8 each. I *could* afford plastic dinosaurs, however. Occasionally, I would have enough for a bag of brightly colored plastic dinosaurs made by MPC, which the convenience store nearby carried. These I would put in my dinosaur box, which had other MPC dinos, a few Tim-Mee dinos, a few Frito-Lay premiums and two or three dinosaurs by the true rulers of prehistoric times, the Louis Marx Co.

I had no idea where my treasured, large, gray Tyrannosaurus rex came from. It was well-worn and obviously heavily played with, for its left toes were smoothed-down to the point it tended to fall over if not judiciously placed so its left foot rested on higher ground.

I do remember where another Marx I had came from. I literally dug it up. At one house where we lived, in an older suburb around Denver, I was engaging in a favorite activity, which was digging in a dirt pile in the backyard. I imagined I was digging for dinosaurs and was thoroughly startled to actually find one. At the time I deeply pondered the differences between these toys and the slightly less elaborate ones made by MPC. I had no way of digging into

toy prehistory and finding out about Marx's fabulous Prehistoric Times play sets. Although Marx was still making them at the time, it would be decades before I would see one.

In 1958, Marx gave this description to entice children—as if they needed any enticements other than the plastic dinosaurs and cave people themselves: "You take off in your Time Machine, headed for prehistoric times. There's a dizzying sensation as it hovers over your home—and suddenly the buildings are gone. Instead, you see forest landscape below. Palms and ferns are everywhere. There's a waterfall, and that splash of color is a clear blue pool. Drinking from it are a group of strange, monstrous animals. Dinosaurs! You gasp as you see a big Allosaurus move off in leaping bounds. And there's the Dimetrodon, its spine adorned by a giant 'sail'—the Stegosaurus, with its double row of bony plates—the Brontosaurus, hugest of all saurians! There's the Pteranodon, a flying reptile, with dagger-like beak and 27-foot wingspread.

"And now you gasp again, for you recognize other primitive figures. They're cavemen, attired in shaggy furs and battling a duck-billed Hadrosaurus with stones, spears, and primitive

**March of the ancients.** *Instead of elaborate Marx play sets, most Boomer kids grew up with dinosaurs bought by the bag at dime stores, made by Marx or other toy companies. Other children put together the fabulously popular dinosaur-skeleton models released by ITC Modelcraft, the hobby division of Ideal Toy Corp. Plastic dinosaurs, MPC, 1960s.*

**Shadows of the past.** *Marx's Prehistoric Times play sets combined all ancient eras into one. Cave people, prehistoric mammals, dinosaurs and even earlier reptiles walked and crawled side by side. Marx, 1950s.*

clubs. And they're winning, too—until another battler enters the fray. It is the huge Tyrannosaurus —50 feet long, 20 feet high and eight tons of fighting fury! The cavemen flee, but the big monster is gaining. Gunning the Time Machine to top speed, you catch up, then hover just above the Tyrannosaur's head, distracting the awful beast until the cavemen can reach the shelter of their caves. Then, with a friendly wave at the grateful cavemen, you roar off—headed for new adventures!"

The first Prehistoric Times set had appeared in time for the previous Christmas, and was available for less than $5. The 47 pieces included plastic palms, ferns and a rocky landscape made of thin, brittle plastic, with a simulated pool at its center. The set returned the next Christmas with 44 pieces, a form it stayed in for several years.

Through the rest of the Boomer period, Marx sold dinosaurs. They came on cards, in bags and in play sets—including, in 1961-62, the Flintstones play set. In that set, dinosaurs were simply a part of the Stone Age suburban scene— much as they were in the Boomer suburban scene. ■

Marx: Prehistoric Times play set, #3389, $180
Marx: Prehistoric Times play set, #3398, $150

# HONEY WHEAT
# DINOSAURS

|S IT that the best things come in small packages, or that the small things come in the best packages? A kid growing up in the late 1950s had trouble with this axiom, especially when trying to convince mom to buy yet another ("You haven't finished the last one, kid!") box of Nabisco Honey Wheats, just to get another Honey Wheats Dinosaur. When mom finally gave in, the dinosaur inside ended up being one the kid already had. Of course.

The colors of the dinosaurs, issued around 1958 in Honey Wheat and Rice Honey cereal boxes, were glorious: a swirled, honey golden color; a swirled, cranberry-relish red color; or a swirled, yellowish green.

The dinosaurs themselves were small—2 inches long, or less—and stylized, a bit chubby and just the slightest bit cute, even though they were dinosaurs: Brontosaurus, Tyrannosaurus, Stegosaurus, Triceratops, Trachodon, Ankylosaurus and Parasaurolophus, as well as the Plesiosaur, the swimming reptile.

The slightly later group of kids being raised in the 1960s had their chance at the same creatures but with darker and duller black and gray colors in packages of Frito Lay corn chips. ■

**Prehistory, Honey Wheat style.** *Dinosaur premiums appeared in boxes of Honey Wheats and Rice Honeys in the late 1950s, making children dig into their cereal with paleontological fervor. National Biscuit Co., late 1950s.*

Honey Wheat Dinosaurs, various, $5-$10

**Sinclair dinos.** *Dinosaur toys served as premiums for Sinclair, too. Stations gave away free bags of tiny toys with fill-ups. 1960s.*

# SPOONMEN

I N THE late 1940s, Nabisco was looking for a way to move into the lucrative children's cereal market, which was dominated by Post, Kellogg's and General Mills. Deciding on Shredded Wheat as the cereal to promote, the company hired an advertising company to create a new radio show, which led to the Mutual Network's *Straight Arrow*, featuring an Indian hero. Soon, Injun-Uity Cards, carrying tidbits of American Indian know-how, appeared in Shredded Wheat as a premium.

In the 1950s, Nabisco hit on a new way of winning its way into children's fancies and cereal bowls. Included in packages of Spoon Size Shredded Wheat were the Spoonmen, who were a trio of plastic spacemen whose heads looked like the Nabisco logo and who had slots in their seats that would fix them to the handle of the average cereal spoon. They even had names: Munchy, Crunchy and Spoonsize. The cereal, like the Spoonmen, took off.

## ADVOCATE OF OUTER-SPACE EATING.

The Spoonmen appeared on the packages of "Spoon Size" Shredded Wheat Juniors riding on spoons through outer space. National Biscuit Co., 1950s.

### SPOONMEN SUPPLEMENTS

The plastic cereal premiums were not the only Spoonmen playthings of the 1950s. Kids could play with Spoonmen stuffed toys made by Schwartz Toy Mfg. Corp., of Brooklyn, N.Y. Or they could put on Spoonmen space helmets, made by Arant & Co., Inc., of Sausalito, Calif. Even Halloween could be a Nabisco experience, with Spoonmen costumes made by Collegeville Flag & Mfg. Co. of Collegeville, Pa. ∎

Spoonmen, $35-$50

**Sitters and hangers.** *Winnie the Pooh spoonsitters were issued as premiums in boxes of Wheat Honeys and Rice Honeys in the mid-1960s. Packages featured Nabisco figure Buddy Bee promising, "Inside! One of seven Breakfast Buddies!" The Breakfast Buddies could not only sit on spoons but also hang onto the edges of cereal bowls. National Biscuit Co., 1960s.*

# LIGHTS! SOUND! A-C-T-I-O-N!
# JAPANESE BATTERY TOYS

PEOPLE shopping for toys in 1953 could find a wide variety of metal toys that would have given them the satisfaction, had they considered the issue at all, of supporting domestic industry. American companies were making the toys, and the actual manufacturing was taking place in American cities by American workers.

Matters were rapidly changing, however. In 1954 and '55, toy imports began appearing in greater number, especially toy imports from West Germany and Japan. While the export activities of those two countries was a means of funding their recovery, it seemed as they were making a consumer-goods retaliation for their military defeats. Mail-order catalogs gave increasing space to these toys, and department stores began to carry them as a matter of course. They were typically inexpensive, brightly colored, well-designed ingenious toys.

The occasional flow of imports into this country, in 1955—remote-control speedsters from West Germany, for instance, and friction-motor truck fleets from Japan—soon became a steady stream and then a flood.

By the time Barbie appeared on the scene, it was hardly a matter of comment that an American manufacturer would package Japanese-made items under the American trade name. By the time G.I. Joe appeared, many American toy manufacturers had grown dependent on overseas production facilities.

Among the most visible imported toys were the battery-operated models of the later 1950s and 1960s. Most of them were manufactured in Japan, and many of them had a charm that reflected their country of origin. That a culture with so long a tradition of expert handcrafts should prove extremely adept at metal fabrication and tin-litho design should have come as no surprise.

The 1950s Japanese import Battery Operated Super Susie is an exceptional example of these toys but also a typical one. Super Susie is a bear, which is one of the animals most frequently used in these toys. Colorful tin-litho was used in Super Susie's check-out counter and cash register. Plastic was used in her snout and hands, as well as in the grocery items that

**Super Toy.** *The Linemar Super Susie was one of the many battery-operated wonders imported from Japan through most of the Boomer years. How many such toys were imported may never be known—nor even the number of different designs that were made, since many toys were made for only short periods of time or were gradually altered because of changing material availability or shifting fashions. Since many toy parts were made in mom-and-pop shops, which were then assembled by the putative "manufacturers," it is remarkable that some toys remained essentially the same for the period of a year or more. Linemar, 1950s.*

**50**

move on the conveyor while she rings up the sale. She was made with cloth blouse, collar and bonnet. And the fur of her head helped give her that brown-bear look.

She was not the sort of toy to be manipulated by a child, but rather the sort of toy to be turned on for sheer delight. Her hands moved, the grocery items moved along the counter, she punched up different prices from the cash register—and she moved her head, sometimes looking at the items being sold and sometimes at the register.

The prices around the sides of her colorful counter has preserved for us the happily low prices of her world: orange juice on sale for 10 cents a can; apples, 50 cents a basket; soap, 4 cents. This particular Super Susie also preserves her own low price. The box has its Up-Town Toyland price sticker: $3.98. The "Your Save-Mor Store" string-tag on the toy itself confirms the price.

To give some perspective, here are a few toy prices from the *Sears Christmas Book* for 1956. Robert the Robot cost $5.69. A Structo Cattle Transport cost $3.59, and the 21-5/8 inch Structo Ready-Mix Concrete Truck cost $6.98. A 10-piece Auburn Rubber set of vinyl fire trucks and firemen cost $1.79. A set of eight Argo cars also cost $1.79. A Marx Automatic Power Shovel cost $3.79. The smallest American Skyline set cost $3.59. A 51-inch vinyl Punch Me cost $2.98. A Roy Rogers two-gun holster set cost $3.79.

It was a price many American companies could not compete with for that kind of toy. Super Susie was a complicated toy automaton with numerous small parts. Her manufacture required delicate assembly and ready access to a variety of cheap materials—and to cheap skilled labor, too.

That some companies simply took advantage of the situation and developed ties with Japanese manufacturing and export firms is certainly clear, too, from the example of Super Susie, who was a Linemar ("Best by Far") toy. The line on the bottom of the box ends gives away the toy's true origin: "One of the many Linemar Toys ... Do you have all of them?" That line echoed similar lines found on the packaging of toy after toy manufactured by Louis Marx & Co., whose Japanese affiliate was Linemar.

Some companies had the clout and wherewithal to set up such arrangements in the 1950s and '60s. Others were simply forced to give in and give up the toy business. ■

> **Yonezawa: Space Saucer Mercury X-1, $175**
> **Yoshiya: Space Dog, 1950s, $250**
> **Zoomer Robot, 1950s, $300**

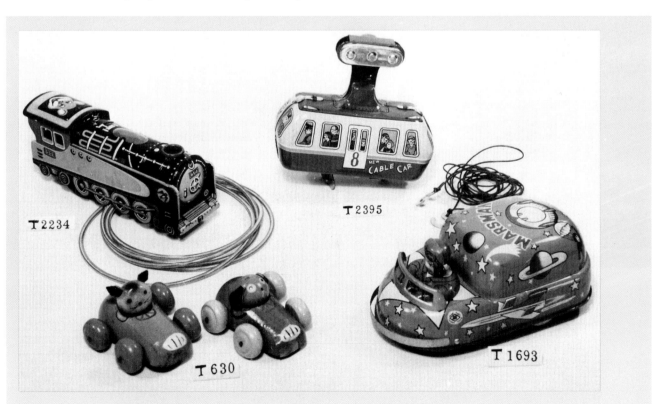

*Miscellaneous tin toys imported by Minamoto Trading Co., Los Angeles, in the 1950s.*

# THE LONE RANGER
## AND THE PLASTIC OLD WEST

THE LONE RANGER was among the first wave of television serials. First appearing in September 1949, and having a remarkable run lasting nearly a decade, the show ended in September 1957.

Unlike Roy Rogers, who started in movies, or Hopalong Cassidy, who had his origins in pulp magazines, the Lone Ranger was a child of prewar radio. The Lone Ranger began his days as John Reid, a young member of a posse of Texas Rangers chasing desperadoes. The bandits lured the Rangers into a canyon and ambushed them. Left for dead, Reid managed to crawl to the safety of a water hole, where he was found by a friendly Indian whom Reid had once helped. Tonto, the Indian, said to Reid, "You kemo sabe. It mean 'trusty scout.'" Vowing vengeance on the outlaws, Reid became the Lone Ranger and set out in pursuit of his enemy Butch Cavendish.

Clayton Moore played the Lone Ranger for much of the TV show's run, first in 1949-'52, and again 1954-'57, with John Hart playing the masked man in the middle years. Jay Silverheels, part Mohawk, played Tonto.

*The Lone Ranger* was originally created for radio before the war by George Trendel and Fran Striker, who also created yet another masked crime fighter, the Green Hornet. The mask itself was apparently a family tradition: the Green Hornet's father was John Reid's nephew.

While playing the Lone Ranger was commonplace before World War II—a mask and cowboy hat were easy to come by, after all, and Lone Ranger cap pistols were made even in the cast-iron toy days—young Boomers in the 1950s saw a new world open with the Marx Western play sets. While playing cowboys and Indians never entirely vanished from school

*Marx Western pioneer and Indian figures, 1950s.*

**Hi-Ho Silver, and away!** It only took two accessories— a hat, and a mask—to make any child one of the great Western heroes. Lone Ranger and Silver plastic figures, 60 mm., Marx, 1950s. Courtesy Ken Boyer.

playgrounds and back yards, a new tradition based on plastic figures was born on play-room floors. Marx released Lone Ranger sets, in addition to many other Western sets through much of the 1950s.

Other companies, including Tim-Mee, Stuart, MPC and Lido helped Marx ensure the Boomers spent hours at a time with bellies flat to the floor, surveying their vast but miniature Old West dominions. ◾

Hartland: Tonto plastic figure and horse, miniature series, $75
Hartland: Paladin plastic figure and horse, MIB, $250
Marx: Fort Apache Carryall, #4685, play set, $75
Marx: Lone Ranger play set figure, 60 mm, $20
Marx: Tonto play set figure, 60 mm, $20
Marx: Rin Tin Tin, #3628, play set, $300

*Tim-Mee Western pioneer figures, 1960s.*

**Faithful companion.** *Friendly Indian characters of the 1950s included radio's Straight Arrow; Red Ranger's friend Little Beaver; and Tonto, the most imitated Indian figure of the Boomer school yard. Tonto plastic figure, 60 mm., Marx, 1950s. Courtesy Ken Boyer.*

"BIG NEWS LIKE BLOCK CITY TRAVELS FAST. THE TRADE SECRET WE WOULDN'T TELL BEFORE IS THE TALK OF THE TRADE TODAY ... YES, BLOCK CITY IS THE MOST THRILLING CONSTRUCTION TOY EVER CREATED! IT'S COLORFUL. IT'S TIMELY. AND THERE'S NO LIMIT TO ITS APPEAL TO BOYS AND GIRLS OF EVERY AGE!"

—ADVERTISEMENT FOR BLOCK CITY, TRI-STATE PLASTIC MOLDING CO., HENDERSON, KY., 1949.

# Real-Life Make-Believe

At the end of the 1960s, children were playing with a selection of toys that included the newest alongside the oldest.

Television shows were still inspiring the creation of popular new playthings, including Talking Gentle Ben and Talking Captain Kangaroo Doll, soft dolls made by Mattel for the youngest kids, and the same company's Buffy and Mrs. Beasley dolls, for all TV-watching young girls. With gosh-wow TV spots selling toys by the millions, it was inevitable a backlash would occur, especially from toy retailers who faced increasingly heavy post-Christmas returns of toys. Too many were failing to live up to their hype. In 1968 and '69, however, the worst of that backlash was largely still in the future. Toys that played well on the TV screen were still the ones making kids clamor for ever more toys — even though they already owned more toys than any previous generation of kids ever had.

It's just like playing in a real game!

At the same time, many tried-and-true playthings kept appearing on store shelves. These old-fashioned items brought pleasure in an old-fashioned way. Usually, too, they brought a much more lasting pleasure to children than did the TV-advertised toys, which were often disappointingly low in play value.

Even the big companies kept old-fashioned toys in their lists. Mattel was still making the jack-in-the-box, at the end of the '60s. Hassenfeld Bros. was making ring-toss games and bagatelles. Such other companies as Alox Mfg. Co. of St. Louis, Mo., and Chemical Sundries Co. of Chicago were making jack-and-ball sets not too different from the ones enjoyed by the Boomers' parents and grandparents. A few, such as Louis Marx and Smethport Specialty Co., were even still releasing tin-litho toys evocative of older times. While the flashy toys waxed and waned in popularity, the standards steadily held their place on the playroom floor.

### Child-Height Appliances
Sturdy Fiberboard
Were 4.44 each **3.99**

**6-9 MATCHING APPLIANCES.** Sturdy corrugated fiberboard. Doors on wood dowel hinges, plastic pull handles. Sink and range have plastic counter top. Easy to assemble. Accessories included. Were 4.44 each last Christmas.
(6) CUPBOARD. 2 sliding doors for top storage; 2 shelves, silverware tray. 34 Y 5921E—18x42x12½-in. overall size. Ship. wt. 8 lb. Mail...........3.99
(7) SINK. Realistic plastic faucet pump. 18x12½x28¾-inches overall. 34 Y 5923E—Accessories included. Shipping wt. 7 lb. Mail...........3.99
(8) RANGE. "See thru" window. 18x12½x28¾-in. 34Y5922E-6 lb. Mail. 3.99
(9) REFRIGERATOR. Large sep. freezer, metal door catches. 42x18x12½-in. 34 Y 5920E—Plenty of shelf space. Shipping weight 8 lb. Mailable....3.99

# GO TO THE HEAD OF THE CLASS

AN APOCRYPHAL STORY goes this way: A pious man of the cloth stopped the young businessman Milton Bradley on the street. The clergyman had heard some disturbing gossip.

"I hear," said the horrified clergyman, "you're making a game of cards!"

"It's true."

"But Bradley—you're a *Methodist*."

Bradley smiled and showed the clergyman his game. It had a quaint and proper name: Curious Bible Questions.

"A sure-fire thing for a Sunday afternoon," said Bradley. "I think it will stimulate Bible reading, don't you?"

Many "educational" cards of the time simply had snippets of information or religious patter on each otherwise normal playing card, which made them more palatable for those who professed to have religious beliefs counter to card playing. Milton Bradley's Curious Bible Questions, however, was simply a trivia game without suits and numbers. It pretended to be nothing but what it was.

Abashed, the clergyman tried to communicate that perhaps Bradley had indeed produced a positive and maybe even uplifting game, albeit with cards. Soon thereafter, Bradley introduced another version with a brazen name aimed directly at churches: Sunday School Cards.

Trivia games kept appearing through the years. During the middle Boomer years, the trivia quiz game of choice was Go to the Head of the Class, produced in the 1950s and '60s by the same Milton Bradley Co.

The board was designed to look like a school room. It showed desks occupying the bulk of the space and the teacher's chalkboard at one end. The playing pieces were cardboard images of children and adults, set in wooden bases in the '50s, and in plastic ones in the '60s.

The trivia quiz was divided into Junior, Intermediate and Senior sections, which allowed people of all ages to struggle forward to the head of the class. Or slip back to the dunce's chair. ■

> **Milton Bradley: Go to the Head of the Class, various versions, $10-$15**

## GO TO THE HEAD OF THE CLASS

## TRIVIA QUIZ

from the *New Triple Quiz Book*, 1955

1. Complete this line: Little Polly Flinders ...
2. Complete this line: A Dillar, a Dollar ...
3. What is the name of Dixie Dugan's little niece?
4. Who is Joe Palooka's little friend who can't talk?
5. A young hare is called ...
6. Which letter of the alphabet do Bridge players often use?
7. What royal comic strip character never talks?
8. What comic strip character agrees with everyone?
9. TV Slogan: What gives you "No unpleasant after-taste?"
10. TV Slogan: What "Guards against throat scratch?"
11. TV Slogan: What is "Look sharp, feel sharp, be sharp?"
12. TV Slogan: What fights headaches three ways?
13. TV Slogan: What does L.S.M.F.T. stand for?
14. TV Slogan: "What'll you have?"
15. Automobile: My model name is Land Cruiser, but what is my real name?

16. Automobile: My model name is Firedome 8, but what am I usually called?
17. Automobile: My model name is Hornet, but what is my common name?
18. What is the popular name of the F4U made by Chance Vought?
19. What is the popular name of the F80 made by Lockheed?
20. How big a crew does a B-36 bomber have?
21. What is the popular name of the C-119 manufactured by Fairchild?
22. Who led the American League in hitting in 1951?
23. Who was the top pitcher in the National League in 1951?
24. What is the number one U.S. magazine in both circulation and advertising revenue?
25. What is the number two U.S. magazine in advertising revenue?
26. Within 105,000, what was the circulation of *Life* magazine in 1951?
27. In playing Easy Money, how much money does each player start off with?
28. What company makes Lux toilet soap?
29. What company makes Mobilgas?
30. What company makes Crayrite crayons?

**Not just skill.** *The aim of "Go to the Head of the Class" is to move from desk to desk, grade to grade, and win by graduating first. Players move not just by answering questions, but by drawing "Luck" cards. "You are a general nuisance," says one. "GO BACK 7 DESKS." Although simple in concept, the board is an attractive one, evocative of the one-room schoolhouses that were disappearing in the early Boomer years. Milton Bradley, mid-1950s.*

## THE DUNCE'S CHAIR
## (ANSWERS)

1. Sat among the cinders.
2. A ten o'clock scholar.
3. Imogene.
4. Max.
5. A leveret.
6. W (double you).
7. The Little King.
8. The Timid Soul.
9. Chesterfield.
10. Pall Mall.
11. Gillette Blue Blades.
12. Bromo Seltzer.
13. Lucky Strike Means Fine Tobacco.
14. Pabst Blue Ribbon.
15. Studebaker.
16. DeSoto.
17. Hudson.
18. Corsair.
19. Shooting Star.
20. Fifteen.
21. Flying Boxcar.
22. Ferris Fain - .344.
23. Preacher Roe. 23-3, for Brooklyn.
24. Life.
25. Saturday Evening Post.
26. 5,297,000.
27. $2,000.
28. Lever Brothers.
29. Socony-Vacuum Oil Co., Inc.
30. Milton Bradley Co.

# THE ROAD TO MILLIONS
# MONOPOLY

TO ANY AMERICAN emerging from the trying years of the Great Depression, the opportunity to make money—great, heaping piles of it—must have seemed irresistible. A Germantown, Pa., man named Charles B. Darrow apparently entertained himself during the Depression years with a homemade game that involved traveling in a circle without reaching any discernible goal. It also involved real estate and those great, heaping piles of money. The game arose from a long tradition of finance games popular in America since the last century when games such as McLoughlin's Bulls and Bears offered players a Wall Street experience, and The Monopolist, also by McLoughlin, put players into "the great struggle between Capital and Labor (which) can be fought out to the satisfaction of all parties." If the players were successful, they could "break the Monopolist and become Monopolists themselves."

After initially rejecting Darrow's game and then watching him successfully sell it through Wanamaker's in Philadelphia, Parker Brothers of Salem, Mass., acquired Monopoly and released it in 1935, with four waxed-wood, chess-style pawns for playing pieces. In its first year, it rose to be the best-selling game in the country.

Parker Brothers attempted a monopoly over finance games by releasing Monopoly Jr., Finance, and Finance and Fortune in the next few years. They could have saved themselves the effort, since Monopoly did it all by itself.

In 1937 the company made the decision that helped Monopoly become an American institution. Parker Brothers turned to Dowst Mfg. Co. of Chicago to produce a set of die-cast playing pieces that are now familiar around the globe. Dowst, a name well known in die-cast manufacturing circles in this country from the 1890s, had combined with its fellow Chicago die-casting company Cosmo in making various trinkets, food premiums including Cracker Jack prizes and game pieces. For many years Dowst, under its far more famous Tootsietoy brand name, issued the familiar pieces independent of Parker Brothers in bubble-pack assortments through dime stores.

Wartime restrictions forced Parker Brothers to use wooden pawns again. By 1947, however, the company returned to the metal pieces. Offered alongside its $2 Monopoly with wood pawns was the restored $3.50 Monopoly with the full complement of die-cast playing pieces, some of which did not survive through the entire Boomer period: cannon, thimble, iron,

**LONELY AT THE TOP.**

The famous Scotty dog stands atop a board now globally famous. Most Boomers can hardly imagine childhood without Monopoly. The game had also been enjoyed by the generation before them. Parker Brothers, 1950s-60s.

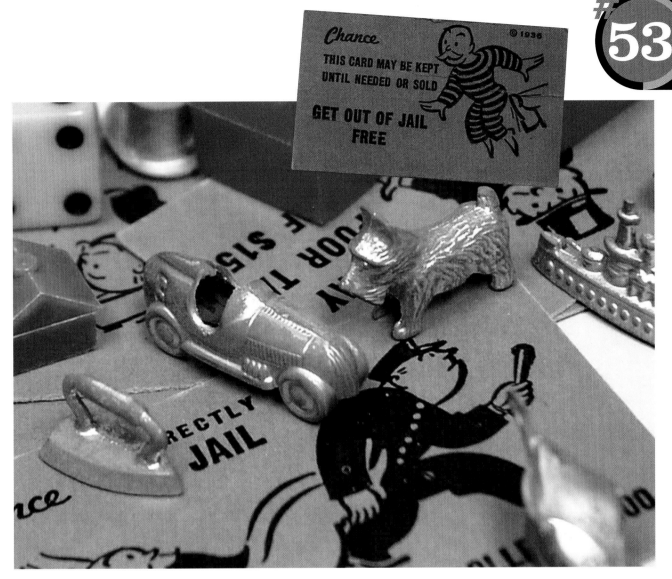

top hat, wheelbarrow, Scotty dog, battleship, racing car, airplane and man atop a rearing horse.

For the first postwar game players, Parker Brothers also issued the well-established Finance game and Dig, the game of gold-mine shares, which made its debut just before the war. Parker also introduced a new finance game, featuring a familiar figure called Rich Uncle. "Fast action, big business! Watch the market quotations shift luck fast!" The new game had, of course, lots of play money.

Monopoly, however, was clearly a special game. Consistently Parker Brothers' best-seller, Monopoly became an international success by 1958, when Charles Darrow took a three-month tour of Australia, New Zealand and the Far East to help promote the game. As the president of Parker Brothers at the time, Robert Barton, noted, "Human nature's pretty much the same the world over. Everyone would like to be a millionaire."

Baby Boomers played Monopoly games by the millions. Parker Brothers eventually became famous for variant versions of the game. Perhaps the most notable of Boomer years was the 1964 underwater set built for New England Divers, Inc., with its cellophane-laminated steel board. It weighed 95 pounds.

Probably a good measure of the game's popularity can be measured by events of the 1970s, years when most Baby Boomers were maturing and beginning to define their adult interests. In 1973, the World Championships began for dedicated Monopolists, and in 1978 Monopoly had its sweetest moment when Nieman Marcus offered a $600 full-size solid chocolate version of the game.

Probably the most telling moment had already occurred, however, in 1972. That year the City Commissioner of Public Works promoted a facelift for Atlantic City that would change the names of some streets—including Baltic and Mediterranean Avenues to Fairmont and Melrose. You can imagine the public's reaction.

Edward P. Parker, then president of Parker Brothers, wrote to the commissioner. "Go directly to Jail," he said. ∎

Parker Bros.: Monopoly, 1950s-60s editions, $20-$25

# THE LIFE-SIZE KITCHEN

AMERICA'S LOVE AFFAIR with "convenience" intensified in the 1930s, becoming so obsessive it led some to observe that everyone was working too hard saving up for labor-saving gadgets. Convenience was important nowhere more than in the kitchen. Partly through the influence of catalog stores, kitchens rose in prominence from closed-door, my-eyes-only rooms to the gathering place for friends and neighbors, for kitchens were starting to fall subject to house-decorating whims. As catalog stores spread their vision of what middle-class lives should look like, the kitchen increasingly became a source of pride within the home.

The modern kitchen remained utilitarian, but now it was beautiful in its usefulness, with shiny surfaces, linoleum floors and counters, and color-coordinated appliances.

Just as real-life kitchens turned this corner, so did play ones. Catalog stores gave the same care and attention to younger homemakers, issuing child-size, color-coordinated kitchen sets. These were not the foot-high tin versions suitable for larger dolls, such as the ones made by Wolverine. These were large appliances, three and four feet high. Children could stand at them without crouching down. All sets had the same components—cupboards, refrigerators, ovens and sinks. Children could store canned and dry goods, open the fridge for a Coke, cook in the stove and do the dishes. Many times the insides of the doors, especially of the refrigerators and freezers, had beautiful lithography depicting various foods.

Never again were children embarrassed to have a friend step into their kitchen. It worked out well for the catalog stores, too. What better way, after all, for those stores to prepare young homemakers for the responsibilities of adulthood? This, of course, would include the purchasing of identical appliances, only now scaled for adults, not children.

## EVERYTHING INCLUDING THE KITCHEN SINK

Companies used a variety of materials in making child-sized kitchens. Toymaster Products Co., Inc., of Clifton, N.J., for instance, used fiberboard to make playroom toys, including its Super Market and Sheriff's Office, in the middle 1950s—as well

**ALL THE CONVENIENCES.**

Not all the kitchens of Boomer youth were made of lithographed metal. Some were made of even cheaper board, with plastic handles and faucets. *Alden's Christmas* catalog, 1968.

as the RightSize range, refrigerator and cupboard.

Dolls had the equivalents of child-size appliances, too. Small, realistically painted metal refrigerators and stoves were commonplace toys during the 1950s, many of them made by Wolverine Supply & Mfg. Co. of Pittsburgh, Pa. Wolverine was also one of leading manufacturers of housekeeping toys, under the Sunny Suzy name. Kiddie Brush & Toy Co., of Jonesville, Mich., was another, using the Susy Goose name.

An usual series of toy appliances appeared from a company more famed for its metal trucks. Structo Mfg. Co. of Freeport, Ill., introduced a line of realistic, scale-model, live-action toy appliances at the end of the 1950s. The first in the line was the Sparkle Bright Washer-Dryer, a 10-inch-high automatic appliance that could wash and spin-dry doll clothes.

The leading manufacturer of household toys that actually worked—especially toy ranges, flat irons and ironing boards—was the Metal Ware Corp. of Two Rivers, Wis. Metal Ware had been one of the leading companies of the 1930s producing working toy stoves and toy steam engines, both of which appeared under its Empire trade name. By the end of the decade, it adopted the Little Lady trade name for its toy appliances, which included electric stoves, nonelectric stoves and even toy kitchen sinks. In the postwar years, it reestablished itself with both Empire steam engines and Little Lady appliances.

In 1950, the electric ranges cost from $2.95 to $9.95, depending on the number of burners and utensils. The "play stoves for tiny tots" cost from $1.50 to $2.95. A Little Lady

ironing board, 28 inches high, cost $2.65, while a working electric flat iron ranged from 39 cents to $2.50. "Streamlined, lustrous chromium finish, heavy cast aluminum sole plate, heating element, fully insulated. Perfect for ironing dolls' clothes, hankies," said the company.

By the mid-1950s, the stoves became the Little Lady Bakerette. At the same time, Metal Ware's regular, domestic appliances now included electric corn poppers—a development that foreshadowed some of the company's toy hits of the 1960s, when toys began emphasizing novelty elements, due in large part because such toys made more effective TV advertising spots.

Other 1950s companies specialized in toy versions of such household items as sweepers and dust pans, including Norstar Corp., of New York City, and Kiddie Brush & Toy Co., of Jonesville, Mich., with its Susy Goose house-cleaning and dish-washing sets.

*Life-size.* Ward's Life-Size Kitchen appliances markedly improved the standard of living for America's youngest suburban homemakers. Ward's, 1960s.

Child-size kitchen, $50-$80

*Imported refrigerator toy, Minamoto Trading Co., 1950s.*

# FURNISHING DOLLHOUSES
# THE RENWAL WAY

HARD PLASTIC proved to be an ideal material for making dollhouse furniture, toy makers discovered immediately after the war. At the time, traditional dollhouses were still popular playthings. The houses themselves aspired to realism, with windows, shutters, tiled roofs, realistic wall decorations and floors inside and the semblance of bricks outside. Usually they were multistory and evocative of upper middle-class style.

The children either lived in this style themselves or aspired to it, having seen it on TV. Children spent hours of imaginative playtime with these houses, with or without dolls, arranging and rearranging the contents in the various rooms. The accessories seemed as real as the houses.

Companies including Banner Plastics Corp. and Plastic Art Toy Corp. of America, with its Plasco line, both of Paterson, N.J., made the toys, as did New York City's Irwin Corp., Louis Marx & Co. and Ideal Toy Corp. Plastic miniatures during the early Boomer years represented every household item. Telephones, vacuum cleaners, toilets and claw-foot bathtubs all became available for tiny household use.

None of the other lines rose to quite the same level of excellence that Renwal Mfg. Co., of Mineola, N.Y., achieved with its couches, chairs, dining room sets, cabinets, chests of drawers and bathroom sets. Renwal paid careful attention to detail, consistently used moving and movable parts, and designed its plastic items with sturdiness in mind. That the toy furniture was made in

realistically colored plastics also made Renwal the manufacturer of choice for furnishing dollhouses in the early Boomer years.

Its ambitious range of products was evident from the first. In 1948 the company was offering miniature playground equipment including swing, slide, see-saw and tricycle; home appliances including washing machine with turning crank and ironing board with iron; full bedroom, kitchen and dining room furnishings. Many were sold in boxed sets, complete with plastic baby: Nursery Set, School Room Set, Music Room Set and Bathroom Set, among others. The company produced an amazing array of miniatures, with some of the most fascinating being the smallest items: mantle clocks, table radios and bathroom scale.

The advantage some companies had over Renwal was their ability to produce tin dollhouses. Louis Marx & Co. made a specialty of producing elaborate, up-to-date, multistory, and multiroom doll houses of attractively lithographed metal, which came equipped with abundant furniture. Plastic Art Toy Corp. of America, of East Paterson, N.J., and Palmer Plastics, Inc., of Brooklyn, also made combinations of doll houses with plastic furniture in the 1950s.

Banner Plastics introduced one of the most interesting tin dollhouses in 1950. Not only was the furniture movable, but the rooms were, too, for they were sold individually, room by room. The bedroom, kitchen, living room and dining room were separate sets, to be purchased by themselves or as a complete five-room house. ■

**Treadle machine.** *Renwal's sewing machine was its most complex doll house accessory, having a moving treadle, a lid that lifted to become a work surface, the machine that could be hidden or raised, and a moving control wheel that caused the sewing needle to raise and lower. Renwal, 1950s.*

Renwal: Doll house mantle clock, $10
Renwal: Doll house radio phonograph, $25
Renwal: Doll house sewing machine, $40
Renwal: Doll house telephone, $15

# SUBURBAN BUILDER
# AMERICAN PLASTIC BRICKS

URING the same period LEGO was developing its building blocks in Europe, Halsam Products Co. of Chicago was selling a set of wooden bricks that interlocked to create buildings very much like the brick houses springing up in the spreading American suburbs.

Halsam changed the building pieces to plastic by the 1960s, making them a bright red, and issued them as Halsam's American Plastic Bricks. The sets featured pieces that allowed the placement of a roof, and doors and windows that opened and closed. Part of their charm was the extreme ease with which they went together to form attractive toy buildings: perfect, neat and tidy, just as all suburbia was supposed to be.

Another part of their charm came from the nature of the building materials themselves. The lightweight hard-plastic pieces were more durable than the easily chipped American Skyline pieces and much more attractive than Lincoln Logs. Plus, after the building was taken down, they mixed together in the box with a clattering sound that was strangely pleasant—a sound that, insignificant as it is, remains clear in memory to all the millions who played with the toy. ■

**CHILD'S-EYE VIEW.**
Much of the attraction of the Plastic Bricks came from their highly detailed, brick-like texture.

Halsam: American Plastic Army Bricks, $100
Halsam: American Plastic Bricks #715, $100
Halsam: American Plastic Bricks #725, $75
Block City, 1950s, $35-$45

**Houses of wood.** *At first, Halsam continued issuing sets of wooden American Bricks alongside the plastic sets. Halsam, 1950s.*

**Red-brick construction.** *American Plastic Bricks were the plastic building blocks of choice for the generation raised before LEGO came to America with its more versatile but less detailed construction toys. American Plastic Bricks, with plastic pickup truck by Irwin, 1960s.*

# GIRDER & PANEL

### INDUSTRIAL HIGH RISE.

Kenner's Girder & Panel sets were to building toys what Structo and Doepke construction trucks were to vehicle toys. Girder & Panel and Bridge & Turnpike combined set, Kenner, 1959.

QUITE DIFFERENT in concept from other architectural toys, Kenner's Girder & Panel and Bridge & Turnpike construction sets of the 1960s combined a variety of materials. Thin, brittle plastic was used for angular braces, building panels and road sections. Heavy cardboard formed the foundation panels. Polyethylene was the material for the vertical and horizontal girders.

The Girder & Panel sets created play spaces evocative of the world of heavy construction and urban industry. Lacking the elegance of American Skyline or the suburban simplicity of American Plastic Bricks, the advantage of the Kenner structures was that that they could rise quickly from the floor, easily achieving heights that could only be reached through dedicated, piece-by-piece assembly of the other construction toy sets.

The Bridge & Turnpike sets also included roads, which could spread across the floor below or rise into the air held aloft by red plastic beams. These held a special attraction for kids during those Matchbox years, since they provided two-lane networks of the proper size. ∎

Kenner: Girder & Panel, #3, 1958, $50-$60
Kenner: Girder & Panel Constructioneer Set, #8, $85
Kenner: Girder & Panel Hydro-Dynamic Single Set, #17, $150
Kenner: Girder & Panel Skyscraper Set, #72050, $50
Kenner: Sky Rail Girder & Panel, 1963, $125

*Planning Book, Girder & Panel Building Set, 1958.*

# ARCHITECT'S TRAINING GROUND
# AMERICAN SKYLINE

SOME KIDS were content to be frontier builders and got out their American Logs or Lincoln Logs. Others were content to be urban and suburban builders and pulled out their American Bricks. Yet others put their hands on their hips and went to Mom saying, "Listen, Mother. There have been modern skyscrapers in the United States since the beginning of this century. It's two generations and two world wars later. So tell me. Where is *my* modern skyscraper building toy?"

Luckily for such architecturally sophisticated kids, a plastics company named Elgo teamed up with Halsam, a company best known as a maker of wooden blocks for tykes, and developed a construction toy called American Skyline. The toy must have seemed stunning to kids in the 1950s and '60s. As a mass-marketed architectural construction toy, in fact, American Skyline probably has never met its equal.

The building pieces were all an up-to-date, antiseptic white. Posts fitted together for corners or vertical wall supports. The pieces for the foundations, walls, windows and doors slipped into slots in the posts. The touch that made the buildings come alive was the use of plastic panes in the windows. The panes were separate sheets of translucent plastic, colored a deep sky-blue. With these panes inserted, the sky-reaching towers lost their cathedral aloofness and seemed to breathe with life—a distinctly modern city life.

Other details were equally effective: stiff plastic sheets of checkerboard floor, flagpoles, flags, and—best of all to me as a child—staircases, wide and narrow. I could lay on my belly and watch tiny, imaginary feet going up and down those steps hour after hour. ■

Halsam/Elgo: American Skyline, #92, $50
Halsam/Elgo: American Skyline, #93, $115
Halsam/Elgo: American Skyline, #94, $300

**BUILDER OF MODERN BEAUTY.**

The American Skyline sets could be assembled into such wonders as the handsome "Elgo Apartments" or luxurious "Halsam Apartment Hotel." Sets were numbered from 1 to 96, with each one a progressively larger selection of the pieces. Set #93, for instance, contained about 800 pieces. Halsam/Elgo, 1950s.

**How To Build with American Skyline.** *"Your American Skyline set is the most fabulous construction toy of its kind," the booklet trumpeted. Many young builders agreed. Since the building pieces were in HO scale, with 1/8 of a toy inch equaling one real foot, the sets also found favor among enthusiasts of HO trains, which were gaining popularity in the postwar years.*

# PIONEER BUILDER
# LINCOLN LOGS

**Western housing.** The huge interest in all things Western among kids, inspired by movies and TV, helped keep Lincoln Logs among the best-selling construction toys in the Boomer years. Box detail, Lincoln Logs, 1950s-'60s.

DID ANY of us examine why we so enjoyed fitting logs together, making earth-brown buildings of the simplest sort, and then setting in place the roof supports, followed by those wonderful green planks? Did we just like building? Or was there something special about the log cabin itself?

John Lloyd Wright, son of Frank Lloyd Wright and then a budding architect in his own right, thought so. He came up with the idea for this toy in the Woodrow Wilson years, reputedly while watching the construction of the Imperial Hotel in Tokyo.

Is it a coincidence? The elder Wright devised an innovative system of interlocking beams for that hotel in Japan. The younger Wright then devised an innovative toy using interlocking wood "logs" to make toy log cabins for American kids. Whether the connection is real or just a quaint story, the younger Wright introduced a construction toy that was successful from its introduction. He gave it a name meant to conjure the most positive associations possible. The name Lincoln Logs evoked the brightest image of pioneer life, even if it referred to a time when the West was only as far as Illinois.

Lincoln Logs stood poised to greet the new crop of children in the late '40s. Unlike many manufacturers who suspended toy production or significantly altered the nature of their toys because of government-imposed shortages of materials, Lincoln Logs made its toys of plentiful wood, with only the production of metal figures to go with its log cabin sets affected. These metal figures appeared after the war: slush-metal frontier people, Indians, horses and livestock.

The pioneer and Western spirit had already hit Boomer kids hard. They happily embraced Lincoln Logs, imagining themselves as Davy Crocketts, Daniel Boones, and Rebecca Boones, raising timbers and families in the wilderness. Since most later Boomers never owned the metal figures, the toy company became associated almost exclusively with the "Logs" part of its name. Later, adolescent log cabin builders had to provide their own frontier populations, usually mined from Marx or MPC play sets.

Lincoln Logs saw spirited competition in the '50s and '60s from Halsam, which had likewise specialized in wooden construction toys since 1917. "American Logs reproduce the natural effect of the rough cut logs," Halsam claimed, "hewn with the adz and ax of the early American pioneer."

Halsam proved the more forward-looking and dynamic of the two companies. It ventured quickly into the world of plastic and created some of the most characteristically Boomer-style construction toys of the 1950s and '60s. ■

Lincoln Logs, 1950s-60s sets, $35-$50

# ERECTOR SETS

**M**ETAL CONSTRUCTION sets were a growth industry in the 1910s, when such companies as A.C. Gilbert, of Chicago, Ill., and Structo Mfg. Co. of Freeport, Ill., issued sets of electroplated steel girders and die-cast pulleys, gears, axles and wheels that could be assembled into almost anything a child could desire.

Toys from several companies preceded the 1913 debut of Gilbert's Erector sets, including the English Meccano construction sets and Kilbourn's Construction Strips, a wooden construction toy W.D. Kilbourn introduced in 1909. Gilbert's toy was the first all-metal construction set to be manufactured in the United States. Within the year it was followed by American Model Builder, American Mechanical Toy Co., and Structo's Structo Building Sets.

Established in 1913, Structo began giving more emphasis to its Auto-Builder Toys in the 1920s, eventually developing a line of large and sturdy vehicle toys that would take it safely through the Great Depression and land it in a position of strength when World War II arrived. After the war, it remained one of the leading toy manufacturers, with its heavy construction vehicle toys consistently strong sellers through the 1950s and early '60s.

The A.C. Gilbert Co. toed the construction toy line, however, with its popular Erector Sets. As with other companies, Gilbert's postwar offerings initially repeated prewar toys, including its famous Ferris wheel. In the late '40s and early '50s, some of its sets were made with aluminum girders because of the combined effects of a steel strike and the beginning of the Korean War.

The company had moved to New Haven, Conn., in 1938. Until the late 1960s, it was located there at Erector Square, making not only Erector and Junior Erector sets but also American Flyer trains, tool chests, chemistry sets, puzzles, magic sets, microscopes and toy motors. The famous construction toys kept changing with the times, featuring plans by the late 1950s for building rocket launchers, robots and space vehicles.

The Boomer years saw as many companies springing up to issue metal construction sets as had the prewar years. Among them were the Urbana Mfg. Co., of Urbana, Ohio, with its Constructioneer of the early 1950s. Later that decade, Toy In A Tube, Inc., of Niagara Falls, N.Y., favored a different metal in its Jack Dandy Toy in a Tube, which it described as an "aluminum construction set which makes over one hundred toys from one kit." ■

**SPANNING GENERATIONS.**

The Gilbert Erector sets satisfied the building urge for children from early in the century through the entire Boomer period. Erector set building, 1950s-'60s, with 1954 advertisement from *Boy's Life* magazine.

**Structo 66.** *In the 1910s, Structo started in the construction toy business, as its name suggests. By the Boomer years, having sold the construction toy part of its business, Structo was known for its fine line of pressed-steel toy trucks. Ironically, by entering into a distribution deal with American Flyer, Structo found itself allied with its old competitor, Gilbert. Tin bank, Structo, 1952.*

Gilbert: Erector No. 10092, 1958, $650
Gilbert: Erector No. 10063, 1960, $35
Gilbert: Erector No. 10211, 1962, $35

**Dime store King.** *One of Renwal's dime store hits was its series of hard-plastic versions of the Speed King race car. Renwal, 1949 to mid-1950s.*

> "Movable accessories and firemen provide added interest and have educational value for children. Equipment and men (11 pieces in all) can be moved and secured in 24 different positions. Many interesting combinations are possible—this feature alone gives children unexpected thrills."
>
> **—ADVERTISEMENT, NOSCO PLASTICS OF ERIE, PA., 1949.**

A FEW YEARS before the World War II, plastic toy cars started rolling out of factories from toy companies including Kilgore and Lapin. Those in the plastics industry saw this as a sign of things to come. Plastic was a happening medium. It had a versatility that made it a perfect match with the toy industry.

But plastic remained out of reach until the end of the war. Soon thereafter, hard-plastic airplanes, ships, trucks, cars, trailers and helicopters started filling dime store bins and even appearing in Christmas catalogs. Plastic became so popular and useful a material that even pressed-steel and cast-metal outfits such as Wyandotte and Hubley made use of some plastic vehicles in their toy assortments.

One of the first companies off the postwar starting block was Renwal Manufacturing Co., which had operated from a factory on Broadway in New York City since 1939, originally as a manufacturer of glass knives. It leapt into plastic toy making in 1945, when the company turned out hard-plastic World War II airplanes. In the following years a wide variety of plastic vehicle toys appeared, some of them complex affairs with multiple movable (and easily breakable) parts, others no more than hollow shapes of cars with wheels beneath.

Renwal's Motorcycle with Sidecar Construction Kit, for instance, appealed to the kids with a can-do attitude. The kit's eight pieces of colorful hard plastic snapped together into a toy. "You be the mechanic," the package exhorted the child. "Build it—fix it—take it apart—put it back together again!" Competing companies Ideal and Marx also made their multipiece Take-Apart and Fix-It toys, perhaps as a challenge to the patience of parents.

Few plastic toys captured the imagination as well as a simpler toy Renwal made: the Speed King. This racing car had a blunt nose, tires covered with prominent, swept-back, teardrop-shaped fenders and a small, forward-placed covered cockpit. While the smaller versions came in only one color, the larger sizes had different colors for the bodies and fenders, and often simple paint applications.

Speed Kings offered everything an imaginative kid could want. Shiny and bright, they evoked the excitement of the race track. They were made of that wonder material, plastic.

And they were inexpensive, too. Released in a variety of sizes from 1949 into the mid-1950s, these breathtaking baubles sold for 79 cents, tops, which bought the biggest version, more than 10 inches long. It came with the bonus of a whining friction motor. What if you didn't have 79 cents? How about a nickel? For that, you could have the smallest version, a little over 3 inches long.

Dime store aisles had plenty of companies to fill them with bright, colorful, hard-plastic toys. Venerable toy makers Marx and Ideal produced more complex toys, sometimes costing as much as $2 or $3, while Thomas, Acme, Banner, Wannatoy, Pyro and Renwal fought to fill the dime to 39-cent bins.

## THE GYROFRICTION CAR

Irwin Corp. of Fitchburg, Mass., started in the 1920s as a manufacturer of novelties—probably the sorts of things you would pick up at carnivals and five-and-dimes: celluloid pinwheels, rattles, dolls and general whatnots.

Novelty companies tend not to develop much of a profile

within the industry, even if they are dependable suppliers, as Irwin was for decades. Or maybe it is exactly because they *are* dependable suppliers. The novelty market has little need for brand names or the kinds of toy innovations that can make a brand name famous. It just needs stuff good enough to attract the eye for a few seconds or to satisfy some lucky mark at a midway shooting gallery.

Irwin was not entirely a bit-part player, however, as it did its best to prove in the years after the war. One such effort came in 1953 with the copyrighted "New 'Gyrofriction' Motor." Friction motors were not exactly news by this time. Louis Marx had popularized them with its early versions of the Dick Tracy Squad Car No. 1, which had gone to children across the country thanks to Marx's presence in catalog stores. To give it credit, Irwin's Gyrofriction Motor was a smoothly running mechanism attached to the rear axle that made enough of a pleasing whirring sound during operation to lead the company to claim its cars had a "powerful screaming siren." Toy claims at the time could stretch truths at least a little. The "siren" was neither powerful nor screaming. Yet it was a good sound to a child's ears.

Irwin also claimed that the Gyrofriction car "travels a long distance"—again, a bit of a stretch. If rolled forward and released, the friction of the motor's turning parts soon brought the toy to a halt. An example I have with a dysfunctional Gyrofriction Motor rolls much, much farther. Yet kids could figure it out: if they never removed their hands from the toy, they could, indeed, make it travel a long distance. After all, it had come all the way from Fitchburg.

The Irwin Hard Top Convertible, with its sheet-metal under-chassis and two-piece plastic top, turned out to be a good toy. It had several features to speak for it. For one, it used a clear plastic dome over the seats. Surface black paint covered the "hard top" part, which could either be depicted as pulled all the way forward or partly pulled back. The part of the top meant to be windshields, of course, Irwin left unpainted. The company saved money on the ones with the top pulled forward, leaving out the attractive interior seats and steering wheel found in the others.

More fun than the sounds made by the Gyrofriction Motor were the working wipers—yellow plastic rods that waved together and apart in front of the windshield. The front, free-turning wheels powered these, so they never stopped.

The Hard Top Convertible was a car always in the rain. That must have puzzled at least a few children who owned the version with the pulled-back top. ■

Irwin: Hard Top Convertible, hard plastic, 9", $35
Renwal: Gasoline Truck, 4-¼", $20
Renwal: Speed King racer, 3-¼", $20
Renwal: Speed King racer, 4-¾", $20

**Powerful screaming car!** *By later toy standards, the car with its "powerful screaming siren" was tame and quiet. In the early to mid-1950s, however, it was the latest thrill. It appeared with a variety of paint schemes. Irwin, 1950s.*

**That unbeatable, hot-roddin' Number Two.** *Auburn Rubber Company turned increasingly to vinyl toy production through the 1950s. Toward the end, some toys from the vinyl molds even appeared in cheaper polyethylene. Auburn Rubber Co., 1950s-60s.*

THE UNITED STATES had no rubber toys in its stores during World War II. Auburn Rubber Corp., of Auburn, Ind., had been the largest rubber-toy manufacturer in the country since 1935, when it had entered the field with toy soldiers. During the war, however, it was busy doing work for the government, making gaskets and synthetic-rubber airplane parts.

"Our experience during this war emergency will enable us to better serve our customers," the company announced in early 1945, "supplying better merchandise in greater quantities to all trade channels, just as soon as 'V Day' gives us a green light to resume civilian production on needed items." With the end of war in sight, the executives at Auburn were looking forward to resuming normal operations. It wanted to get back to making those "needed items," including toys.

Yet even when looking forward to getting rubber automobiles, animals, trucks, racers, tractors and novelties back into production, those executives must have been thinking about the great strides the chemical industry had made in devising new synthetic materials. They were already considering how those developments might change their line.

Their words were carefully chosen when they published a notice to the toy industry that was still not yet at the point of making toys again. They mentioned synthetic rubber. They mentioned "better merchandise."

The change did not come immediately. When production resumed, the toys Auburn Rubber was producing were similar to what had come before. They were heavy toys, made of a thick, black rubber. The company added inflated rubber balls by 1950 and soon was expanding its business of providing rubber wheels and parts to other toy manufacturers.

In 1953 the change began. For the next three or four years, the company gradually replaced its various rubber toys with new, more highly detailed vinyl equivalents. The company released vinyl motorcycles, trucks, construction vehicles and automobiles made of the new, flexible material, as well as play-set figures, toy tools and toy weapons.

**Vinylculture.** *Tractors were among the most characteristic toys of Auburn Rubber. In the background of this vinyl example, a Marx tin barn rises. Tractor, 7" long, Auburn Rubber Co., 1960s.*

# 62

**Fire fighter.** *Among Auburn Rubber's most popular rubber toys were its fire engines. When the company began moving to vinyl, it continued issuing rubber fire engines into the later 1950s. When the vinyl versions appeared at last, they were marvels. Cast in a bright red vinyl, with silver detail paint, the toys were highly detailed, lighter in weight and more apt to bend than break. Fire pumper, 7-½" long, Auburn Rubber Co., late 1950s-60s.*

The company, now named Auburn Rubber Co., Inc., used the material as a major selling point. "Vinyl toys sell!" it proclaimed to the toy industry in 1955. "Soft—tough—flexible—brilliant colors."

Of the rubber vehicles, the fire engines were the last to go, remaining in the line until 1956.

Auburn's vinyl cars and trucks proved immensely popular, as did its vinyl farm animals. Few sandboxes in America were without them. As Auburn touted, they were safe, durable, no-mark, scratch-proof, popularly priced and sanitary—although why a toy that did so well on the floor and in the sandbox had to be sanitary was never discussed.

By 1957 the company had hit on the phrase "rubber-like vinyl toys" for selling its products, and had named them the Auburn Safe Play Line. By 1957, too, the rubber fire engines had disappeared, replaced by the wonderful vinyl fire trucks that became standard playthings across the country. ■

Auburn: **Cadillac Convertible**, vinyl, 3-½", $10
Auburn: **Hot Rod**, vinyl, 4-¼", $15-$20
Auburn: **Jeep, with cannon**, vinyl, $20
Auburn: **Telephone Truck**, vinyl, 7", $25

# TOOTSIETOYS

SOMETIMES toys need no gimmicks. After all, kids start out with one power that puts all the rest to shame: the power to imagine things. Thus, the toys that left room for the imagination—that did not drive away every instinct toward creativity and invention—sometimes proved the most rewarding to children, especially when they had to play, as most children did, with the same toy day after day, week after week, month after month.

At the Dowst Mfg. Co. in Chicago before World War II, the company president decided that the already famous die-cast Tootsietoys were "for doodling, not collecting." The company focused on simple, sturdy toys that conjured up the adult life of driving cars and trucks, flying airplanes and riding trains, which all kids yearned for. In the 1950s and '60s, being adult meant being a part of a world of transportation options of every kind.

Sandboxes and sidewalks and driveways: Tootsietoys went everywhere, too. An archaeologist 100 years from now would be able to find this out from looking at the toys themselves. An overwhelming number of them today are not just rubbed and worn, but heavily worn down, often to the point of having only

**ROAD FAVORITES IN MINIATURE.**

Tootsietoy specialized in providing inexpensive models of contemporary cars and trucks for floor-level motorists. Ford pickup, 3", first introduced in 1949.

residues of the original paint left in the cracks and corners.

They also retained their dedication to reality. In spite of being "for doodling, not collecting," new Tootsietoy toy cars kept appearing, year after year, that were based on real-life automobiles. With the Sports Car Assortment of 1958, for instance, toy-store owners could offer a variety of 6-inch 1950s models that taught kids some of the major car-manufacturing names and styles of the decade: Volkswagen, Porsche, Jaguar, Mercedes Benz, Austin-Healy and MG. Even the Midget assortment of smaller toys managed to evoke recognizable real-world automobiles despite the limited amount of detail in their castings.

## DIE-CASTING PIONEER

Tootsietoy's parent company Dowst had roots in the 1800s. More importantly, it was in the prestigious position of being the inventor of the die-cast toy car, which it introduced in the 1920s. It prospered in the toy world and was well positioned in 1945 to hold onto its popularity.

Other prewar die-cast toy companies survived and sometimes thrived in the postwar era, including the Hubley Mfg. Co. of Lancaster, Pa., and Jack Manoil Co., Inc., of Waverly, N.Y. One small company, A. & E. Tool & Gage Co.,

**Old-fashioned space adventure.**
*These spaceships are typical of toys appearing soon after World War II. Although in a sense "futuristic," the 3-¼ inch toys were made of a heavy die-cast zinc alloy instead of plastic and evoked the 1930s even in its design, which was modeled after Buck Rogers vehicles, although unlicensed. Midgetoy, late '40s.*

Inc., of Rockford, Ill., entered the fray just after the war and offered yet more stylized, Art Deco-inspired vehicles under its Midgetoy trade name. Midgetoy gave Tootsietoy serious competition for two decades, although A. & E. Tool & Gage emphasized more of a budget line of toys than did Dowst.

Die-casting companies, including Hubley, Manoil and Dowst, all embraced plastic at various times in the 1950s and '60s. Dowst probably took the biggest step in this direction, even while maintaining its line of die-cast toy cars, trains and airplanes. It did so, in 1961, by purchasing the hobby and toy divisions of the Strombeck-Becker Mfg. Co., of Moline, Ill.

With Dowst history going back to 1878 and Strombeck-Becker history going back to 1911, the purchase joined two venerable toy-making lines. The purchase was of extreme significance to the toy-manufacturing world, for Strombeck-Becker was an important part of the new model road-racing fad with its Electric Road Racing Game.

Tootsietoy die-cast cars gradually grew smaller through the Baby Boomer years. Older Boomers fondly remember playing the heck out of a full range of die-cast toys, including 9-inch tractor-trailers, 6-inch cars and trucks and 3-inch junior assortments of vehicles. By the late 1960s, new 2-inch and 1-inch die-cast cars were becoming the norm. Boomers played with them happily, no matter the size. ■

Dowst: **Tootsietoy Buck Experimental Coupe, 6", $25**
Dowst: **Tootsietoy El Camino Pickup, 6", $12**
Dowst: **Tootsietoy Kaiser Sedan, 6", $30**
Dowst: **Tootsietoy '62 Ford Econoline Pickup, 6", $10**

# TRU-ACTION
# ELECTRIC FOOTBALL

**PLAYERS OUT FOR A RUMBLE.**

The vibrations of the rumbling, shaking game surface kept the players moving in the Tru-Action Electric Football Game. This set cost $6.95 in the mid-1950s, the price it stayed at for the remainder of the decade. Tudor Metal Products, 1954.

TUDOR METAL PRODUCTS CORP. of New York City was a 1930s maker of metal toys and games that gradually moved itself in the direction of musical toys—harmonicas, in the late 1930s, and then xylophones and toy pianos as the 1940s arrived. Toy banks were another important product.
The company survived the war years mainly by making all-wood Victory xylophones painted red, white and blue. Afterwards, it returned to its strengths: xylophones, budget banks and pianos. Then it moved to Brooklyn and took a step back to metal games.

Tudor's 1949 Tru-Action Electric Football Game was as strange and unlikely as a game could be. It was large, arriving in a box measuring roughly 17 inches by 27 inches. The game board was a raised platform with a flat metal sheet lithographed to resemble a football field. The players were pieces of metal cut in a shape that more or less resembled football players. On their undersides were two small tin strips, the only part of the football players that touched the metal field when they were set down for the game. With these strips bent so they pointed slightly backwards, the football players moved forward.

**Straight-arm, fumble, kick and pass.** *Later football players were molded from soft plastic. They looked more realistic and still scooted across the board, still powered by the vibrating playing surface. Tudor Metal Products, 1960s.*

Why? Because the whole board vibrated. Once you set up the players, you plugged in the game, flicked the switch and watched the fast-jiggling guards and tackles have at it.

Strange as it was, the game did well for Tudor. The company went into the 1950s advertising itself as a maker of xylophones, budget banks and pianos, while its Tru-Action games, which encompassed not only football but also baseball and horse-racing, quietly grew to take a larger share of the company's output. The Sports Car Race joined the Tru-Action line by 1959. De Luxe Hockey, with miniature hockey players controlled by knobs and levers that ran beneath the "ice," also soon joined the line and caught on. While xylophones and Ready Money banks were still vital to the company, the sports-related games had become at least as important to the company's profitability.

The new decade would prove the most important for the Tru-Action games. Their popularity was helped by a massive advertising campaign early in the decade. Rather than taking the TV approach, Tudor advertised in magazines with readerships in the many millions: *Sports Illustrated*, *Boys' Life* and *The New York Times Magazine*.

By then, Tudor had stopped making the players of metal. Now they were realistically molded in plastic with four plastic hairs on the underside replacing the earlier strips of tin. The game was no less strange than before, yet somehow kept winning over new kids who loved to watch the players run around the board as if alive. ■

All prices subject to change without notice. Some items slightly higher in some sections of the South and West.

It's just like playing in a real game!

**ELECTRIC**
6⁹⁸ **FOOTBALL GAME**

"Hey, I'll bet I can beat you in football," says Chipper. "We can actually kick and pass the ball, the players can run and tackle." There's line plays, end runs, forward passes, field goals . . . all the color of a real game right in your own home. 25 x 15¼ inches. By Tudor Metal. Ask for 35BR4.

*Tudor Electric Football advertisement, Billy & Ruth, 1952.*

**Cadaco-Ellis: Foto-Electric Football, 1965, $15**
**Tudor: Tru-Action Sports Car Race, 1950s-60s, $25**
**Tudor: Tru-Action Electric Football, various, $10-$25**

# CHAPTER 7

# Bash! Wow! More Sixties and Seventies Toys

**B**irthrates peaked in the mid-1960s for the Baby Boomers, then declined rapidly enough that by 1969 the nation had about as many preschool children as it did in the early 1950s—a little more than 17 million, as opposed to the high of 20-plus from 1959 through 1964.

The lowering birthrate would take longer to be felt among school-aged children. The nation's peak population of children ages five to fourteen came in 1969—only a few hundred thousand short of 41 million kids, or roughly twice the number of kids filling schools as before World War II.

Toys were now not just big business—they were *huge* business. And the number of important properties in the biz just kept multiplying. A report in *Playthings* magazine assessed the big sellers of the 1968 season.

A survey of retailers produced the information that, despite delivery problems, the new Hot Wheels cars from Mattel were the best-selling toys. Matchbox cars followed in second place. The drawing toy Spirograph-Spirotot took third place. Fourth went to Parker Bros. hit novelty puzzle, Instant Insanity. Mattel's Tippee-Toes doll captured fifth place. Sixth went to activity game Skittle Bowl, made by Aurora Plastics Corp., with Aurora's Speedline following right behind in seventh place.

Also a top-seller for 1968 was Remco's Rudy the Robot; Marx's Marvel the Mustang talking horse, an imitation of the English Mobo Bronco; and Billy Blastoff.

For many vendors, it was not just a matter of single toys. Some entire lines seemed stellar: Tonka, Madame Alexander, Fisher-Price and Parker Bros. earned praise. It was this way every year through the Boomer years. Every year had a different top ten.

# RAT FINK CHARMS

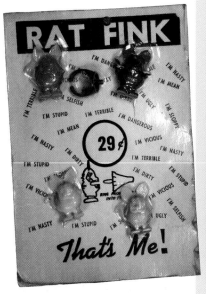

**NASTIER THAN YOU—
BUT COOLER, TOO.**

Rat Fink charms were carried around in the pockets of countless children who otherwise looked like perfectly well-adjusted suburban sorts. Store display card, 1960s.

**The face only a Mutha could love.**
*Rat Fink charms, 1-¼" tall, 1960s.*

**W**HY DID kids of the '60s respond so favorably to bulging, blood-shot eyes, ratty shirts and crooked teeth emerging from really wicked smiles? We may never know. Maybe it had to do with the disillusionment of the 1960s. In one part of the adult world, an optimistic public watched the Kennedy Camelot spring into being, only to see it shake in response to race riots, shudder beneath the threats of the Cuban Missile Crisis and finally shatter with assassination. In another part, older brothers died in Vietnam or returned strangely altered in personality. In yet another, people Dropped Out and Turned On, decried the War Machine and celebrated the plain old Human Condition, Rock and Roll and Hippydom. Some of these last turned up occasionally with blood-shot eyes, ratty shirts, and ... a connection might be drawn.

Whatever the origins and whatever the reasons for the attraction, kids shoved nickels into gumball machines for plastic Rat Fink charms or shoved dimes across the counters of the new convenience stores springing up everywhere to buy their Rat Fink rings. These rings were crazy to some, cool to others. To me, they were Oh-Wow Neat, just as were the plastic Batman rings.

Who was Rat Fink? As a kid, I never knew. As a character, Rat Fink simply existed. I had no idea what he did. I had no

idea, or at least no clear idea, what he represented. He was simply what he was. A rat. And a fink. If I had ever given it thought, I might have perceived that Rat Fink was a kind of scummy guy. But that was just how he was, and that was OK.

And even though the heyday of the dime store was quickly waning, this whip-tailed figure somehow rose into the Convenience Store Empyrean to become a part of the magic pantheon already there. It was quite the spectacle: Davy Crockett, Bullwinkle, Batman, Cat Woman, Wonder Woman and ... Rat Fink.

The secret to Rat Fink's appeal was not actually so secret. His personal characteristics were printed on the cards of Rat Fink charms sold in dime stores. Behind the four plastic-sealed Finks—and the plastic ring that could inserted into the back of one of the charms for those who like more refined jewelry—were Rat Fink's claims for himself: "I'm terrible. I'm stupid. I'm mean. I'm nasty. I'm dirty. I'm selfish. I'm vicious. I'm sloppy. I'm dangerous. I'm ugly." He was proud of these things, too. "Rat Fink—That's Me!" was all the slogan it took to make kids snap them up.

### HOT ROD MANIA

The T-shirt designs and custom hotrod designs of Ed "Big Daddy" Roth proved to have massive influence in the toy world of the 1960s. Roth had started painting T-shirts in the '50s as a way of raising funds to produce his eye-catching, Fiberglas-bodied automotive creations. Since his T-shirt designs involving monster-driven cars sold at a good clip, the characters of those monster drivers naturally developed. Roth's fertile and warped imagination—warped, as they would have argued in the 1960s, in a good way—produced and perfected the wickedly grinning Rat Fink. One of his best creations, it would become an emblem of an era that still seems luridly airbrushed in fluorescent colors in the minds of those Boomers who would have happily adopted the names of Roth's early hotrods: Outlaw and Beatnik Bandit.

Two model companies especially benefited from Roth's oddball—and flaming eyeball—vision. The company directly benefiting was Revell, Inc., a specialist in plastic hobby kits based in Venice, Calif. As a company that had made its name in the 1950s as a maker of automobile kits, its decision to release a Beatnik Bandit kit in 1963 was perfectly in character. Yet the company had engaged in some off-beat kits, such as the 1959 kit Norval the Bashful Blinket, based on a Dr. Seuss design. Firmly within that tradition fell the other Roth-inspired kits issued in the early and middle '60s: Drag Nut, Mr. Gasser BMR Racer, Brother Rat Fink and Angel Fink among them.

A second model-maker capitalized on the exuberant car-crazy culture centered in California. Hawk Model Co., of Chicago, Ill., was a company with a longer pedigree in the business than California's Revell. It was firmly established by the late 1930s under the name Hawk Model Aeroplane Co., although oddly enough, its model railroad construction kits were its lead items.

Around 1951, when it updated its name and started making its scale-model airplane kits out of plastic, the company was located at a Chicago address that seems prophetic: North California Street.

By the mid-1960s, the Hawk Model Co. name seemed almost synonymous with another, much newer one: Weird-Ohs. The number of Hawk's absurd and outrageous hotrod kits was astonishing: Digger—the Wayout Dragster, 'Daddy'—The Suburbanite, Endsville Eddy, Drag Hag and Huey Hut Rod were among them.

"King of the Uglies is this serene, quiescent contained Endsville Eddy—the Eddy to end all," Hawk said of that model kit. "All brake and no brain, Eddy's ready for whatever the task—bedlam, ruin, riot. But underneath it all he has a heart full of chaos and calamity."

Hawk emphasized zany, backwards-thinking humor. Of 'Davey'—The Motorcyclist Road Blaster, the company had this to say: "A miserable person with all the charm of a hissing rattlesnake—a scary scamp who scoots in and out of traffic creating the biggest jam since strawberries."

The Weird-Ohs appeared on water-applied decals, also produced by Hawk. Other companies—Dennis & Dorst of San Mateo, Calif. and Standard Toykraft, Inc. of Brooklyn, N.Y.—joined in on the fun, too, producing novelty items that devotees of the Rat Fink era still treasure when they are lucky enough to find them.

Even some of the heavy-hitters of the toy world joined in, with Ideal Toy Corp. issuing a Weird-Ohs game and Fairchild Variety Products, Inc. of Rochester, N.Y., making puzzles.

Standard Plastic Products, Inc. of South Plainfield, N.J., the company that was making the vinyl doll-cases for Barbie and Skipper, was making such useful items as Weird-Ohs pencil cases and ring binders.

Probably the oddest—well, weirdest—toys had to be the *Plush* Weird-Ohs made by Jee-Bee Toy Creations of Kansas City, Mo.

## NUTTY MADS

Rat Fink was not the only outrageous creature whose soft-plastic figure was treasured by Boomer kids, for there were Nutty Mads, too. While Rat Fink charms were ugly-cute and had some appeal across the Toyland gender-gap, Nutty Mad figures were more distinctly of the gross-out-cool type of toy aimed at boys. Made by Louis Marx & Co., that multinational among toy companies, the Nutty Mads were part of that first, 1963 wave of eye-popping weirdness. Being 6 inches tall, they had wonderfully unappealing detail: veins in the eyes, slithering tongues and devious-looking furrows in their foreheads.

For many boys who thought charms were too girly and model-kits too much work, the Nutty Mads were a source instant gratification for their gross-out needs. ■

Marx: Nutty Mads Bagatelle, 1963, $45
Marx: Nutty Mads Car, $225
Marx: Nutty Mads Indian, 1960s, $125
Marx: Nutty Mads Target Game, 1960s, $70
Rat Fink plastic ring, $15

**Weird Waldo.**
*The larger Marx plastic figures, made in single-color plastics, invited painting, especially at a time when everyone was accustomed to assembling plastic model kits and then painting them. The Nutty Mads, like models, were more display pieces than toys, although they probably lived imaginary lives in kids' minds. The original clay-green hue of this Waldo the Weight Lifter peeks through some child's vivid paint job. Louis Marx & Co., 1963.*

# DREAM PETS

**Quick Draw McGraw.** *The popular comic character was made in Dream-Pet-like form by one of the many smaller companies that imported toys from Japan. Photo by Martha Borchardt. Herman Pecker & Co., 1960s.*

NOT ALL of the imports from Japan in the 1960s were battery-operated tin-litho mechanicals. Some were an entirely traditional sort of plaything: the stuffed toy. By means of imports from Japan, one California manufacturer found a way in the early 1960s to compete with the long-established doll and stuffed-toy industry based in the East Coast around Manhattan.

R. Dakin & Co. of San Francisco, Calif., inaugurated a line of Dream Pets and Dream Dolls. Designed as impulse sellers, with price tags normally at a dollar, the Dream Pets and Dolls sold well and made them favorites among the later Boomers. They were distinctive in part for their charming design and in part for how unusually firm they felt.

Dakin's Dream Pets and their kin were a far cry from the soft and cuddly standard of the stuffed-toy world. They were tightly stuffed with "wood byproducts," a term accepted by the toy industry in lieu of sawdust. The outer materials were likewise usually stiff. While often it was felt or a similar cloth material, leatherette vinyl was also used.

Other companies joined Dakin in selling these charming toy animals, including Kamar, Inc. of Inglewood, Calif., which sold

its hard-packed animals alongside mechanical toy animals and action dolls, and Animal Fair of Chanhassen, Minn., which sold Animal Fair Pets. Other importers included Takara, Herman Pecker & Co., and Circle Importers, with its Treasure Pets.

Manufacturers in Japan took a decidedly whimsical turn with these toys, issuing pink rhinos, rose-colored wiener-dogs, beret-sporting skunks and fire-engine-red reindeer.

Stuffed toys were distinctive products of the 1960s. During the toy-safety scare of the early '70s, toys stuffed almost to the bursting point with sawdust were abruptly considered fire hazards.

It was the firmness of these toys that helped make them stand out, however. They were unusual: stuffed toys that stood up pertly. No other stuffing quite had that pertness. While Dakin continued its Dream Pet line through the 1970s, the ones from the toys' first decade were the perkiest and most irresistible. ■

> **Dakin: Dream Dolls, miscellaneous, $8**
> **Dakin: Dream Pets, miscellaneous, $8**

# SUPER BALL

**RUBBER JEWELS.**

Colorful Super Balls bounced their way into, and often out of, children's hands and hearts. Wham-O or unknown manufacturers, 1960s.

Wham-O: Cheerios box, 1969,
    Super Ball and Frisbee offer, $30
Wham-O: Super Ball, multicolored, small, $5-$10

WHAM-O'S DAYS in the sun were coming fast and furious at the end of the 1950s. The San Gabriel, Calif., company began the 1960s not only with the Hula Hoop but also a Flying Saucer horseshoe game and the Sputnik Sailing Satellite, soon to be known everywhere as the Frisbee. By mid-decade, its lead items had solidified into a strong quintet of toys: Frisbee, Slip 'N Slide, Water Wiggle, Hula Hoop and Limbo.

Then, in the 1965-66 season, kids started bouncing their Super Balls. Wham-O finally had a toy that worked exactly the way the company's name sounded. The Super Ball was no more than a ball made of a superbly bouncy rubber. Yet the power of its performance—the impressive and neck-bending heights of its rebound—surprised everyone.

While it did not sweep all of America into a sudden, thunderous fad, Super Ball nevertheless proved an inspired addition to Toyland. Absolutely every child played with a Super Ball, or one of its imitators, at least once during the later 1960s. If they did not have one of the large ones made by Wham-O, they had one of the balls made in smaller sizes. If they did not have one of a solid, dark color, they had one made with a wavy mix of colors. If they did not have an opaque Super Ball, then

they had a transparent one made by a competitor, with shiny metal flecks inside. Super Ball led to the notion that there was a generic category, called superballs. Super Ball may have ended up being a phenomenon here today and gone tomorrow, but the superball itself proved to be a perennial staple on the toy scene.

I remember having one particular Super Ball, somewhat opaque and whitish, with reflective sparkles inside. I guarded it carefully. Super Balls were so lively on hard surfaces that living in the midst of so much suburban pavement made me cautious.

The original Wham-O Super Balls were completely opaque and issued in either solid colors or attractively swirled combinations of color. I remember the largest being a large, heavy, black ball—intimidating in its weight, solidity and bouncing power.

*I* felt intimidated, at least. Maybe it was because that was the Super Ball that was always wielded by the bigger boys and by the schoolyard bullies. *You* remember the ones; if they ever got hold of your Super Ball, why, then, over the school building it went. *Way* over. And Super Balls did not have to be thrown very hard to be lost forever. ◾

# SPY TOYS

**T**HEY APPEARED by the dozens—not only the Super Spy characters of movies and TV, but the toys that transformed the everyday boy or girl into the thrilling realm of the Secret Agent. The Secret Sam Bomb Binoculars in the Topper Toys line was just one of the many toys of the 1960s that looked like some ordinary object, but when placed in the hands of the Secret Agent Kid, became a devastatingly effective weapon. One moment, a bird-watcher. The next ...

"They look like ordinary binoculars—you sight through them—they really work—then press against nose and—BANG—your Secret Sam Bomb Binoculars shoot an exploding Bomb," Topper's sales literature boasted.

The Secret Sam Camera Book, cunningly entitled *Spy Dictionary*, could shoot real pictures—or bullets. The Secret Sam Pipe Shooter fired with a squeeze of the teeth. The bizarre Sixfinger was that extra finger in the secret agent's hand that could fire a bomb or bullets.

Secret Sam could look like a sporting man carrying around the Secret Sam Bazooka Bat that fired an "exploding grenade"—or like a dandy, leaning nonchalantly on the Secret Sam Cane Shooter.

## THE MAN FROM U.N.C.L.E.

"'Let me get out of this lei and into something more comfortable,' was what she'd said. And then abruptly she was dead. Napoleon Solo stood immobile, staring at the bewitching corpse without a face. Deceptively slender, no more than of medium height, he had the smart appearance of a young intern, a Madison Avenue account exec. He looked like anything except what he was: a diamond-hard, exhaustively trained enforcement agent for perhaps the most important secret service in the world, the United Network Command for Law and Enforcement. His jacket and slacks were impeccably tailored with a Brooks Brothers quality, but the disarming cut concealed a strapped-down Berns-Martin shoulder holster housing its hidden U.N.C.L.E. Special, 37 ounces of deadly weapon, including silencer."

Harry Whittington's opening for one of the Man from U.N.C.L.E. books of the mid-1960s captures much of the bizarre, tangled and far-fetched nature of television's greatest spy series. Running from September 1964 through January 1968, NBC's answer to the popular James Bond movies combined the high-tech thrills and essential silliness that seemed intrinsic to the super-spy genre. Far more than the TV series *I Spy* or *Get Smart*, *The Man from U.N.C.L.E.* balanced its spoof element with an intense fantasy world of danger and intrigue.

Part of its success came from the light-and-dark main characters of dark-haired and calmly urbane American agent Napoleon Solo, played by Robert Vaughn, and the blond, quiet and mysterious Russian agent Ilya Kuryakin, played by David McCallum, who together combated the evils of the international crime syndicate THRUSH.

While most kids played being Napoleon and Ilya by simply pretending they were handsome and incredibly cool—or incredibly beautiful and cool, if *The Girl from U.N.C.L.E.*—others were lucky enough to have plastic guns, badges or Marx plastic figures to evoke the colorful and wonderfully weird show.

In some ways, games were the best ways of returning to favorite TV shows, for they could be played again and again. And, as on TV, the good guys always won. ■

### IMPRISONED IN THRUSH HEADQUARTERS!

The Ideal Toy Corporation capitalized on the super-spy phenomenon with its The Man from U.N.C.L.E. Game. "The word is out," Ideal told its apprehensive players. "THRUSH is planning something big. Quickly, U.N.C.L.E. is alerted and counters by assigning men to capture the THRUSH chiefs!" Players, beset by THRUSH agents at every point, were given their missions: "You must battle your way back to U.N.C.L.E. headquarters through overwhelming odds!" Ideal, 1965.

**Agent Zero M.** *The harmless-looking "Transistorized Portable" radio snapped open to turn into Agent Zero M's rifle! Mattel, 1964.*

**Just press against nose.**
*Secret Sam Bomb Binoculars, Topper Toys, 1966.*

King Seeley Thermos: Man from U.N.C.L.E. lunch box, 1966, $275
Lone Star: Girl from U.N.C.L.E. Garter Holster, 1966, $125
Miner Industries: Secret Agent 86 Pen Radio, 1960s, $70
Topper: Secret Sam Shooter Pipe, $10
Watkins-Strathmore: Man from U.N.C.L.E. coloring book, 1965, $35

A PARODY OF the suburban life so many families of the Boomer years were living, Hanna-Barbera's *The Flintstones* was television's first prime-time television cartoon, making its debut the evening of Sept. 30, 1960. Lasting through 1966, it was also the longest running prime-time animated series of the Boomer years.

The Flintstone family of Fred and Wilma, later joined by baby Pebbles, experienced all the joy and turmoil of modern suburban life in a campy prehistoric setting. They drove rock-wheeled cars, played a record player with a bird loaning its beak for the stylus and kept a buzzard beneath the sink for a garbage disposal. They kept pets, including a dinosaur. They quarreled, made up, had barbecues and went on outings with their friends and neighbors, the Rubbles. Until the cartoon appeared on their televisions, people never knew how far they had not come since the Stone Age.

Alan Reed provided the voice for Fred; Jean VanderPyl for Wilma and Pebbles; Mel Blanc for Barney Rubble and Dino the Dinosaur; Bea Benaderet for the first Betty Rubble, Gerry Johnson for the second; and Don Messick for Bamm Bamm. Numerous cameo characters spoofed famous TV personalities, including Perry Masonry and Ed Sullystone.

The Flintstone family entered the playroom through games, battery-operated toys and plastic figures. Perhaps the most enduring fun through the years came from a series of simple but entertaining toys from the Kohner company. Based on the wooden push-puppets the parents of the Boomers had enjoyed before the war, Kohner's plastic push-puppets were figures that could bend, wave their arms, nod and bow. ■

**YOU'LL HAVE A YABBA-DABBA-DO TIME.**

Push-puppets, still being made of wood as the Boomer era began, later proved popular in plastic. Fred, Pebbles and Bamm-Bamm, Kohner Brothers Inc., 1960s. Toys courtesy Becky Stubbe.

**Yogi.** *Kohner Bros., 1960s.*

**Dancer.** *Even less famous Hanna-Barbera characters made their way into toy form. "I'm Dancer the Dog Push-Button Puppet," the label of this one reads. Kohner Brothers, Inc., 1960s.*

Kohner: **Atom Ant Push Puppet, $40**
Kohner: **Pebbles Push Puppet, $35**
Kohner: **Fred Flintstone Push Puppet, $30**
Kohner: **Bamm-Bamm Push Puppet, $20**
Marx: **Play set figure, Fred Flintstone, $10**
Transogram: **Flintstones Stone Age Game, 1961, $45**

# THE ADDAMS FAMILY
## GAME

WHILE MANY of the names everyone came to know and love were not to come until later, the characters who were to become TV's Gomez, Morticia, Uncle Fester, Wednesday, Pugsley, Grandmama and Lurch first appeared in the sophisticated pages of *The New Yorker*.

Charles Addams stood out among the cartoonists of that often witty and usually elevated magazine. His cartoons, many of them set within a moldering, many-spired mansion, took a distinctly grotesque and often morbid turn.

John Astin, Carolyn Jones, Jackie Coogan, Ken Weatherwax, Lisa Loring, Blossom Rock and Ted Cassidy played in the starring roles when the cartoon inspired the 1964-66 TV show. Cassidy also played the role of the helpful hand named Thing.

Felix Silla occasionally appeared as the all-hair Cousin It.

*The Addams Family* and its competitor *The Munsters* fit neatly into the burgeoning interest in all things monstrous among America's youth. Ideal's The Addams Family Game gave kids the chance to wander a little deeper into the America's most morbidly funny mansion.

"The moon, half hidden behind dark gray clouds, casts weird shadows around the Addams Mansion," the 1964 game tells players. "It is a perfect night for the Addams Family to go on their annual midnight picnic at the nearby cemetery. The only trouble is that the family is scattered all over the house. You must have them meet in front of the house so that they can all leave together."

Based on the abc TV series

### ALTOGETHER OOKY.

Composer Vic Mizzy wrote lines that vied with toy jingles in the minds of the TV-bound children of the 1960s. "They're creepy and they're kooky, mysterious and spooky, they're altogether ooky: The Addams Family." Former child star Jackie Coogan, here peeking from behind the chair, was turned down for the role of Uncle Fester until he showed up bald and dressed to resemble the crazed man of Charles Addams' original cartoons. Ideal, 1964.

**#70**

Early toys tying into the TV show also included "caricature figures" by Remco.

Milton Bradley soon had an Addams Family game, too, while Aurora Plastics made an Addams Family: The Haunted House kit, and Colorforms issued Addams Family sets. Before the fuss ended in the late 1960s, Bantam-Lite released the perfect toy for haunted-house explorations, an Addams Family flashlight.

A house with a carnivorous houseplant, Wednesday's headless doll, a dashing and debonair gentleman in love with a pallid but beautiful witch, a wide-eyed lunatic capable of lighting light bulbs with his ears ... In a world gone half crazy anyway, it made its own kind of sense.

Ideal: Addams Family Game, 1965, $75
Ideal: Gomez Hand Puppet, 1965, $50
Milton Bradley: Dastardly & Muttley, 1969, $40
Milton Bradley: Beverly Hillbillies Set Back Game, $20
Milton Bradley: Bullwinkle Hide & Seek Game, 1961, $30
Remco: Hawaii Five-O Game, 1960s, $75
Transogram: Dragnet Game, 1955, $50-$60
Transogram: Eliot Ness and the Untouchables Game, 1961, $70
Whitman: Family Affair Game, 1967, $35

## DASTARDLY AND MUTTLEY IN THEIR FLYING MACHINES GAME

One of the late hits for Hanna-Barbera Productions in the 1960s was *Dastardly and Muttley in Their Flying Machines*, featuring an animated duo with voices by Paul Winchell and Don Messick. The characters had already gained fame in the simple yet popular *Wacky Races*, which debuted in 1968.

"Once upon a time there were four great pilots who flew their beautiful, specially built flying machines in great precision formations," Milton Bradley told kids who played their tie-in game. "They were called, for their daring, Vulture Squadron. Their mission, to knock from the air Yankee Doodle, a carrier pigeon who flew a mailbag full of enemy secrets." The other two pilots, Klunk and Zilly, never quite stuck in memory the way Dastardly and Muttley did.

The popular *Wacky Races*, with its large cast of cross-country racers designed by Jerry Eisenberg and Iwao Takamoto, had been inspired by such similarly wacky movies as *The Great Race* and *Those Magnificent Men in Their Flying Machines*. *Wacky Races* also led to the spin-off series *The Perils of Penelope Pitstop*. ■

**Drat and double drat!**
*Dastardly and Muttley vie to capture the bugle-blowing Yankee Doodle Pigeon. Milton Bradley, 1969-70.*

**Astronaut's dream girl.** *TV comedies involving the fantastic also included Bewitched and I Dream of Jeannie, the latter being especially interesting for featuring the U.S. space program in its background story. I Dream of Jeannie Game, Milton Bradley, 1965.*

# PLASTIC POWERHOUSES
# ELDON'S BIG POLY

ONE OF the toy-making revolutions of the late 1950s was led by Eldon Mfg. Co. of Los Angeles, Calif. It was not the sort of revolution that anyone truly noticed, besides the toy-buyers of department stores and the parents who thought very deeply about the toys they were buying their children. It was another of the revolutions coming out of the still-developing plastics industry.

In 1957 and '58, Eldon began advertising a new line of big toys. The toys were not unusual for their size, because they were toy trucks and aircraft, after all, and large-scale toy trucks and aircraft were nothing new to the toy industry. Rather, earlier toys of this sort had been made of metal or occasionally of earlier, harder plastics.

"This is Big Poly!" said Eldon advertisements in 1958. Showing the $2.98 Cargo Plane, a large aircraft whose nose opened to unload smaller military vehicles, the ads made two points. "Two feet long," was one of them. "Unbreakable polyethylene toys," was the other.

What Eldon was grasping, along with a few other companies, was what direction large toys were going to go in the 1960s and beyond. In 1958, most such toys were metal. But the handwriting was on the wall: polyethylene was the way to go.

By 1960, Eldon had chalked up a number of successes of the Big Poly sort. Even though the big polyethylene toys lacked the heft and brute sturdiness of pressed-steel toys, they succeeded for at least three reasons.

They were good indoor toys. If a child rammed one into the kitchen cabinets, neither cabinets nor toy were the worse for it.

Less clanging and banging, too, meant more peace for parents.

They also seemed good deals to parents. When the Eldon Tow Truck was being sold in the 1960-61 season, it cost $1.99, which was cheaper than the pressed-steel trucks half its size.

To the industry, these big plastic toys must have offered one further allure. At a time when overseas imports were taking over even the tried-and-true steel truck, polyethylene promised continuing competitiveness. Pages of mail-order catalogs would be featuring truck toys in which all the steel trucks were imports and only the polyethylene and vinyl ones were made in the United States.

Eldon was not quite alone in this corner of the toy field. Plastic Toy & Novelty Corp. of Brooklyn, N.Y., was also issuing its Polyethylene Giant Trucks by 1957.

Eldon achieved its lead through extensive advertising and placement in countless chain department stores across the country. That lead was later taken over by other companies, notably Louis Marx & Co., which had a series of big-plastic truck hits during the middle 1960s—notably the large, white tow truck named Big Bruiser, which seemed almost an homage to the tow-truck toy Eldon made at the beginning of the decade. ■

Eldon: Big Poly Wrecker, $75
Irwin: Barbie's Mercedes Roadster, 1964, $150
Irwin: Ken's Hot Rod, 1963, $175
Irwin: Skipper's Sports Car, 1965, $175

**World wrecker.** *The toy world would never be the same. The Eldon Tow Truck was one of the toys spelling the end of the big, metal truck. Increasingly, that niche would be filled by plastic toys. Eldon Mfg. Co., ca. 1960.*

I N THE early 1960s, HO-scale motoring appeared to be the wave of the future. In 1961, Eldon Industries, the new Hawthorne, Calif., company under whose umbrella Eldon, Ungar and Knickerbocker toys were being made, was buying TV advertising for its Eldon Deluxe Road Race and the Eldon Cup Auto Race, alongside its memorable Yakkity Yob, the Red-Headed Robot. New York City's Ideal Toy Corp., meanwhile, was buying TV spots for its Electric Roadway. In that year, too, the A.C. Gilbert Co. of New Haven, Conn., was banking heavily on miniature racetracks, with its Gilbert's Autorama Highway System.

These were toys not so much for kids as for fathers, even though fathers would be buying sets for the children, much as previous generations of fathers had bought their children railroad sets. The price-points alone ensured that

these would be toys of the more privileged families or for adults indulging their own model-miniature fancies. The smallest Gilbert set was the Daytona Beach Tri-Oval, at $19.98, featuring 1940 Ford Coupe stock cars that sped around a tri-oval raceway. In other words, the cheapest of these sets were at the premium price for many other kinds of playthings.

The largest set from Gilbert was the Highway System, with a Corvette and pickup truck, at $39.98. Even the accessories were not cheap. Roadway sections were 50 cents apiece. Extra Fords and pick-up trucks cost $6.98, and extra Corvettes, $7.98.

The Gilbert sales department projected that miniature, remote-controlled cars would become the most profitable item in the toy industry in the 1960s. That department helped ensure that the projection would become reality by investing more heavily

**For more ZOOM**

**Slot car magic.** *For a few heady years, every toy catalog was filled with the sinuous images of slotted tracks and the lightweight racers that spun around the curves. Besides Aurora, such companies as Strombecker, Eldon and Topper developed followings of their own. Sears Toys, 1967-68.*

**Best of two worlds.**
*The Prop Rod by Thimbledrome showcased the sleek body of a racer and the clear-plastic, covered cockpit of the airplane, plus the spectacle of a spinning rear propeller. It burned real fuel while friends looked on, burning with jealousy. L.M. Cox Manufacturing Co., 1960s.*

**The real rip-snortin' stuff itself.**
*Cox gas-powered vehicles operated best on the company's own formulation, which it sold in attractive tin cans. Cox, 1960s.*

in TV advertising for the Autorama than the company ever had before for any single Gilbert toy. Soon every kid wanted grooved track sets, down which wedge-nosed cars raced, skidded and flew off the track.

Train sets had done fairly well in maintaining the popularity they had enjoyed before the war. One of the best strategies for survival had been the move Gilbert had taken with its American Flyer HO sets toward smaller-scale tracks and trains.

Slot cars, however, threatened to take the place of even HO railroads, since they occupied the same place on the den floor a toy train might otherwise take and had an unbeatable advantage: kids could compete. If a train took a corner too quickly, it just fell over. If a racing car took a corner too fast and leapt off the track, it meant losing the race.

The enthusiasm for slot-cars was ignited in the United States in 1959 by Strombecker Road Racing Sets of Strombeck-Becker Mfg. Co., Moline, Ill. The sets did so well they were selling out of stock by the 1960-61 season, inspiring others, including Gilbert, Ideal and Eldon—and, later, Aurora Plastics of West Hempstead, N.Y., to join in.

An indication of the intense level of excitement about the new hobby can be found in developments at Dowst Mfg. Co. of Chicago. Not long after it purchased Strombeck-Becker's toy and hobby division in 1961, the company decided to rename itself. Even though it had called itself Dowst since the 1800s, the strong performance of electric racing sets during the early 1960s inspired the name-change to Strombecker Corp.

As huge as the phenomenon was to be, by mid-decade, it proved to be not quite as long-lived as the toy industry expected. By the late 1960s and early '70s kids were ready for something even more exciting, easier and quicker to set up—and cheaper. Mattel gave it to them in Hot Wheels.

## THIMBLEDROME

Even before the appearance of electric racing sets in 1959, race-car toys with working motors were an exciting and important part of the toy scene. A variety of companies worked with such engines immediately after World War II, including Dooling Brothers of Los Angeles, Calif. Dooling produced internal-combustion engine models and a working open-cockpit racer made of cast magnesium. Riding on semi-pneumatic wheels, its two-cycle gasoline motor could propel the 8-½ pound car at up to 90 mph.

To go even faster, another company named McCoy issued a teardrop-shaped car of the same weight with a ram-air-intake gas engine. In tests it clocked over 115 mph. For powering toy planes and boats, Minijet Motors, of Pasadena, Calif., created a "real jet motor, not a toy" that produced 3 pounds of thrust.

The Minijet Motors warning hit the problem on the head. These were designed for adults, not children. Their cost was similarly adult-scale: the Dooling Bros. and McCoy racers cost $70 or more, and the Minijet Motors jet cost $35. In contrast, a 19-inch car from Buddy L, still made of hardwood due to wartime materials restrictions continuing into postwar times, cost only $6 in 1946.

The company to bring gas-powered toys within reach of the most children during the 1950s was L.M. Cox Manufacturing Co. of Santa Ana, Calif. Its Thimbledrome miniature racers, introduced nationally around 1951, became mainstays of the toy-manufacturing scene. Even though the company's powered airplanes would prove equally important, it was Cox's line of Prop Rods, Dune Buggies, Red Hot Drag Racing Buicks and Corvettes that gave early Boomers some of their most lasting memories. What could have been better than a gas-powered car that could go streaking away, causing havoc down the streets of their lucky owners? ◼

Cox: Baja Bug, 1968-73, $65
Cox: Thimble Drome Prop Rod, $75
Eldon: Power 8 Road Racer Set, 1960s, $75
Revell: Rat Fink slot car, 1966, in original box, $250

**Le Mans.** *By the mid-1960s, sales of electric road-racing sets was at a peak. Even Louis Marx & Co. jumped into the fray with sets, including the Le Mans Speedway. Sears Toy Book, 1963-64.*

# BASH!
## THE DECADE OF LOUD GAMES

**BASH!**

By mid-decade, games relying on keeping things in a delicate balance were transforming the games market. Ideal Toys, 1967.

THE TREND that started in 1961-62 reached its crest a few years later. Games once designed for family enjoyment, fairly quiet for the most part and often dependent on mental agility and knowledge, gave way to bright, brilliantly designed, fast-paced, noisy games of impulse and chaos.

Many games gained their feeling of mounting tension by creating an imminent disaster, which one player would set off. No one could tell at the beginning who that player would be—who would be the winner or loser.

In Ker-Plunk, a 1967 Ideal game, players sat around a clear plastic tube filled with marbles suspended by plastic straws. The players had to pull out the straws without letting the marbles drop. In The Last Straw, Schaper's 1966 hit, players kept adding plastic straws to the camel's basket, wondering whose would be the one to tip the balance and break the camel's back. In the same company's Don't Break the Ice game, players took turns hammering out chunks of ice, trying to leave just enough to keep the hapless ice-fisherman from falling through.

The games came out in profusion: 1965's Booby-Trap, a wooden spring-bar game from Parker Brothers; Operation, from Milton Bradley in 1965; Tip-It, a balancing game, Hands Down, described as "the slap-happy game," and KaBoom!, a balloon-popping device from Ideal in 1965; Don't Spill the Beans and the Voodoo Doll Game from Schaper in 1967.

Bash! was another Ideal game issued in 1967. The Bash! man was a stack of plastic disks, with the man's head on top of the stack and his large feet bracing the stack from below. Equipped with a plastic hammer, players took turns knocking pieces out of his body, making him progressively shorter—or making him totter over, sending the pieces crashing down, which was what all the games were about.

Time Bomb, issued at mid-decade by Milton Bradley, may have touched at the heart of the matter. Anything connected to the word "bomb" was connected to a notion new on Earth, made vivid in America by events in Cuba a few years earlier: Everything hung in a delicate balance. "Duck and cover!" Kids had to learn it somehow. ■

Ideal: Bash!, $10
Ideal: Ker-Plunk, 1967, $10

# ROMANTIC GAMES #74
## FROM BEN CASEY TO MYSTERY DATE

ROMANTIC FANTASIES played a role in board games of the 1960s, especially the ones based on popular TV hospital shows. Even though the TV networks in the early 1960s were moving toward sitcoms and generally goofy programming, several series focused on serious topics, including the medical drama *Ben Casey, M.D.* from ABC, the same network that would later release *Marcus Welby, M.D.*, the top-ranking TV medical series of the end of the Boomer period.

*Ben Casey* won audience loyalty not only through realistic depiction of the daily life of a doctor in a busy, demanding metropolitan hospital environment, but also through the visual charisma of its star, Vince Edwards. Young women enjoyed the show. So did kids, who had always gotten a kick out of playing hospital with their Hassenfeld Bros. or Transogram doctor and nurse bags. Suddenly, they had a specific TV-star character to role-play.

Knowing the show's popularity, toy manufacturers produced a variety of goods. Transogram issued a *Ben Casey, M.D.*, game, as well as *Ben Casey, M.D.*, play-hospital sets.

*Ben Casey, M.D.* aired from 1961 to 1966, a run NBC matched with *Dr. Kildare*, starring Richard Chamberlain as Dr. James Kildare. That TV character had his toys, too, including a Dr. Kildare ambulance made by A.J. Renzi Plastic Corp. of Leominster, Mass.

Probably the oddest TV-doctor items were manufactured by Bayshore Industries, Inc., a New York City novelty and costume company that produced both Ben Casey and Dr. Kildare Autograph Fractures for kids who wanted to show that their bones were set by only the very best.

If Milton Bradley, with its long history, had simply rested on its laurels during the Baby Boomer years, that in itself would have been newsworthy. But the company remained a dynamic presence in the business, as demonstrated by such entries as 1965's Mystery Date, a game that appealed to young girls because it mirrored what they saw around them and ahead of them in their lives. Mystery Date was not a game based on cartoon characters or a TV show. Too many such games were fairly lame, interesting mainly because of the characters depicted on the box-tops. This was a real game, one that stimulated involvement, often in the form of laughter, fits of jealousy and moments of wishful thinking.

At that point in the decade, every game manufacturer, including Milton Bradley, emphasized action games that threatened players with collapses, explosions or general breakdowns of some variety. Mystery Date offered a different kind of general breakdown. Players each had their chance to open the door, where their date had come knocking. Maybe they would be lucky and get the cool ski dude wearing the turtleneck sweater and exuding wealth and confidence … or maybe not. ■

> Ideal: Dr. Kildare Game, 1962, $25
> Lowe: Dr. Kildare & Nurse Susan paper dolls, 1962, $50
> Milton Bradley: Mystery Date, 1965, $75
> Milton Bradley: Mystery Date, 1972, $35
> Transogram: Ben Casey MD Game, 1961, $20

**Ski bum, or just a bum?** *Girls responded with mock thrill or dismay after opening the plastic door at the center of the Mystery Date game board. Milton Bradley, 1965. Photo courtesy Sharon Korbeck.*

**"X-Ray Report—Positive!"** *With a handful of diagnostic cards and a few cardboard stand-ups representing their favorite TV doctor, kids re-created the "drama of life in a big metropolitan hospital." Ben Casey M.D. Game, Transogram, 1961.*

# THE ROAD TO HAPPINESS
# THE GAME OF LIFE

**Plastic people.** Players in the 1960s wandered the sinuous path through Life in pastel-colored plastic cars filled with soft plastic people and their plastic children. The Game of Life, Milton Bradley, 1960s-70s.

**The player with the most money WINS THE GAME!** *The Game of Life had some of the best play money to be found. The face of Ransom A. Treasure graced the $500 note, and that of G.I. Luvmoney, the $20,000 bill. The face on the highest denomination bill of $50,000? Bearded old Milton Bradley himself. Bradley, 1960-70s.*

I N 1960, Milton Bradley created a hit board game that was not an action game or TV tie-in. It was in some ways brand-new but in other ways exactly 100 years old.

In 1860, the young Milton Bradley took inspiration from an English board game and drew on his skills as a designer and lithographer to create a new game he called The Checkered Game of Life. He made several hundred copies of the game and took a laborious trip in September from Springfield, Mass., to New York City, where he found the stationery and department stores receptive. He sold every example he had of this "highly moral game" and through the following winter sold a remarkable 40,000 copies.

For its centennial year, the Bradley company revived this road-to-happiness concept. Its new Game of Life was updated and revised to match a Boomer vision of reality. It featured a molded plastic landscape, a white plastic spinner and plastic automobiles in which plastic stick-people traveled forward full of hope.

Bradley revised the game's goal, too. The new Game of Life was not really about the road to happiness, but rather the road to wealth. Should it be surprising that Boomers now remember it almost as fondly as they do that other millionaire-making game, Monopoly? ■

Milton Bradley: The Game of Life, 1960s, $40
Milton Bradley: Candyland, 1949, $50
Parker Bros.: Clue, 1960s, $15-$20

# JOHNNY ASTRO

**P**RETENDING TO BE at the controls of jets, spaceships, missile systems and rocket launching pads became easier in the later Boomer period, thanks to De Luxe Reading Corp., also known through the years as De Luxe Topper and Topper Toys. The company produced large, plastic, battery-enhanced dashboards of cars, with steering controls and endless dials. The equally large Jimmy Jet had the U-shaped steering control of an aircraft cockpit, firing plastic missiles and a screen that lit up to reveal the shadow of a military jet traveling across the landscape.

Best of all may have been Johnny Astro, which De Luxe Topper announced as "The Most Exciting Toy Ever! Johnny Astro really flies!" Relatively simple in concept, it used the same principle that had appeared in 1950s "satellite" toys, in which the "satellite," much like a ping-pong ball, floated above the battery-operated space car or electric train car. The ball floated within a cone of rising air created by a small fan.

In Johnny Astro, a large fan, guided by a pair of control levers, made the spacecraft take off. The suspended spacecraft were simple balloons with markings on the sides such as "Luna 3 USA" and "Mars 2." They stayed upright due to being weighted on the bottoms with small landing platforms. The plastic control unit came with a cardboard landing field where the spacecraft could land—after extraordinary adventures several feet above the ground. ■

Topper: Johnny Astro, $75

**Space-age balloon launcher.**
*De Luxe Topper admitted ordinary balloons will work, but "may not perform as well." It offered to send six extra balloons for 50 cents, postpaid. Johnny Astro, De Luxe Topper, 1960s.*

**Hybrid vigor.**
*While Eldon was best known for its slot cars, it made an important contribution to space toys with Billy Blastoff, a combination space-themed child doll and battery-operated toy. Although given relatively few accessories, Billy was the first successful fashion doll for younger boys. Eldon, late 1960s.*

**Switch 'N Go.** *Sears Toys, 1966-67.*

### DOWN THE BATTERY TRACK: GRIPPIDEE GRAVIDEE

Several other toys matched Billy Blastoff in its combination of Space Age ideas and battery-operated cuteness. At the same time the fad for HO and 1:32 scale model racing was raging, a less heralded but still popular series of vehicle toys relied on tracks of quite a different sort.

Where little slot cars were zipping along, these larger vehicles were slow and sometimes even ponderous. Also unlike the slots, half the fun of these was in the moving around of the more versatile tracks into different configurations and to different places, even outdoors. Being battery-powered, with the power packs located in the vehicles themselves, kids were no longer restricted to the reach of the power cord.

Batteries were admittedly expensive. Even so, the toys won a welcome from parents, who had long been nervous about the idea of their children putting anything into electrical sockets. With households moving away from the easygoing pace of prewar times, parents had less time to play with their children and to supervise the use of wires, plugs and transformers.

Mattel's Switch 'N Go vehicles, which included a Ford racer, Batmobile, *Lost in Space* crawler and dump truck, had the most flexible of tracks, in that it consisted of a simple plastic tube that could be placed anywhere, over almost any terrain. A grooved wheel on the vehicle's underside kept it on track.

Unlike the Switch 'N Go *Lost in Space* crawler, Grippidee Gravidee was a contemporary Space Age toy, using a more realistic design resembling the future space shuttle. The track, which came in segments, could be built into various three-dimensional configurations, with the spacecraft equally able to travel right-side-up or upside-down.

IN THE SECOND HALF of the 1960s, space action figures took over where plastic space people left off in the 1940s and '50s. While they came in all shapes and sizes, the majority were dressed in current NASA style.

Gilbert's 1966 Moon McDare and his Space Mutt, for instance, wore sterile NASA white tube suits with round space helmets. Unlike his real-life NASA counterparts, however, the 11-inch McDare was billed as never being without his space gun, which shot soft pellets. Sears, in 1966, said of McDare, "Who knows what creatures he may find in outer space?"

In the same year, Hassenfeld's G.I. Joe also went into orbit or at least came back from it in his "splashdown" set, with Mercury-style space capsule, rescue-party Frogmen, and zippered space suit of metallic plastic.

Mattel's smaller, 6-inch figure, Major Matt Mason, made a notable debut in 1967. He was a bendy, unlike other action figures. He appeared with his peg-wheeled Space Crawler and jet-propelled Space Sled. In the following year the Astro-Trac Space Missile Convoy, the eight-wheeled Space Mobile and Matt's double-sized friend Captain Lazer appeared.

Soon the semirealistic space universe gained more dimension with the addition of strange beings: the green, translucent Callisto ("transparent skull reveals his superior humanoid brain!") and Scorpio, an insectoid alien.

An even smaller figure than Major Matt went farther off the beaten path, fittingly enough for a space explorer. Billy Blastoff was "America's first boy in space," according to the ads. He wore a white NASA-style suit with air tanks on the back that held batteries. These powered not Billy, but his vehicles—a peg-wheeled crawler like Major Matt's, a second crawler equipped with treads and a space capsule.

For a change, kids could play with a space figure that was not an adult make-believe character, but one they could imagine being themselves. With NASA's space efforts at a peak by the end of the 1960s, they all wanted to go to the moon—not in 10 or 20 years, when they might have been old enough, but right then. ■

Eldon: Billy Blastoff Space Base, $80
Eldon: Billy Blastoff Space Scout Set, $150
Eldon: Billy Blastoff's Robbie Robot, $60

## GOING BONKERS.

THE THRILL of the illicit, the banned, the black-listed: it still hangs over the mere word, Klackers. Klackers were simple toys designed for the irritation of parents, teachers and other kids who were not allowed them. Consisting of a pair of hard-plastic balls connected by a yo-yo type string, with a tied-in ring at the middle for a grip, Klackers were excellently named, as they made noise, and lots of it, sounding exactly like the name—*clack, clack, clack*—as the balls bounced against each other, perhaps gently at first and then with increasing force until the balls bounced not only against each other underneath the player's hand, but first below, then above, and up and down again and again in rapid succession. This could be carried on for so long and with such force that the balls cracked and flew apart in pieces or simply detached from the strings, crashing through a window or into another kid's head.

In a time of anti-war protests, folk music and the Beatles, did kids protest when the ban was announced? I don't recall myself. I only remember a greater sense of safety going down the school halls. So brainwashed was our entire generation with the notion of consumer safety that those of us already denied Klackers by our parents, for those same safety reasons, were mainly glad to see everyone else denied too. ■

**Various Mfrs.: Klacker-type toys, $10-$15**

Klackers were easily imitated and appeared from many novelty manufacturers under a variety of names. Pictured packaged are Zonker, by C&K Novelty, and Ker-Knockers, by the Ker-Knockers Corp. Loose is a pair of Klackers or similar brand item from the late 1960s to early 1970s.

"WE'VE PLANNED THE BIGGEST ADVERTISING AND PUBLICITY CAMPAIGN IN JURO HISTORY TO HELP PROMOTE THIS EXACT REPLICA OF THIS IMPISH DUMMY OF NATIONALLY FAMOUS VENTRILOQUIST PAUL WINCHELL. RADIO, TELEVISION, NEWSPAPERS, MAGAZINES AND PERSONAL APPEARANCES ... WE'RE GOING TO COVER THEM ALL! WATCH FOR THE 'JERRY MAHONEY' DOLL DEBUT THROUGH PAUL WINCHELL'S NATIONWIDE RADIO AND TELEVISION SHOWS—WHEN HIS MILLIONS OF FANS GET WIND OF THE WHIMSICAL 'JERRY MAHONEY' DOLL, IN STYLES RANGING FROM THE LARGE TO THE MARIONETTE AND HAND PUPPET MODELS, THE STAMPEDE WILL BE ON!"

—ADVERTISEMENT, JURO NOVELTY CO. OF N.Y.C., N.Y., 1949.

# Squeakers and Squealers

**A**s the 1960s waned and the larger part of the Boomer generation moved beyond their toy years, they may have noticed how their younger siblings were sometimes playing with new sorts of toys.

There was the Kohner Busy Box, a cradle toy for the new generation. There was the Fisher-Price Play Family Farm, a popular new play set featuring the company's increasingly popular Little People. There was Mattel's series of See 'N Say toys, which were plastic, talking, educational toys. There was the Lite-Brite, a new, electronic design toy from Hassenfeld Bros. These were the toys that would become standards for the

"Generation-X" kids who would follow the Boomers.

At the same time, the Boomers were probably amused at how many of their own toys were reappearing in the small, chubby hands of the new kids in the neighborhood. Easy-Bake Ovens, Wooly Willy magnetic drawing toys, Changeable Charlie blocks and Give-A-Show Projectors kept reappearing in toy stores. Tonka, Structo and Nylint trucks remained on the scene, as did Matchbox and Tootsietoy cars. Bozo the Clown, Barbie, Zip the Monkey and even Howdy Doody dolls and figures kept reappearing, even though in some cases the TV-show originals were now unknown to children.

# VINYL-FACED BEAR
## FROM CHUBBY TUBBY TO YOGI

ONE OF the important innovations of the early Boomer years was the introduction of the plastic-faced stuffed toy. Ideal's 1951 Algy, the Bear, for instance, was a plastic-faced teddy bear. About 18-inch tall, it was a bedtime toy with a plush body and "friendly plastic face." New York City's M. & S. Doll Co. was another important pioneer, issuing plastic-faced dolls with cuddly, terrycloth bodies.

At the time, teddy bears made by The Rushton Co., of Atlanta, Ga., also known as Atlanta Playthings Co., looked very much the way teddy bears had for decades. They were plush toys, top and bottom. Yet the company was quickly introducing a new line of At Play stuffed toys that were markedly different. They had the same, soft bodies, but now they had distinct, doll-like features that were made possible by combining vinyl faces with the plush bodies. Lambsie-Wamsie was a vinyl-faced lamb. Floppy Poodly, Dan-D-Lion and Curly Purr Cat all combined vinyl features with pastel-colored plush. Some, like Chico Monkey, not only had vinyl faces but also vinyl feet and hands, too—and, in the case of Chubby Tubby, vinyl paws.

Chubby Tubby was the teddy bear of the line. He came in three sizes, at 9, 12, and 17 inches high, costing from $3 to $8. For teddy bears they were unusual not only for their irresistibly charming vinyl faces, but also for the fact that they, unlike other teddy bears, had claws.

Alongside Chubby Tubby in the 1953-54 season was Ideal's strongest entry in the vinyl-and-plush category: a 15-inch Smokey the Bear.

Chubby Tubby, one of the most successful plush toys of the early 1950s, was used as a symbol for the company in its advertising into the 1960s, taking the place of the older-style, all-plush teddy bear that had served before.

### SMARTER THAN YOUR AVERAGE BEAR.

Knickerbocker made its 18" Yogi Bear "with two-tone real bear markings," the company boasted. "All the fun of a college cut-up!" Yogi, one of many stuffed, plush toys with vinyl heads made by Knickerbocker and its competitor Rushton, originally cost less than $5. Knickerbocker, 1960s; photo by Martha Borchardt.

By the middle decade, other vinyl-faced toys such as Stinky Winky, the skunk, and Daisy Belle, the cow, had also risen to toy stardom,. Most popular of all, however, was Zippy Chimp, modeled on the source of mischief that had appeared on the *Howdy Doody Show*.

### HEY, BOO-BOO!

In 1957, the team of Bill Hanna and Joe Barbera left MGM superstars Tom and Jerry behind and started pitching simple, original cartoons to the TV networks. Their first was *The Ruff and Reddy Show*, followed in 1958 by their first TV hit, *The Huckleberry Hound Show*.

*Huckleberry Hound* featured a half hour of the Southern-talking blue hound dog, with voice by Daws Butler. In his onscreen life, Huckleberry went through every occupation possible, from sheriff and farmer to mailman and lumberjack. In his offscreen life, he was an Emmy Award winner, as of 1959.

Besides Huckleberry's own cartoons, the show included segments for Pixie and Dixie, both voiced by Don Messick, and Yogi Bear, voiced by Butler. When Yogi and his college-style, pork-pie hat proved popular enough to spin off into his own series, a new duo, Hokey Wolf and Ding-A-Ling, took his place.

*The Yogi Bear Show* debuted in 1961 with a cast of Yogi Bear (Butler), Boo-Boo the bear cub (Messick) and Ranger John Smith (Messick). The show included two additional segments,

**Claws.** *Chubby Tubby, who came in three sizes, was perhaps the most important early plush-and-vinyl toy. The teddy bear became a symbol for Rushton, its parent company, lasting into the 1960s. The small vinyl-nosed bear with the googley eyes was made by Expert Doll & Toy Co., N.Y.C. Chubby Tubbies, The Rushton Co., 1950s.*

one featuring Snagglepuss (Butler), and the other Yakky Doodle (Jimmy Weldon) and the bulldog Chopper (Vance Colvig).

Among the most popular toys of the early 1960s were stuffed animals in the Famous Plush TV Characters line by Knickerbocker Toy Co., Inc. of New York City. It included a selection of television's best in "DuPont crush resistant plush," feather foam stuffing and, with the exception of the mice, vinyl faces: Ba Ba Looey, Snooper Sleuth, Blabber Detective, Quick Draw McGraw, Mr. Jinks, Doggie Daddy, Augie Doggie, Huckleberry, Yogi, and Pixie and Dixie, none much more than 20 inehes tall.

Knickerbocker had other popular stuffed-toy items, too: Cuddle Bears, Kewpie Dolls, Baby Santa and Betsy McCall's Pets. For a while, Knickerbocker's series reigned supreme in the playroom, surrendering its top place only when Mattel's plush figures turned talkers. ■

Knickerbocker: Huckleberry Hound, plush and vinyl, $40
Knickerbocker: Yogi Bear, plush and vinyl, $35
Marx: Yogi Bear, play set figure, 60 mm, $30
Rushton: Chubby Tubby, 17", $50

# VINYL SQUEAKERS

## SUN RUBBER GETS THE SQUEEZE FROM COMPETITORS

People thinking back to their squeeze-toy childhood years may have toys in mind made by other companies than Sun Rubber, which was far from the only specialist in these toys.

Toy distribution was more regionally oriented then than it is now. A California child in 1957, for instance, may have been more apt to play with a Vinfloat than a Sun Rubber squeeze-toy.

Others operating in the 1950s included Mail Pouch Toys of Wheeling, W.Va., with its Uncle Robbie's Animal Friends; Dreamland Creations, Inc. and Gloria Toy Co., Inc. of New York City; Tinkle Toy Co. of Youngstown, Ohio; William G. Minder Industries, Inc. of Atlanta, Ga.; Topstone Rubber Toys Co. of Bethel, Conn.; Eastern Moulded Products Co. of Norwalk, Conn.; Vinfloat Co. of Los Angeles; and Irwin Corp. of Nashua, N.H.

Unlike the rubber-toy industry, vinyl-toy production was not heavily centered in Ohio.

### POLKA-DOT CHARMER.

*Famed children's illustrator Ruth E. Newton designed several dolls for Sun. Wearing the ever-present polka dots of the time, this girl doll, 8-½" tall, is made of soft vinyl, with a squeaker in her left foot. Sun Rubber, 1950s.*

Smith consulted the artist about his company's masks. Gas masks, he realized, were unappealing objects at best and frightening objects at worst. How did kids see them? Would they understand that the masks meant safety and protection, when they looked so alarming? After the meeting with Disney, Sun Rubber started manufacturing its most unusual item: the Mickey Mouse Gas Mask.

As the years passed, Sun Rubber notched up a number of toy-making innovations. The company made the first cry-and-wet dolls, setting the stage for one of the doll hits for later Boomer kids, Ideal's Betsy Wetsy. In 1949, Sun introduced the first mass-produced black doll, named Amosandra, daughter of Amos and Ruby of the popular *Amos 'N Andy* radio show.

Perhaps its most important contribution to the toy world was its development around 1953 of the rotational casting machine, which let the company produce dolls seven times faster than before using a vinyl called Plastisol. The method and the material also allowed exceptionally good detail.

Sun Rubber may have overinvested in the new technology. It also overextended in defending its patent in court and went into bankruptcy, closing its doors in 1958. The company reopened in 1960, however, after the Ohio court ruled in Sun's favor.

MILLIONS OF children in the 1950s and '60s took for granted squeezable, shiny, highly detailed toys made of vinyl, available by the armload at Woolworth's and other dime stores. Many of these toys were one-piece, doll-like figures, sometimes based on the works of famed children's artist Ruth E. Newton.

The company making these dolls started its successful toy-making business in the 1920s, when a man named Tom Smith traveled from Pennsylvania to Barberton, Ohio, to sell off the unprofitable Avalon Rubber Co., but instead stayed to make the company a leader in rubber toy manufacturing, under the name The Sun Rubber Co. Its first toy hit, a rubber hot-water bottle for dolls, helped see the company through the Great Depression.

At the outbreak of World War II, Sun Rubber gave up toys and turned to production of wartime supplies, including gas masks for civilian use as a safeguard against possible coastal attacks. Having gotten to know Walt Disney in the 1930s,

Sun Rubber's Barberton plant was peremptorily closed by then-owner Talley in early 1974, during a labor-management dispute. While some operations continued in Georgia, the rubber and vinyl toy giant's days were ending after having provided well-loved playthings for the parents of the Baby Boomers and for the Boomers themselves. ■

Arrow: Squeaker animals, $10-$15
Sun Rubber: Squeaker dolls, $15-$25

# VINYL STICK-ONS
# COLORFORMS

**G**IRLS not playing with a Barbie in 1959 may have been too busy with a different kind of fashion toy: Colorforms. They may even have had the new Sleeping Beauty set, released to coincide with the Walt Disney animated movie.

While paper dolls never died out, even enjoying a renaissance of sorts with the regular releases of Betsy McCall paper dolls within the pages of *McCalls* magazine, Colorforms were the true Boomer incarnation of paper dolls. The pieces were all flat—and usually vinyl. The sets came with a backing board, typically decorated with figures that could be dressed and accessorized with the colorful vinyl cutouts. Better than paper dolls, the vinyl tended to cling, which eliminated worry about folding and tearing tabs, as happened with paper dolls.

A New York City couple, Harry and Patricia Kislevitz, invented the toys after receiving a fortuitous—if odd—gift from a friend of a roll of pliable vinyl. Their simple observation that cutout pieces stuck to the semi-gloss paint in their bathroom made toy history.

The Norwood, N.J., company they founded

thrived especially during the 1960s, issuing Winnie the Pooh, Popeye and Superman sets alongside such fairy-tale sets as Cinderella and Little Red Riding Hood. By the end of the decade, its line included Raggedy Ann, Popeye and Chitty Chitty Bang Bang sets—as well as Outer-Spacemen bendy toys. ◼

Colorforms: Barbie's 3-D Fashion Theatre, 1970, $10
Colorforms: Barbie Sport Fashion, 1975, $5
Colorforms: Bugs Bunny Cartoon Kit, 1950s, $75
Colorforms: Huckleberry Hound Cartoon Kit, 1962, $100

**Vinyl-ly Ann.** *Raggedy Ann was one of the popular dolls issued in two-dimensional cardboard-and-vinyl form by Colorforms in the 1960s. Liddle Kiddles and Barbie were others. Raggedy Ann Dress-Up Kit, 1967.*

**Dancing Dolls.** *While Colorforms was a pioneer in the use of vinyl in toys, it did acknowledge tradition in such sets as Dancing Dolls, which used heavy cardboard figures of ballet dancers with a wardrobe made of coated paper. The clothes attached to the plastic-surfaced dancers with adhesive tabs. Suspended from elastic bands, the figures could be made to dance on the stage hidden behind the striped panels. Colorforms/United Productions of America, 1950s.*

# PLASTIC-AGE CANDY DISPENSER
# PEZ

THE IDEA of packaging candy in toy-like containers was nothing new in the 1950s. For decades, candy makers had made attractive glass animals, boats and cars to hold sweets. But a new candy holder was about to explode on the scene.

In the late 1920s, Austrian Eduard Haas III created an intense peppermint candy, which he called PEZ, as a short form of the German word for peppermint, "pfefferminz." Eventually it came to be sold in a package not toy-like at all: it resembled a cigarette lighter, which helped sell the mints as anti-smoking aids.

When the company tried to market the product in the United States, it failed to attract much attention. Haas changed the candy to fruit flavors, even while retaining the peppermint-associated name, and he changed the containers as well. In some cases, the entire PEZ dispenser was reshaped, as was the case with early Santa Claus and Space Robot dispensers. More often the company simply changed the top of the dispenser, which retained its cigarette-lighter thinness.

Those tops made the dispensers immensely attractive, for they featured the heads of famous cartoon characters, fanciful animals and such miscellaneous oddities as whistles and eyeballs. ■

PEZ: Chick in egg, no feet, $20
PEZ: Spider-Man, no feet, $15
PEZ: Pluto, no feet, $10
PEZ: Penguin (Batman villain), soft head, $135

**Mr. Ugly.** PEZ candy dispensers became a more widespread item in the 1970s, when such characters as Mr. Ugly and this skull-headed PEZ appeared. PEZ, made in Austria, 1970s.

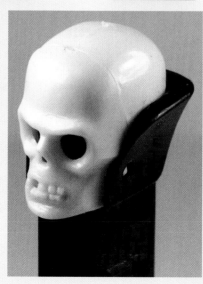

**Kris Kringle.** From the late 1800s well into the Boomer period, candy containers often appeared in the guise of toys. While glass was the material of choice for most of the century, the postwar rise of plastic led to an increasing number of toy-like candy containers in the new material. The most famous of these were PEZ dispensers. PEZ, made in Austria, 1950s.

# THE YO-YO

THE HISTORY of Boomer toys is partly the history of frustrated kids: kids trying to make a perfect Spirograph design without a slip of the pen ... kids trying to keep hula-hoops from sliding down around their knees and then their feet ... and especially kids trying to make their yo-yo do tricks. Eventually they learned. But sometimes, as was the case with me and the yo-yo—and a lot of my friends were the same way, too—it just never took.

As old as some of the ideas behind other popular Boomer playthings are, yo-yos, also called "return tops," are among the oldest of all. Although many people think of it as a 20th century toy, it had inspired fads in Europe and Asia long before finding its way to America. Yo-yos provided entertainment to the playful ancients of Egypt, India and China. If an Aurignacean yo-yo turns up, carved from bone by prehistoric, fun-loving Neanderthals, I wouldn't be surprised.

The first large-scale American fad for the toy took place in the 1920s, the decade that saw the revival of table tennis in this country, the worldwide craze surrounding the Chinese game Mah Jong, and the arrival of the wild dance moves of the Charleston.

Even though the yo-yo had appeared in many cultures down through the ages, the toy in Flapper-era America was considered of Philippine origin. Americans had a perfectly good reason for believing this, for they were being entertained by touring shows of experts from the Philippines. One such expert was Pedro Flores, who is the single individual most credited for making the toy an American hit and for making the Philippine word "yo-yo" commonplace here.

Companies quickly sprang up to manufacture the toys, including Flores' own, The Yo-Yo Mfg. Co., in Santa Barbara, Calif., in 1928. In the same year, Donald F. Duncan, inspired by Flores, started his company in Chicago, Ill. Cheerio Toys and Games, Inc., of Kitchener, Ontario, Canada, was another late-1920s entrant, followed by Cayo Manufacturing Co. of Buchanan, Mich., in the early '30s.

**Plastic spinners.** *By the later Boomer period, most smaller spinning toys were made of plastic. Duncan Butterfly, Duncan Genuine Gold Award Yo-Yo and Mattel Mini Whiz-z-zer, late 1960s to early '70s.*

Duncan purchased Flores' The Yo-Yo Mfg. Co. in the 1930s, beginning the process of making the words "Duncan" and "yo-yo" almost synonymous among kids during the Boomer years.

While prewar and early Boomer-era yo-yos were mostly made of wood decorated with paint and decals, colorfully lithographed tin yo-yos also appeared, especially Cayo's Musical Ka-Yo.

The Baby Boom revitalized the world of yo-yos. Duncan took the lead with a variety of wooden yo-yos, including the Butterfly versions that evoked the "bandalore" tops of earlier centuries.

Duncan also introduced Duncan Imperial Yo-Yo tops by the mid-1950s. These were solid-plastic yo-yos of new weight and durability. The material also gave the manufacturer greater freedom: the toys could now be translucent, opalescent, transparent, colored, plain, glitter-flecked and molded with a variety of new imprints and designs.

The toys themselves were only half the phenomenon in the 1950s and '60s. Corner competitions sprang up everywhere among kids eager to compare skills at fancy tricks. Duncan and other companies sponsored many competitions, giving out embroidered badges that yo-yoists prized above anything. Walking the dog, 'round-the-world, playing dead ... yo-yo tricks were what made the toys a source of excitement.

Yo-yoing was not automatic with many children, just as Frisbee-flying skill proved elusive to many. Me, I mainly remember trying to untangle the string on a wooden yo-yo that I was sure didn't work. It was fun anyway. ■

Duncan: Autograph Yo-Yo, 1950s, $20
Duncan: Bosco Bear wooden yo-yo, $8
Duncan: Chief Yo-Yo Return Tops No. 44, $25
Duncan: Expert Award, 1960s, $15

# 84 HOPPITY HORSE

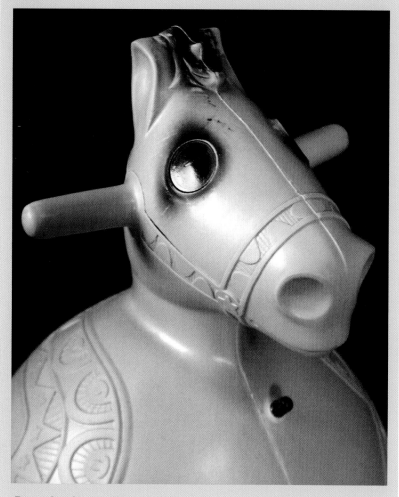

MUCH AS the doll form of Barbie came from Germany or as the massive Tiddly-Wink fad of the mid-1950s came from England, the last hit toy for the Sun Rubber Co. came from abroad.

On a trip to England, Sun Rubber executive Richey Smith spotted a toy he had not seen before. He quickly developed a new line of toys based on it after his return to America. The new Hoppity Toys included a horse, Donald Duck, and Mickey Mouse.

The simplest of riding toys, the Hoppities were inflatable balls of heavy rubber with heads that served as handles for the small rider. A child wrapped legs around the toy, hung on tightly and bounced.

Sun Rubber introduced the toys to the last of the Baby Boomers in 1968 with an advertising budget of $40,000. Hoppity Horse and his fellow Hoppity toys then brought Sun Rubber $2.5 million in sales. Makers of trampolines, moon-shoes and pogo sticks had long known that kids love to bounce. ∎

**Sun Rubber: Hoppity Horse, $45**

**Bouncing innovation.** *The Sun Rubber Company introduced a new kind of riding toy when it released its Hoppity Toys in the late 1950s. Hoppity Horse, Sun Rubber, 1968. Photo by Martha Borchardt.*

## RUBBER: BOUNCING THROUGH HISTORY

Hundreds of years before rubber was known in the rest of the world, Central and South Americans used latex, a sap harvested from native trees, for various functions such as making waterproof cloth, fastening handles to tools and fashioning bouncy balls for games. When Spanish Conquistadors first encountered the balls, they were so amazed at their bounciness that they feared they were demon possessed.

Europeans soon recognized latex's magnificent characteristics, however, and brought it back to the Old World, eventually giving it a new name. Latex is believed to have first been nicknamed "rubber" in 1770 when Englishman Joseph Priestley noted how well it rubbed out pencil marks.

Rubber production evolved over the years. One of the key improvements occurred in 1830s when Charles Goodyear developed the process known as vulcanization. The technique involves adding sulfur to heated latex to enhance elasticity and resiliency. In the mid-20th century, inventors created synthetic rubber compounds with various properties to meet the increasing demands of technology. The post-World War II toy industry, rapidly expanding to meet the needs of a new generation of toddlers, formed a significant part of that demand. Thus, rubber came full circle, from the bouncing latex balls of ancient Aztecs and Mayans to modern bouncy toys—like the Hoppity Horse.

# COMICS-PAGE 'POSSUM
# POGO

THE QUIZZICAL 'possum of the *Pogo* strips made his debut in the first issue of *Animal Comics* in December 1941. The character's creator, Walt Kelly, was working for Dell Comics after a stint at Disney, where he had worked on *Snow White*, *Fantasia* and *Dumbo*.

Not until after the war did the 'possum and his fellow Okefenokee Swamp critters take on their most characteristic forms, however. On Oct. 4, 1948, the first funny-pages strip featured a turtle, a worm and the round-headed 'possum with his up-swung nose and vertically striped shirt. It appeared in the *New York Star*, where Kelly had a gig as political cartoonist.

Pogo's talky and intelligent misadventures, together with Albert Alligator, Beauregard Montmingle Bugleboy III, Churchy La Femme, Porky Pine, Howland Owl and other memorable figures, soon became mainstays of newspapers across the country, with the daily adventures giving rise to a widely popular series of books.

As happened with *Peanuts*, the paperbacks, printed in sizes larger than standard mass-market editions, gave the characters and their comic commentaries a permanent place in Boomer culture. Issued from 1951 through the cartoonist's death in 1971, they established Kelly and Pogo as much-needed voices of reason, even fearlessly taking on the McCarthy witch trials and blacklists.

While Pogo toys that combined vinyl with fake fur appeared in 1968, the 1969 premiums from Proctor & Gamble were the form in which they entered the most late-Boomer households. All vinyl, they effectively evoked the original comic-strip figures—and they seemed free, coming as premiums in boxes of detergent. They were good, clean fun. ■

**Milton Bradley: Snoopy & the Red Baron, 1970, $35**
**Miscellaneous: Pogo figures, $8-$12**

## OKEFENOKEE FRIENDS.

Pogo and pals Albert, Beauregard and Churchy spoke loudly to both children and adults at a time when many other creative voices were being stifled, censored and blacklisted. Earlier figures had been made in 1968 by Alabe Crafts, of Magic "8" Ball fame. Proctor & Gamble detergent premiums, 1969.

## ... AND "PEANUTS"

Intelligent and well drawn, Charles Schulz's "Peanuts" strips attracted readers young and old from their debut in newspaper comic pages of the 1950s. Yet they never reached their full measure of popularity until a series of specials on TV featured the same characters. Slowly Peanuts toys began to appear: a Peanuts game from Determined Productions, Inc. of San Francisco; Peanuts coloring books from Saalfield Publishing Co.; and the Peanuts Talking Bus, made by J. Chein & Co. of Burlington, N.J. Chein also made Peanuts spinning tops and drums. At the end of the decade, Aviva Enterprises, Inc. of San Francisco began making Peanuts jewelry, turning the beloved characters into fashion accessories.

The strip changed through the years, introducing new characters and sometimes letting others slip away. The basic cast, however, remained the same: Charlie Brown; Lucy; Linus; Schroeder, the musical genius; and Pig Pen.

# 85

**Marbles, for Peanuts.** *In Snoopy and the Red Baron, one child tried to sneak marbles down the plastic raceway, while the other tried to catch only "his" color inside the doghouse, the roof of which opened for catching or closed for blocking marbles. The number of "Peanuts" toys and games greatly increased in the last years of the Boomer period. Snoopy and the Red Baron, Milton Bradley, 1970.*

Increasingly, the Peanuts strips focused on the imaginary life of Charlie Brown's dog Snoopy, who from the beginning was the jolt of lightning, laughter and occasional lunacy in that child-high world.

A true postwar child, Snoopy lived in a world deeply affected by war. In his mind, he "relived" his days in World War I, sometimes as foot soldier and often as pilot of his airborne doghouse, which he flew against the dreaded Red Baron.

He was no different from the millions of boys in their sandboxes, who even by the 1960s were still playing with plastic soldiers colored green and gray, to depict the Americans versus the Germans. In some ways, Snoopy was a child Walter Mitty, living a life detached from the ordinary one, sustained by illusion. In this, he may have helped the generation see itself.

Eventually we grew and learned that the romantic picture we cradled in our minds of World War II was illusory. Daily in the 1960s, radio announcers gave body counts, as if quietly relating the changing score of a years-long ball game. Increasingly, we saw war as a disturbing and incredibly repellent reality—especially for those of us growing up, but truly, deeply, not wanting to grow up, because growing up meant facing the draft.

Snoopy had just been playing us all along. We were the ones atop those flying doghouses, our fists raised against the comic-book enemy. Games such as Snoopy and the Red Baron submerged kids in the beagle's world of wartime fantasy.

The number of Peanuts items rose gradually through the end of the Boomer years—so much so, in fact, that they may actually be more characteristic toys of the post-Boomer generation. Even so, a great many Boomers grew up knowing the Peanuts gang—especially Snoopy—belonged to them.

# RECORDING STAR
# BOZO!

**W**HILE SOME Boomer era characters entered TV from newspaper cartoons, Hollywood or radio, one of the most durable entered from vinyl. Bozo the Clown was the creation of Larry Harmon and Alan Livingston. While Harmon provided the voice, Livingston, a Capitol Records executive, not only helped create the clown concept for Capitol's line of children's records but wrote the lyrics of the "Bozo Song" of 1948.

Livingston enjoyed other hits in his life, being the person who signed the Beatles to Capitol and who then brought them to the United States for their first appearance.

In the early days of television, Bozo was no one particular person. Local stations had local talent play the clown, using the official Bozo music and Bozo costume. In 1959, WGN-TV in Chicago started airing a regular Bozo show featuring Bob Bell, who went on to play the famous clown for a quarter century.

Bozo the Clown dolls, which would remain available in various forms throughout the Boomer period, were probably born as soon as the original recordings were pressed. Early dolls were made by Knickerbocker Toy Co., with the other major toy being Bozo the Clown Changeable Blocks, by Gaston Mfg. Co. of Cincinnati, Ohio. These funny-face toys continued to be made into the later 1950s, with Chas. Wm. Doepke Mfg. Co., Inc. of Rossmoyne, Ohio, the manufacturer at the end.

By 1952, Whitman was issuing Bozo books, and Spin-A-Wheel Toy Co., Inc. of Fitchburg, Mass., had a Bozo the Capitol Clown novelty toy. With the new decade, Renall Dolls, Inc. of Los Angeles was making Bozo the Capitol Clown dolls.

Bozo came full circle in the 1960s, when toys started incorporating record-player technology. Audio Creations of Millbrae, Calif., made a large push in this direction in 1961 and '62, with its series of Bozo Talking Books. For many Boomers, however, the most familiar version was the 1960s Mattel Bozo, proud possessor of a Chatty Ring, with what was essentially a Bozo record inside. ■

**OVERJOYED!**

After Knickerbocker, Renall Dolls made the "Bozo the Capitol Clown" cloth-and-vinyl doll on the left, from about 1960-65. The doll on the right was Mattel's version.

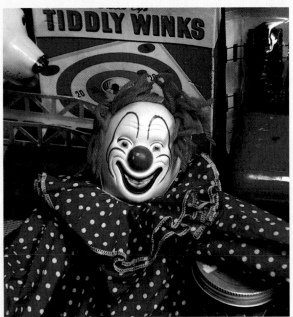

Capitol Records: Bozo the Clown doll, $45
Knickerbocker: Bozo the Clown Push Button Marionette, 1962, $25
Mattel: Bozo the Clown doll, talker, $75

**Changeable Bozo.** *Blocks with changeable faces were popular toys before the war. The endless possibilities—over a million different faces were possible, according to one manufacturer—continued to attract (and distract) children during the Boomer years. Bozo the Clown Changeable Blocks, Gaston Manufacturing Co., 1940s-50s.*

**Bozo, the recording star.** *Bozo's television presence grew strong enough in the 1960s that eventually few Boomers remembered the clown's origin in a recording studio. This early doll is marked "A Genuine Bozo, 'The Capitol Clown,' Capitol Records, Inc." Renall Dolls, Inc., ca. 1960-65.*

# THE MOUNTAINS OF THE MOON
# MAGIC ROCKS

**EDUCATIONAL—FASCINATING—EXCITING!**

Packages of Magic Rocks boasted the contents produced "all the colors of the rainbow in fantastic shapes and sizes." Despite the claim of being educational, the composition of the growing salts and their dyes were closely kept secrets. Magic Rocks Co., 1971.

NOVELTIES WERE important to every child of the Boomer years, whether they were such oddball items as Mexican Jumping Beans, kits of a vaguely scientific nature such as Uncle Milton's Ant Farm or game-like question-and-answer devices such as the Magic "8" Ball.

One of the most interesting of novelties was Magic Rocks, originally called the Magic Isle Undersea Garden when brothers James and Arthur Ingoldsby first introduced them in southern California in 1945. These activity kits consisted of colored salts that "grew" quickly—in roughly a half hour—when placed in water and the Magic Growing Solution.

Aside from the fun of watching them develop in glasses and fish tanks, people considered Magic Rocks not so much toys as decorator items and accessories for the "far-out" lifestyle.

Various companies farmed out and administered Magic Rocks rights during the Boomer years. B. Shackman & Co., an enterprising and long-lived toy-import and distribution firm, was selling Magic Rocks in 1966, followed in 1967 by Park Industries, a Cleveland, Ohio, firm that emphasized it specifically.

That year, as it happens, was also the time Honey Toy Industries, Inc. of New York City, was making news selling Magic Sea-Monkeys ("Alive in only five minutes! Incredible but true!"), another offbeat 1960s oddity kids grew to take for granted.

While the novelty of Magic Rocks tended to wear off, they remained one of the striking memories for countless Boomers. The pleasure of watching the marvelous, mysterious rocks transform stuck in Boomer memories, becoming part of the body of toy memories most of them held in common. ■

**Various Mfrs.: Magic Rocks, $15**

# SILLY PUTTY

" AS SEEN in *Life*," some toy packages said. "As Seen on TV," said a lot of others. "As Seen in the Pages of *The New Yorker*," a very few *might* have read, although the chances are against it. It would have been true, though.

You would think Silly Putty would be the last item to have benefited from an appearance in that urbane weekly. Yet mention of the rubbery curiosity in a 1950 "Talk of the Town" column of the magazine, which was then available through Doubleday book stores in the city, made the unlikely toy bounce high from obscure curiosity to nationally embraced novelty.

A formulation of boric acid and silicone oil sold in plastic eggs, Silly Putty stretched, flattened, rolled into a ball, bounced and picked up images off newsprint. Although it performed no useful function that anyone could determine, the substance came into existence through a government contract to develop an inexpensive synthetic rubber.

James Wright was working in New Haven at General Electric's labs when he happened to combine the necessary materials. The results surprised him. Not only did the rubbery stuff bounce higher than rubber and stretch farther, but it retained its properties over a wide range of temperatures. By the end of the war, however, the U.S. War Production Board had dismissed it as being of no interest as a rubber substitute. Since Wright and others found his bouncing putty entertaining, it became the center of attention at New Haven cocktail parties, where it caught the attention of toy store owner Ruth Fallgatter and ad man Peter Hodgson.

The bouncing putty sold well through the catalog Hodgson produced for Fallgatter's store. While the shop owner decided to let the substance go, Hodgson persevered, hiring Yale students to shape pieces to put in multicolored plastic eggs. Selling the new product was an uphill battle before the mention in *The New Yorker*. Within days afterwards, Hodgson's orders topped tens of thousands of dollars, and then hundreds of thousands, surpassing a quarter million dollars in half a week. ∎

Photo courtesy SeriousToyz.com

Ernie Bushmiller's *Fritzi Ritz*

Silly Putty on original store card, $25-$35

Superman

# CHAPTER 9

# Tinkers and Whiskers

I n the last period of Boomer Toys, from roughly 1962 to 1969, animated cartoon characters took over the roles played earlier by puppets and marionettes. Toy manufacturers made toys to match the new TV stars, using not only cartoon characters but also the cartoon style. New toys were bright, loud and absurd. With the escalation of the Vietnam War, war toys proliferated, as did anti-war sentiments. G.I. Joe made his debut the same year students protested in Washington against the bombing of North Vietnam. The Beatles, who had changed rock and roll when they arrived the year before, helped usher in psychedelia. First people, then toys, started to let it all hang out.

The toy years of the last Boomers continued into the 1970s, as the kids born in the earlier 1960s were entering their teens. Many toys stayed true to trends set in the

1960s. Yet many of the successes and innovations of that and the prior decades were forced to change or retreat in 1969 and subsequent years. The epitome of safe indoor toys, the Nerf Ball, conceived by Twister inventor Reyn Guyer, made its debut. The sharp-pointed pieces that attached accessories to Gumby and Mr. Potato Head fell victim to child safety laws. For the same reason, the Cootie bug lost much of its rangy bugginess, Klackers were banned and the lead-based paint jobs of the early Hot Wheels and Johnny Lightnings lost their glitter.

In perhaps the surest sign of the end, Barbie, who changed through the 1960s from a perfectly poised and utterly sophisticated model to a Tammy-like wholesome American teen, lost her calm and started, albeit hesitantly, to smile. Things would never be the same.

# TINKERTOYS

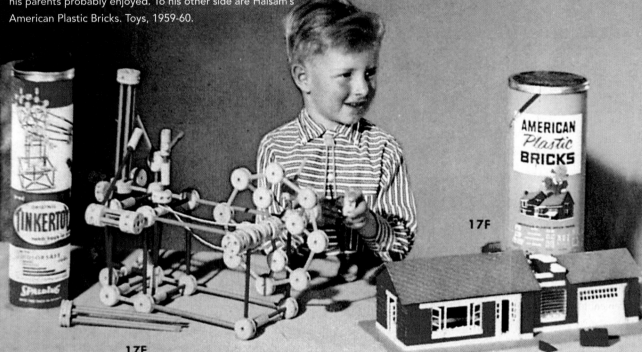

**Boy tinker.** A young construction enthusiast, decked out in classic shirt and bolo, enjoys the same stick-and-spool toy his parents probably enjoyed. To his other side are Halsam's American Plastic Bricks. Toys, 1959-60.

IF YOU were to try to find one toy that everyone in the 20th century played with, one of the best candidates would be the construction toy named the Toy Tinkers made by an outfit based in Evanston, Ill., from early in the 20th century and into the Boomer years.

If you talk to many Boomers, you'll find it is one of the toys that keeps coming up in conversation. It meant something to them. It occupied long hours during their youngest playing years. It usually gave them their first complex construction experience after graduating from such playthings as the Playskool peg-bench sets and Fisher-Price plastic beads. They fondly remember fitting the sticks into the wheel-shaped connectors. They remember the sound of the sticks rattling and tumbling out of the cardboard tubes.

In 1914, a tombstone manufacturer named Charles H. Pajeau started the Toy Tinkers after meditating on the pleasure children find in playing with sticks and spools. He soon brought in a friend, Robert Pettit, member of the Chicago Board of Trade. The two of them settled on the tube-shaped container for their toy set. Their Thousand Wonder Builder sold well locally, thanks to creative window displays in Chicago, and then nationally, thanks to a traffic-stopping display at the Grand Central Station pharmacy in New York.

In the first year, they manufactured and sold 900,000

Tinkertoys. Baby Boomers started off with essentially the same kits kids had played with for 30 years.

In 1952, A.G. Spalding & Bros., Inc. of Evanston, Ill., acquired the still-growing company. Changes then became the name of the game. Beginning in 1953, red sticks were mixed with unpainted ones. In 1955, green, blue and yellow sticks followed.

Besides adding colors in the 1950s, the Tinkertoy line gradually expanded during the Boomer years. Tinkertown Trains, which were wooden take-apart toys, arrived by the end of the 1950s, followed by Tinker Zoo in the 1960s.

Unchanged through the Boomer period, however, was one of the original principles applied to the design book children found inside each tube. In earlier years, the booklets might have had designs for such things as a Cream Separator or a Bi-Plane. In the Boomer era, these changed to reflect the times. Children were now shown how make Tinkertoy versions of the Television Camera and Jet Plane. But the Tinkers stuck to their guns—so to speak—and never used designs for weapons in their instruction books. ■

A.G. Spalding & Bros.: Tinkertoys canister, 1960s, $10-$20

A POPULAR PARLOR recreation early in the 20th century involved stereoscopic viewers, through which photographic stereo images took on three dimensions. With people so accustomed to 3-D viewing, the advent of 35-millimeter filmstrips in the 1920s led naturally to stereoscopic filmstrips.

The first stereoscopic film viewer arrived from an unexpected source: the Rock Island Bridge and Iron Works, in Rock Island, Ill., which formed the Tru-Vue Co. around its new viewer and filmstrips, consisting of 14 stereo frames.

Another unexpected source developed the next viewer. William Gruber of Portland, Ore., who has been variously identified as a piano tuner or organ maker, took his invention to Harold Graves, the president of Sawyer's, Inc., a company specializing in picture postcards. The two produced the first commercial View-Masters in time for a debut at the New York World's Fair in 1939, where they were sold as a tourist curio.

While Gruber's View-Master films featured only half as many stereo views as did Tru-Vue films, the films came in an incomparably convenient form: the frames were arranged in a circle, on a card easily popped in and out of the viewer. The cards had an appealing name, too, that evoked the glamorous film industry. Sawyer's called them "reels."

View-Master, sold through stationery and photo shops, appealed largely to the adult market, with Sawyer's reels providing 3-D images of national parks and other scenic wonders up to World War II.

Much as Walt Disney filmmakers found themselves busy with instructional films related to the war effort, View-Master photographers worked on educational and training reels for the government. Some reels, for instance, helped Army gunners train for anti-aircraft range estimation and Navy personnel train for ship-to-ship identification.

Even if Tru-Vue came first, View-Master came to ascendancy after the war. Sawyer's issued color reels, forcing Tru-Vue to introduce Stereochromes. Then, in 1951, View-Master bought its competitor and moved Tru-Vue production from Illinois to Oregon.

View-Master reels covered every desirable subject imaginable through the Boomer years, from cartoon favorites to such TV pop figures as Pinky Lee, Captain Kangaroo, Rin Tin Tin, Hopalong Cassidy, the Lone Ranger, Roy Rogers, Flipper, the Munsters, the Green Hornet and *Lost in Space* characters.

General Aniline and Film Corporation (GAF) bought View-Master in 1966 and introduced such innovations as the Talking View-Master and the View-Master Projector.

I remember as a child being a little frustrated at these reels. They were fascinating and fun, yet they ended so quickly.

**Reel entertainment.** *Most Boomers grew up with piles of View-Master reels like this, with combinations of scenic and entertainment reels. This pile includes Sawyer's reels "Grand Canyon National Park" and "Mickey Mouse in 'The Brave Little Tailor,'" alongside such new GAF reels as "Love Bug," "Bambi," and "Charlie Brown's Summer Fun." Reels from any period of View-Master history could be viewed through any of its viewers.*

Then you had to put in another one. This must have worked in Sawyer's and then GAF's favor. Kids always needed new reels, and Sawyer and GAF were always happy to provide them.

Also working in their favor was the long-lived utility of Gruber's original View-Master. Sawyer's never changed its fundamental design, which meant that if a child in 1969 was given a new reel but only had a Bakelite 1939 Model A viewer handy, the two would still match.

Unlike much of the rest of the toy industry, which relied on constant change for survival, View-Master at its core never changed. That saved it and made it a fixture in the childhoods of not only the Boomers but of their own children and grandchildren. ◼

Captain Kangaroo, reel B-560, 1957, $30
Time Tunnel, reel B-491, 1966, $50
World of Liddle Kiddles, reel B-577, 1970, $70
Zorro reel B-469, 1958, $30

# YOGI BEAR
# SCORE-A-MATIC

**Score-A-Matic.** *Few Boomers remember this Yogi Bear skill game, even though many of them played with it—for it was sold across the country through much of the 1960s. Transogram, 1960s.*

ONE OF the characteristic materials of toys during the 1960s was thin, brittle, vacuum-formed plastic. It's hard to imagine an American child in that decade not getting to know the feel of this material, since cartoon-character masks of the material appeared at Halloween in dime stores across the country.

One toy that relied on the material achieved widespread and long-lived popularity: the Yogi Bear Score-A-Matic Ball Toss game. It was made for much of the decade by Transogram Co., Inc., a New York City outfit that enjoyed considerable success throughout the Boomer years with such playthings as games for children and adults, craft sets, play-doctor and play-nurse kits, weaving looms and doll furniture.

The Score-A-Matic was a large affair, being over a foot and a half tall—but a lightweight one, as it was mostly hollow, with the vacuum-formed plastic Yogi face supported in back with cardboard. It served its function in the playroom, for it was a skill toy, of sorts, for younger kids.

The kids could aim brightly colorful balls at Yogi's wide-open mouth, and rack up points—with the Score-A-Matic keeping count as the ball dropped into the mouth and struck a star-shaped wheel, also made of the same, thin plastic. Numbers painted on the turning wheel appeared through a yellow-rimmed hole next to Yogi's tie, revealing the score.

As is the case with many of the toys the youngest kids played with, the Yogi Score-A-Matic, and its partner toy, the Popeye Ball Toss, evoke somewhat less nostalgia among Boomers than do the toys they played with at ages 7 to 12. Even so, it was an important part of the toy scene. The young children who loved Yogi TV cartoons no doubt squealed with joy when their ball fell into the Yogi Score-A-Matic's wide, inviting mouth. ■

Transogram: Yogi Bear Score-A-Matic, $35
Transogram: Popeye Score-A-Matic, $45

**When Polly's in trouble, I am not slow!** *Brittle plastic masks were a vital part of childhood in the Boomer years. Even kids whose mothers created homemade costumes would go to school for the Halloween parade and be surrounded by countless images from ageless fairy tales to contemporary TV, including Cinderella, Zorro, the Lone Ranger, Batman and Wonder Woman. Underdog mask, Ben Cooper, mid-1960s.*

### BEN COOPER MASKS

*TV cartoons and vacuum-formed plastics seemed perfectly fitted to one another. The company that fit the two together and then fit the resulting product firmly on the faces of American kids, was Ben Cooper, Inc., a Brooklyn, N.Y., specialist in masquerade and Halloween costumes. The Ben Cooper name became familiar because of the way it kept reappearing every October on the square boxes with the cellophane windows that held character masks painted in the broadest, brightest strokes. In 1965, its masks of "Hairies, Scaries, Cuties & Beauties" cost 29 cents apiece. "TV character masks!" the company trumpeted. "Hair trimmed masks! New wig masks! Frankenstein & the famous monsters!"*

*Racks of Ben Cooper masks showed a cross-section of mid-decade childhood tastes, for Donald Duck would be hanging alongside the Phantom of the Opera, and a sword-skewered skull beside Cinderella. While Disney-character masks, masquerade costumes and Santa Claus suits had been the company's strengths through the 1950s, by the time Underdog cartoons were running on TV, from early October 1964 through early September 1973, Ben Cooper had firmly tied its fortunes to the big staring eye. The company had its hands on an incredible number of top licenses, including Superman, Addams Family, Munsters and Hanna-Barbera characters.*

*As garish, simple, and cheap as the plastic masks were, what child of the 1960s doesn't remember the feel of the elastic strap around the head or the way the smooth insides of the masks grew moist with steam, even on a chilly Halloween outing in search of the neighbors' candy?*

# THE MAGIC WHISKERS OF
# WOOLY WILLY

THE VACUUM-FORMING devices developed by the plastics industry in the late 1940s and early '50s gave rise to Smethport Specialty's hit toy of the Boomer years.

Smethport had been a maker of tops, horseshoe magnets, and other playthings since before the war. One idea for a toy had never quite gotten off the ground in the prewar, early-plastic years. It featured a line-drawn face, over which whiskers and other facial hair made of metal filings could be moved around with a stick magnet. It was a tough task to keep metal filings from leaking out—although another company, Broadfield Toy Co., Inc., of Hempstead, N.Y., had done fairly well with its Whiskers toy, a nearly identical plaything it released back in 1925.

Once it was able to create airtight containers of transparent plastic, however, Smethport Specialty released a series of toys that proved perfect for rainy afternoons and back-seat entertainment on long road trips.

Funny Face, Brunette Betty, Dapper Dan, and Wooly Willy: all were essentially the same. First sold on a test basis through the G.C. Murphy dime store chain, they performed well enough to attract the attention of the nationwide chain Woolworth's.

After that, time went quicker for all of us sitting in the back seats of the family car on summer trips. ■

Smethport: Dapper Dan, $18
Smethport: Wooly Willy, $12

**THE MAGNETIC MAN.**

"Dapper Dan is a secret agent, chosen because of his easily disguised face," the back of the Dapper Dan card says. "Alter his appearance to help him carry out his investigations." Pictures show him as Scientist, Detective, Counter Agent, Dictator and Magician. 10-½" by 14", Dapper Dan, Smethport Specialty Co., 1950s.

**Magnetic sketchboard.** *Magnetic toys played an important role in the 1950s and '60s. A few had staying power, such as Ohio Art's Magnestiks, a magnetic construction toy. Dapper Dan's maker made another stab at magnetic success with the more difficult Doodle Balls. 10-½" by 14", Doodle Balls, Smethport Specialty Co., 1960s.*

# LAMB CHOP

**THE SOCK WHO UPSTAGED EVERYONE.**

Children had a good excuse to be sassy when they played with their Lamb Chops hand puppet. Vinyl and cloth Lamb Chops, 8" tall, Tarcher Productions, 1960; vinyl Hush Puppy, Alan Jay Clarolite Co., Tarcher Productions, 1962.

**Romper Room.** *The same year Hula Hoop took the nation by storm, a small toy company was billing its Bob-A-Loop as "the game sensation of the nation!" Consisting of two pieces of thick wood connected by string, the toy probably knocked the most heads and broke the most windows of any toy before Klackers came along. What helped the toy was its association with another popular young-kids TV show. Romco Enterprises, 1958.*

WHO WAS the only character in the world with the guts to gush over the Queen of England and tell her how much bigger she was than her postage stamp? Lamb Chop, the endearing, ever-sassy sock-puppet creation of ventriloquist and musician Shari Lewis.

Shari Lewis studied piano and violin and attended the New York High School of Music and Art. Following her well-received appearances on *Captain Kangaroo*, she was given her own show on NBC, *The Shari Lewis Show*, which aired from 1960 until the conversion of daytime children's programming completely to animation in 1963.

The show proved an important one for the toy industry, not only for its lovable characters, but also as an advertising showcase for toy manufacturers. Among the most important early sponsors of the show were Remco Industries, an electronics-toys specialist based in Newark, N.J., and American Doll & Toy Corp., of New York City, which was promoting its new, fully-jointed version of the Betsy McCall doll.

J. Halpern Co. of Pittsburgh, Pa., was better known at the time for its holsters sets, including *Have Gun Will Travel* and *Gunsmoke* sets, but it did also make costumes. Halpern responded to the popularity of Shari Lewis puppets by adding Lamb Chop, Wing Ding, Charlie Horse and Hush Puppy to its 1961 masquerade-costume line.

The most important toys surrounding the shows, however, were the ones modeled directly after Shari Lewis puppets, produced starting in 1961 by the stuffed-toy division of Ideal Toy Corp. While miscellaneous toys based on toddler-TV shows appeared in the 1960s, the puppets based on the Shari Lewis characters of Lamp Chop, Charlie Horse and Hush Puppy were the most successful and most beloved of the lot.

The puppets proved to be more than American TV stars. After NBC's cancellation of her show, Lewis took her performances to England, where British Boomers welcomed her with open arms. ■

Lamp Chop hand puppet, $20
Hush Puppy, vinyl, $35

## CAPTAIN KANGAROO

Lamb Chop was born as a result of a suggestion made to Lewis before making an early-1950s TV appearance. It might work out better, she was told, if she used something smaller and less cumbersome than the large, wooden, Charlie McCarthy-style dummy she had brought to the studio. The year was 1952, and the show was *Captain Kangaroo*.

Bob Keeshan, the original Clarabell Clown of Doodyville, had the distinction of being fired twice from NBC's flagship children's program. The second time had been in December 1952. In the summer of the next year, he managed to land another clown job, this time as Carny the Clown on ABC. A formerly struggling station, ABC was undergoing a facelift and revitalization after being acquired by United Paramount Theaters, which had been separated from Paramount Pictures due to an antitrust ruling.

Unlike Clarabell, Carny the Clown talked on camera, showing a more easygoing and gently humorous side of the actor. In 1954, a new show made its debut after Keeshan convinced network execs at CBS that television needed a program for the very youngest.

*Tinker's Workshop* competed against NBC's *Today* and CBS's morning *Jack Paar* show. It soon put ABC neck-and-neck with NBC for early-morning ratings.

The watershed year proved to be 1955, and October was the watershed month. Not only did Walt Disney's *The Mickey Mouse Club*, aimed at older children, begin airing in the early evening, eating into the *Howdy Doody Show* time slot, but Bob Keeshan's new show for young children began airing in the early mornings on CBS.

*Captain Kangaroo* began in 1955 and remained a daily television fixture for 29 years, making Keeshan a legend within the industry and a familiar, favorite-uncle figure for millions of Boomers.

While Captain Kangaroo cloth dolls eventually became popular playthings, the majority of Boomers played with the smallest of toys, usually accessories or activity sets that identified the child's allegiance to the Captain.

Within the first two years of the start of Captain Kangaroo's long-lived TV tenure, the earliest playthings had arrived. Barry Products Co., of Chicago, offered Captain Kangaroo Fun Kits alongside its Winky Dink Pipe Cleaner Art sets. Admiral Toy Corp. produced Captain Kangaroo Hat & Key Sets. Dangles, Inc. of New York City, manufactured small accessories in its Captain Kangaroo Dabbles. These items were vitally important to millions of Boomers, even if few remember that to have been the case. If they were still young, it would all come back.

**Puffy sticker.** *As was true of the television show, "Captain Kangaroo" toys and games were designed to appeal to the youngest children. Most Boomers played with them at so young an age they have few or no memories. Many who had vinyl stickers such as this one would be wearing flower or Weird-Ohs stickers on their notebooks just a few years later. Robert Keeshan Associates, 1962.*

**Safety Belt Team.** *Safety issues became of almost overriding concern in the later 1960s. Captain Kangaroo Safety Belt Team tab button, 2" diameter, Robert Keeshan Associates, 1969.*

# CRAYON MAGIC
# BUGS BUNNY

WARNER BROTHERS created a star a few years before World War II. Its cartoon department had come up with a new character with a voice by Mel Blanc. The character, a rabbit, responded in his opening scene to a hunter pointing a gun: "Eh, what's up, Doc?" When the first audiences roared with approval, director Tex Avery figured the line had better stay.

Bugs Bunny's star kept rising as he appeared in new Looney Tunes and Merrie Melodies films each year. Unlike Mickey Mouse at Disney, Bugs showed no signs of retiring from the theatrical stage after the war and continued taking starring roles until Warner closed its cartoon department in 1963.

Bugs' fellow animated stars were also constant companions to the Boomers: Porky Pig, Daffy Duck, Elmer Fudd, Pepe LePew, Tweety Bird, Sylvester, Foghorn Leghorn, Roadrunner, Wile E. Coyote and many others.

These cartoon stars made ideal subjects for coloring books. Cheaply printed by companies including Whitman and Saalfield, and distributed through every dime store in the nation, coloring books were the artistic teethers for the Boomers. The reusable coloring book was a special fascination for kids of the 1950s, issued by Whitman and also Hampton Publishing Co. of Chicago, with its Rub Clean coloring books.

Bugs Bunny's Magic Rub-Off Pictures were a kind of ultimate—the coloring kit that never ran out of pictures of Bugs and his friends, for you could color and erase, and color and erase.

**BUGS THE MAGICIAN.**

The Warner animated crew was instantly familiar to nearly everyone in the Boomer generation. Bugs Bunny's Magic Rub-Off Pictures, Whitman Publishing Co., 1954.

## COLORING WITHIN THE LINES

Boomers grew up to regard many toy trade names as their own, when they had actually been passed down to them from their parents—or, in some cases, their grandparents and great-grandparents. One such was Crayola, the name Boomers saw in big, block letters on many of the boxes of crayons they scribbled with, broke in half and wore down to nubs in their preschool, kindergarten and elementary-school years.

The brand's story began in the late 1800s when the Binney & Smith Co. moved gradually deeper into the educational market, progressing from slate pencils to dustless chalk, and from there to wax crayons, which previously had been available only in expensive European versions. Alice Binney, wife of company co-owner Edwin, devised the Crayola name. The beginning was based on the French word for "chalk," while the ending suggested "oil."

Crayons proved of immense importance to most children thereafter, especially in the Boomer period—for Crayola Crayons did for books what Winky Dink Magic Crayons had done for TV: they turned a nontoy into a toy. ■

Crayola: crayon boxes, various sizes, 1960s, $4-$8
Whitman: Adventures of Rin Tin Tin coloring book, 1955, $25
Whitman: Magic Rub-Off Pictures, $30
Whitman: Bugs Bunny Private Eye coloring book, 1957, $20
Whitman: Raggedy Ann coloring book, 1968, $10

48 beautiful CRAYOLA colors

Sold by
JOHN C. BALLES
908 So. Saxby Ave.    Freeport, Illinois

**Forty-eight colors ... and all forty-eight tasted the same.** Advertising blotter, 1940s.

**Project Book.** *Binney & Smith did its best to plant activity ideas in the heads of kids. One idea, to make an Indian headdress from a brown paper bag, was used in various forms in elementary schools across the country. Playing Indian in the Boomer years would have been different without those cardboard packs of color. Crayola Crayon Project Book, Binney & Smith, 1958.*

# BOP BAGS AND
# PUNCHOS

I N 1947, parents could encourage a child's natural inclination to hit things in one way only; they could buy a leather punching bag. Ward's offered the classic sheepskin striking bag in a six-panel pattern, double-stitched in the seams, with hardwood frame, steel platform and leather hanger. It also offered Jack Dempsey Boxing Gloves, endorsed by the great pugilist with his signature over the knuckles. The gloves featured backs of wine sheepskin, palms and cuffs of tan sheepskin and padding of selected goat hair. They came with a Jack Dempsey Boxing Chart. Three sizes were available: 8-ounce for youths 10 to 16, 6-ounce for boys 7 to 12, and 4-ounce for boys 4 to 8.

Since the wise souls at Wards knew the kids didn't really want a punching bag for an opponent, they sold the gloves only in sets of four. Children should have a chance at head-battering well before kindergarten, after all.

The onset of plastic toy production changed a great many things. It may have changed childhood boxing most of all. Suddenly it became a sport suitable for everyone, girl and boy alike. This happened not through a change in punching bags, gloves or even the number of gloves, but through the invention of the bop bag. Kids could now have an opponent who never fought back. One they could hit with their bare fists, too. Since their opponent was made of sand-weighted ("for roly-poly action"), air-filled vinyl, fists and the bop-bag could go boppity-boppity-boppity with neither emerging the worse for wear. Even if the bags had a tendency to spring leaks, no one bled.

One of the best-loved of the bop bags was Bobo, a clown figure made by Doughboy Industries of New Richmond, Wis. Built of "Forti-Plyed" vinyl, Bobo featured a squeaker nose that was irresistibly punchable.

Through the latter Boomer years, a wide variety of bop bags made by different manufacturers rebounded to the punches of young pugilists. Usually classed as "inflatable toys," they came under such names as Punch-Me's, Punchos and even Bop Bag. Toy manufacturers always put kids' favorite characters on these bags—Flipper, Gumby, Bozo—as though they imagined the kids really wanted to take it out on the Good Guys. ■

## PICKING ON SOMEONE THEIR OWN SIZE.

A child could punch Hanna-Barbera's Pixie, who holds a book entitled "Diary by Pixie Mouse." Tiring of Pixie, she could turn the bop bag around to Dixie, who holds a sling-shot and a rock. Around the rock is tied the message, "To Mr. Jinx from Dixie Mouse." Standing 18" high when inflated, the Puncho was made by Kestral Corporation of Springfield, Mass., as part of its Air-line Inflatable Toys line. Early '60s.

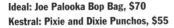
Ideal: Joe Palooka Bop Bag, $70
Kestral: Pixie and Dixie Punchos, $55

# KRAZY IKES

**Ike-A-Doo!** *Whitman declared this to be a "fast-moving game of luck." The first player to complete a figure called out, "IKE-A-DOO." Whitman Publishing Co., 1955.*

**Plastic Ike meets wood.** *Whitman oversaw the Ikes' transition from wood to hard plastic in the 1950s. Its phrase, "Makes Hundreds of Interesting Toys," was a significant toning-down from Knapp Electric's "A Thousand Funny Things." Whitman Publishing Co., 1950s and '60s.*

INTRODUCED in the late 1920s by Knapp Electric Co. of Indianapolis, Ind., Krazy Ikes was a construction toy from which, Knapp promised, children could "build a thousand funny things, all different." The toy remained the same through World War II, having the good fortune to be made of a material with no rationing restrictions. It was one of the first toys to greet young children in the heady days ending the war.

Whitman Publishing Co., better known for a long and illustrious line of children's books, purchased rights to the toy and saw it through the inevitable conversion into plastic, the form in which most Boomers came to know it.

Krazy Ikes consisted of various pieces that could be assembled into people, animals and things best just called Ikes. The slender connector pieces were of about pencil thickness, 1-½ inches long. These could attach to knobs on the body pieces or to the head or feet pieces. The people heads, which were spherical with printed faces in the wooden versions, were slightly flattened and hollowed and had raised features in the plastic versions.

The strange and wonderful beings and things to be made from Krazy Ikes remained unchanged in the transition from wood to plastic: the Kangarike, the Bucker-Ike, the Ike-Hopper, the Ikeville Flier, the Ike-Cycle, the Ikabird, the Crocodike, the Ikosaur, the Gooner-Ike, the Shmike and the Lazy-Ike. In the 1950s and '60s, following Schaper's lead, Whitman issued Ike-A-Doo, in which children could assemble their Ikes with a spinner, instead of the dice that Cootie used. ■

Whitman: Krazy Ikes, wood, $15-$25
Whitman: Krazy Ikes, plastic, $8-$15

I N THE MID-1950S, Joe McVicker invented a compound for his father's soap and cleaning products manufacturing company. Its purpose? Cleaning wallpaper. He had created a nontoxic, putty-like substance that was easily shaped and kneaded. And it did clean wallpaper.

When McVicker's school-teacher sister-in-law mentioned that the school's modeling clay was difficult for her children to shape, he mailed her a sample of his wallpaper cleaner and started a chain of events that resulted in stores across the country carrying millions of canisters of a colored substance that was safe, easy to use and easy to clean up.

The family business, based in Norwood, N.J., changed its name to Rainbow Crafts Co., perhaps thinking the name Kutol Chemicals had an odd sound for a toy maker. While the toy had innate worth, the new company hedged its bets by issuing not just Play-Doh but Ding Dong School Play-Doh. ∎

**COLORS BLEND.**

Play-Doh came in packs of four colors, which, although not pure primary colors, still mixed together under the kneading fingers of the patient child. Play-Doh Modeling Compound four-pack, Rainbow Crafts Inc., 1963.

**Rainbow Crafts: Play-Doh canister, 1960s, $5**
**Rainbow Crafts: Play-Doh Wood-Doh Modeling Compound, 1959, $25**

**Fun Factory.**
*Devices to help shape the modeling compound came almost as soon as the compound itself. Rainbow Crafts package, 1963.*

**NEW! FUN FACTORY JR.**

FOR: LITTLE FOLKS

With *NEW* 2 oz. Miniature Cans

# THE MUSICAL
# TEDDY BEAR

## SWISS MOVEMENTS.

In an earlier age, only the wealthiest owned moving automatons with Swiss-quality music boxes and movements, but they were common to the Boomer generation, however. Parents found the Gund Musical Toy very helpful at bedtime. The slow, hypnotic motions and gentle music lulled countless children to sleep. Other companies making musical plush toys included the Ka-Klar Cloth Toy Co., of Manchester, Conn. Teddy bear, 8" tall; puppy dog, 9" long, Gund Musical Toys, 1950s.

Gund: Musical Teddy Bear, $50

THE GUND MANUFACTURING CO. of New York City was making a dizzying array of stuffed animals and rag dolls by the middle of the Boomer years. The company entered the 1960s with a full line of licensed characters: Popeye, Mickey Mouse, Little Audrey, Casper the Friendly Ghost, Donald Duck, Felix the Cat, Herman and Katnip, Wendy the Good Little Witch, as well as other TV, Walt Disney and Harvey Comics characters. Its lines included TV Tuffets, Scribble Animals, Hand Puppets, Puppetettes and Action Musicals.

The Action Musicals were, in many ways, traditional toys. The success of these toys, including the musical teddy bear, showed that despite the influence of TV and movies and the arrival of such new materials as polyethylene and vinyl, the old materials and old ideas sometimes still worked superbly.

The musical teddy bear contained a Swiss-made music box that could withstand constant use. And although it was constructed with a rugged design, it was made to create a soothing environment. As the music played, the bear's head turned slowly and peacefully.

While the motion seems slight and inconsequential compared to the clattery and elaborate tin windups and battery-operated toys that brightened Christmases through most of the Boomer period and before, the quality of the gear action made these bears more akin to European automata—the playthings and novelties of the wealthy from another age—than to the clever, skittery baubles that tumbled over playroom floors. The motions were appealing to young children. Ideal Toy Corp.'s baby-doll Thumbelina, for instance, moved in a similar way, rolling her head and moving her arms.

The teddy bears are emblems in their own way of the wealth that flooded America in the postwar years. Toys that once would have graced the parlor of only a marquis and marchioness could now be found in nurseries of the American middle class. ■

# THE LITTLE PEOPLE
# SCHOOL BUS

AT THE BEGINNING of the Boomer years, Fisher-Price Toys of East Aurora, N.Y., was known for its inventive, colorful and charmingly noisy pull-toys and push-toys, which the company had been making since the 1930s. Many were quite large, with some being a foot or more long. While a few measured only a few inches, they were in the distinct minority.

In some early toys, particularly vehicles, Fisher-Price incorporated figures made from small wooden columns and spheres, with simple smiling faces painted on. The people were always firmly affixed to the toys, so they were never lost. When the company decided to make freestanding Little People figures, it unknowingly created a new toy category for its own catalogs, one that would become a major factor in Fisher-Price's considerable success in the later Boomer years.

The first of the loose Little People appeared with the Safety School Bus, issued in several forms from the end of the 1950s to the middle of the 1960s, when the most characteristic form was introduced and subsequently kept in constant production.

The Little People themselves changed through time, starting as all wood and ending as all plastic. Since their round bodies fit into round holes inside the Safety School Bus, they were reminiscent of the pegs every child in the 1950s and '60s hammered into wooden benches made by Playskool and Halsam.

But these pegs had heads with charming expressions displaying freckles, smiles and frowns. One was even a dog. In a sense, Fisher-Price had learned what other companies discovered during the Boomer years. The toys with the best chance of acceptance and longevity were toys with accessories. In every other toy line, figures of people were the main toy. In this case, however, the Safety School Bus, with its rattling noises, rolling eyes and turning-head driver, was the primary toy. The passengers were the accessories.

And like Barbie, who often reappeared years later in shoe boxes and sock drawers without clothes or wigs, or like G.I. Joe, who always lost his weapons, hats, uniforms and boots, the Safety School Bus emerged from closets without people. ■

**THE BUS OF 1965.**

Instantly recognizable to the last Boomers, the most popular version of the Safety School Bus rolled from the mid-1960s into the '70s. Fisher-Price, 1965 and on.

**The other Little People.** *Seeing Fisher-Price's success, other toy companies introduced versions of their own. Tootsietoy, 1967-68.*

Fisher-Price: Safety School Bus, #983, 1959-61, $350
Fisher-Price: Safety School Bus, #984, 1961, $225
Fisher-Price: Safety School Bus, #990, 1962-65, $85

**THE STEADY DRONE
OF PROGRESS.**

Fisher-Price, long the bastion of all-wood toys, introduced plastic to its toys in 1950. Buzzy Bee, the standard-bearer for plastic at the company, was later crowned for her effort. Fisher-Price Toys, 1950.

**For pre-schoolers 1-4 years**. *For much of the Boomer period, pre-schooler toys often combined paper-lithographed wood and plastic. "Enormous bill flaps open and shut—fascinating 'craw-aww, craw-aww' sound!" states the box for this toy. "Flipper-like feet rotate with comical paddling motion. Unbreakable polyethylene bill holds toy fish. Solid wood body, non-toxic finish. Preschoolers 1-4 years." Big Bill Pelican, Fisher-Price Toys No. 794, 1961-64.*

FISHER-PRICE wasn't caught sleeping when the 1950s arrived and other manufacturers busily scrambled to be up-to-date. The venerable toy maker, an industry leader in the 1930s and '40s, introduced plastic to its formerly all-wood line in 1950, when it released a toy inspired by an insect: Buzzy Bee, Fisher-Price No. 325.

Buzzy Bee rolled around on standard wooden wheels and had wood-tipped spring antennae. Her top and sides were covered with colorful lithographed paper. It was her wings, spinning rapidly when she rolled forward, that were now being made of a bright yellow acetate.

In the Easter offering introduced for 1951, Buzzy was the only novel Fisher-Price toy. The Donald Duck Cart, Bunny Cart, Chick Cart and Peter Bunny Engine were completely traditional, exhibiting wooden wheeled carts with colorful paper lithography.

Buzzy Bee, at 59 cents, was a successful addition to Fisher-Price's line. After being produced for three years, she was briefly retired, only to reappear in 1956 with a polyethylene crown and the name Queen Buzzy Bee, No. 314. In her various incarnations, she was to toddlers and crawlers of the 1950s what Fisher-Price's Talking Telephone, introduced in 1961, was to the toddlers and crawlers of that next decade. ■

Fisher-Price: Buzzy Bee, #325, 1950-56, $40
Fisher-Price: Queen Buzzy Bee, #314, blue crown, $35-$45
Fisher-Price: Queen Buzzy Bee, #444, red body, 1959-62, $30-$35
Fisher-Price: Queen Buzzy Bee, #444, honeybee, 1962 and later, $10

# THIS LITTLE PIGGY

SOFT POLYETHYLENE TOYS rank among the most played-with toys of the Boomer years—and also among the most forgotten. Why forgotten? Because we so young when we played with them. As we went to kindergarten, we were told, "That's a *baby* toy" and "You're too big to play with *that*," so we expunged from our memories many of the early soft and hygienic toys of the cradle and the playroom floor.

Fisher-Price, which had long specialized in toys for the youngest children, rightly realized that polyethylene presented endless possibilities for the future. It was a soft, nontoxic material that took colors well—perfect for crawlers and toddlers. In 1956, it launched itself and the rest of the toy-making world firmly on the road to soft toddler toys with This Little Piggy, a pull-toy entirely of soft plastic. Fisher-Price reached even more children—maybe even *all* children of the late Boomer years—with squeezable sets of take-apart soft plastic beads.

Soft polyethylene swiftly became the standard for the preschool toy. Sure, Boomers forgot about them. But these toys were the first ones many Boomers played with. The very first. Which makes this a perfectly good place to end. ■

**Went to town.** *Fisher-Price's This Little Piggy marked the company's entry into all-polyethylene toys. A plaything that almost no one remembers, buried as it is beneath memories of more vivid toys that arrived in later childhood, the squeaking pull-toy was popular and long-lived, going through three versions in the 11 years following its introduction in 1956. 16" long. Fisher-Price, 1960s.*

Fisher-Price: This Little Piggy, #900, all pink pigs, 1956-1959, $15
Fisher-Price: This Little Piggy, #905, different colors, 1959-1963, $10
Fisher-Price: This Little Piggy, #910, wood ball inside, 1963-1966, $10

# BOOMER TOY VALUES

To give a halfway decent idea of today's collector values for Boomer-era toys would take another book at least as long as this one. The following list consists of examples that are intended simply as a rough guide. I give values here for toys as they are usually found—in fact, as they *should* be found—in played-with, slightly worn condition. Is a toy really a toy if a child never put hands to it and gave it imaginary life? I think not.

Some of these values are based on personal experience, some on perspective given by various collector guides. Refer to the Additional Reading section for some of them. Remember that all collector values are highly provisional and always approximate. The toy-collector market is a mass of miscellaneous collectors and dealers, all of whom disagree, to greater or lesser degree, about how much their toys are worth. With the popularity of Internet buying and selling, prices are going ever higher—and ever lower. You just never know.

I reserve the right to be wrong about these estimates—sometimes quite wrong. That's part of the fun of the game.

### A.C. GILBERT
| | |
|---|---|
| Gilbert Erector No. 10092, 1958 | $650 |
| Gilbert Erector No. 10063, 1960 | $35 |
| Gilbert Erector No. 10211, 1962 | $35 |

### ALADDIN
| | |
|---|---|
| Disney School Bus Dome, 1968 | $70 |
| Disneyland Monorail lunch box, 1968 | $250 |
| G.I. Joe lunch box, 1967 | $350 |
| Hopalong Cassidy lunch box, 1952 | $250 |
| King Kong lunch box, 1977 | $95 |
| Mickey Mouse Club lunch box, 1963 | $150 |

### ARCHER
| | |
|---|---|
| Robot | $20-$25 |
| Space man | $8-$10 |
| Space woman | $45-$50 |

### ARGO
| | |
|---|---|
| Action Cars, loose, each | $10-$15 |

### ARROW
| | |
|---|---|
| Squeaker animals | $10-$15 |

### AUBURN RUBBER
| | |
|---|---|
| Cadillac Convertible, vinyl, 3-½" | $10 |
| Hot Rod, vinyl, 4-¼" | $15-$20 |
| Jeep, with cannon, vinyl | $20 |
| Telephone Truck, vinyl, 7" | $25 |

### AURORA
| | |
|---|---|
| Frankenstein, built-up kit, 1961 | $30 |
| King Kong, built-up kit, 1964 | $75 |
| King Kong, Glow Kit, built-up | $75 |
| Odd Job, built-up kit | $200 |

### AUTOMATIC TOY CO.
| | |
|---|---|
| Hopalong Cassidy Automatic Television Set | $100 |

### BEN COOPER
| | |
|---|---|
| Batman Halloween Costume, 1965 | $25 |

### BREYER
| | |
|---|---|
| Fighting Stallion, 1961-71 | $150 |
| Lassie, 1958-65 | $40 |
| Running Foal, glossy gray, 1963-73 | $45 |

### CAPITOL RECORDS
| | |
|---|---|
| Bozo the Clown doll | $45 |

### COLORFORMS
| | |
|---|---|
| Barbie's 3-D Fashion Theatre, 1970 | $10 |
| Barbie Sport Fashion, 1975 | $5 |
| Bugs Bunny Cartoon Kit, 1950s | $75 |
| Daniel Boone Fess Parker Cartoon Kit, 164 | $85 |
| Huckleberry Hound Cartoon Kit, 1962 | $100 |

### CONNECTICUT LEATHER
| | |
|---|---|
| Mousketeer Handbag | $50 |

### COX
| | |
|---|---|
| Baja Bug, 1968-73 | $65 |
| Cox Thimble Drome Prop Rod | $75 |

### DAKIN
| | |
|---|---|
| Dream Dolls, miscellaneous | $8 |
| Dream Pets, miscellaneous | $8 |

### DELL
| | |
|---|---|
| Satellite Rocket Launcher punch-out book, 1959 | $40 |

### DILLON BECK
| | |
|---|---|
| Wannatoy Coupe | $20 |

### DOWST MFG. CO.
| | |
|---|---|
| Tootsietoy Buck Experimental Coupe, 6" | $25 |
| Tootsietoy El Camino Pickup, 6" | $12 |
| Tootsietoy Kaiser Sedan, 6" | $30 |
| Tootsietoy '62 Ford Econoline Pickup, 6" | $10 |

### DUNCAN
| | |
|---|---|
| Autograph Yo-Yo, 1950s | $20 |
| Bosco Bear wooden yo-yo | $8 |
| Chief Yo-Yo Return Tops No. 44 | $25 |
| Expert Award, 1960s | $15 |

### ELDON
| | |
|---|---|
| Big Poly Wrecker | $75 |
| Power 8 Road Racer Set, 1960s | $75 |
| Billy Blastoff Space Base | $80 |
| Billy Blastoff Space Scout Set | $150 |
| Billy Blastoff's Robbie Robot | $60 |

### ELGO AND ELGO/HALSAM
| | |
|---|---|
| American Plastic Army Bricks | $100 |
| American Plastic Bricks #715 | $100 |
| American Plastic Bricks #725 | $75 |
| American Skyline, #92 | $50 |
| American Skyline, #93 | $115 |
| American Skyline, #94 | $300 |

### FISHER-PRICE
| | |
|---|---|
| Buzzy Bee, #325, 1950-56 | $40 |
| Safety School Bus, #983, 1959-61 | $350 |
| Safety School Bus, #984, 1961 | $225 |
| Safety School Bus, #990, 1962-65 | $85 |
| This Little Piggy, #900, all pink pigs, 1956-59 | $15 |
| This Little Piggy, #905, different colors, 1959-63 | $10 |
| This Little Piggy, #910, wood ball inside, 1963-66 | $10 |
| Queen Buzzy Bee, #314, blue crown | $35-$45 |
| Queen Buzzy Bee, #444, red body, 1959-1962 | $30-$35 |
| Queen Buzzy Bee, #444, honeybee, 1962 and later | $10 |

### FRISBIE
| | |
|---|---|
| Pie tin | $45 |

### GUND
| | |
|---|---|
| Musical Teddy Bear | $50 |

### HARTLAND
| | |
|---|---|
| Davy Crockett on horse | $550 |
| Paladin and horse (mint in box) | $250 |

Roy Rogers, walking (mint in box) $250
Tonto and horse, miniature series $75

### HASBRO
| | |
|---|---|
| Batman and Robin Game, 1965 | $50 |
| G.I. Joe Action Marine, 1964 | $125 |
| G.I. Joe Action Pilot, 1964 | $130 |
| G.I. Joe Action Soldier, 1964 | $100 |
| G.I. Joe Talking Action Marine, 1967 | $175 |
| G.I. Nurse, 1967 | $1,750 |
| Jumpin' Mr. Potato Head Set, 1966 | $30 |
| Leave It to Beaver Rocket to the Moon Game, 1959 | $45 |
| Little Miss No Name, doll, 1965 | $75 |
| Mickey Mouse Club pencil case, 1950s | $35 |
| Mr. & Mrs. Potato Head Set, 1960s | $50 |
| Mr. Potato Head on the Moon | $200 |
| School Days Potato Head Pencil Case | $35 |

### IDEAL
| | |
|---|---|
| Action Box with space suit, 1968 | $350 |
| Addams Family Game, 1965 | $75 |
| Atomic Rocket Launching Truck, with fair box | $75 |
| Bash! | $10 |
| Batman hand puppet | $45 |
| Batman Helmet and Cape Set, 1966 | $150 |
| Crazy Clock, 1964 | $80 |
| Dr. Kildare Game, 1962 | $25 |
| Flatsy doll, Baby | $10 |
| Gomez Hand Puppet, 1965 | $50 |
| Joe Palooka Bop Bag | $70 |
| Ker-Plunk, 1967 | $10 |
| King Zor, 1964 | $150 |
| Mouse Trap, 1963 | $30 |
| Mr. Machine, 1961 | $125 |
| Mr. Machine, 1970s | $30 |
| Mystic Skull, 1965 | $60 |
| Robert the Robot, opening tool box, 1954 | $200 |
| Robert the Robot, no opening tool box, 1955 | $150 |
| Robert the Robot, no glassy eyes or antenna, 1956-59 | $90 |
| Roy Rogers Fix-It Stage Coach, with box, mid to late '50s | $125 |
| Tammy, doll | $35 |
| Tammy's Dad, in original box | $75 |
| Tammy's Mom, in original box | $75 |

### IRWIN
| | |
|---|---|
| Barbie's Mercedes Roadster, 1964 | $150 |
| Hard Top Convertible, hard plastic, 9" | $35 |
| Ken's Hot Rod, 1963 | $175 |
| Leakin' Lena Boat, 1962 | $50 |
| Skipper's Sports Car, 1965 | $175 |

### JAMES INDUSTRIES
| | |
|---|---|
| Slinky, early | $50 |
| Slinky Dog, 1950s | $35 |

### JAYMAR
| | |
|---|---|
| Bullwinkle & Rocky, frame tray puzzle, 1960s | $30 |
| Mickey Mouse Lotto Game, 1950s | $15 |
| Red Ryder, frame tray puzzle, 1951 | $10 |
| Winky Dink, frame tray puzzle, 1950s | $40 |

### KENNER
| | |
|---|---|
| Easy-Bake Oven, turquoise | $15-$40 |
| Girder & Panel, #3, 1958 | $50-$60 |
| Girder & Panel Constuctioneer Set, #8 | $85 |
| Girder & Panel Hydro-Dynamic Single Set, #17 | $150 |
| Girder & Panel Skyscraper Set, #72050 | $50 |
| Give-A-Show Projector Set, 112 slides, 1963 | $100 |
| Roy Rogers Give-A-Show Projector, with slides, 1960s | $50 |
| Sky Rail Girder & Panel, 1963 | $125 |
| Spirograph, 1960s | $20-$25 |

### KESTRAL
| | |
|---|---|
| Pixie and Dixie Punchos | $55 |

### KING SEELEY THERMOS
| | |
|---|---|
| Man from U.N.C.L.E. lunch box, 1966 | $275 |

### KNICKERBOCKER
| | |
|---|---|
| Huckleberry Hound, plush and vinyl | $50 |
| Yogi Bear, plush and vinyl | $50 |

### KOHNER
| | |
|---|---|
| Atom Ant Push Puppet | $40 |
| Bamm-Bamm Push Puppet | $20 |
| Bozo the Clown Push Button Marionette, 1962 | $25 |
| Howdy Doody Push Puppet, 1950s, wood and plastic | $50 |
| Pebbles Push Puppet Push Puppet | $35 |
| Fred Flintstone Push Puppet | $30 |

### LAKESIDE
| | |
|---|---|
| Gumby figure, 1965 | $10-$15 |
| Pokey | $10-$15 |

### LEE
| | |
|---|---|
| Tom Corbett Space Hat | $50 |

### LESNEY MATCHBOX
| | |
|---|---|
| Alvis Stalwart, #61, 1967 | $30 |
| Bedford Dunlop Van, #25 | $50 |
| Boat and Trailer, #9, 1967 | $10 |
| Hillman Minx, #43 | $40 |
| Leyland Tanker, #32, 1968 | $20 |
| Rolls Royce Silver Cloud, #44 | $25 |
| Safari Land Rover, #12, 1965 | $20 |

### LIDO
| | |
|---|---|
| Captain Video figure, alien or robot, plastic, 2" | $15-$20 |

### LOWE
| | |
|---|---|
| Dr. Kildare & Nurse Susan paper dolls | $50 |
| Jack Barry's Twenty One, 1956 | $30 |

### LOWELL TOY MANUFACTURING
| | |
|---|---|
| Groucho's You Bet Your Life, 1955 | $75 |
| What's My Line? Game | $45 |

### MAGGIE MAGNETIC
| | |
|---|---|
| Sputnik | $75-$100 |
| The Twister | $45 |
| Whee-Lo, with box | $15 |

### MARX
| | |
|---|---|
| Alamo Play Set, #3530 | $300 |
| Davy Crockett Frontier Rifle, 1950s, 32" long | $75 |
| Deluxe Delivery Truck, 13-¼", 1948 | $100 |
| Electric Robot & Son | $500 |

Farm Set, 1958, No. 3948 $250
Farm Set, 1969, No. 3953 $225
Fix-All Wrecker Truck,
    with tools and box $100
Fort Apache Carryall, #4685,
    play set $75
Frankenstein, tin-litho $900
Modern Farm Set, 1951 $150
Modern Farm Set, 1967 $185
Mr. Mercury $350
Nutty Mads Bagatelle, 1963 $45
Nutty Mads Car $225
Nutty Mads Indian, 1960s $125
Nutty Mads Target Game, 1960s $70
Plastic Figure,
    Chief Cherokee, 1965 $150
Plastic figure, Davy Crockett,
    on stand, 60 mm $15
Plastic figure, Jackie Gleason,
    60 mm $50
Plastic Figure, Jane West, 1966 $60
Plastic Figure, Johnny West,
    1960s-70s $75
Play set figure, Bullet (Roy's dog) $10
Play set figure, Dale Evans, 60 mm $10
Play set figure, Fred Flintstone $10
Play set figure, Howdy Doody,
    60 mm $35
Play set figure, Lone Ranger,
    60 mm $20
Play set figure, Prince Valiant,
    54 mm $20
Play set figure, Robin Hood,
    54 mm $15
Play set figure, space alien or
    robot, 45 mm $8
Play set figure, Tonto, 60 mm $20
Play set figure, Yogi Bear, 60 mm $30
Polaris Rocket Ship $300
Prehistoric Times, #3389 $180
Prehistoric Times, #3398 $150
Rex Mars Space Tank, tin-litho $250
Rin Tin Tin, #3628, play set $300
Rock 'em Sock 'em Robots,
    in good box $125
Roy Rogers Double R Bar Ranch,
    #3989, play set $300
Space Patrol Atomic Pistol $95
Sportster convertible, 20", 1950s $70
Squad Car No. 1, windup, 11" $150
Walt Disney's Television Car,
    tin-litho $450

**MATTEL**
Baby Secret, doll, talker, 1965 $45
Barbie & Francie Case, 1967 $35
Barbie Queen of the Prom game,
    Mattel, 1960 $60
Barbie, Fashion Queen doll, 1963 $145
Beany Talking Doll, 1950s $90
Bozo the Clown doll, talker $75
Bugs Bunny, hand puppet, talker,
    1960s $30-$40
Cecil in the Music Box, 1961 $80
Chatty Baby, doll, early issue $85-$95
Chatty Cathy, doll, early issues $125
Christie, talking, 1970 $100
Creeple Peeple Thingmaker, 1965 $95
Dr. Doolittle doll, talker, 1969, 24"
    $130
Hot Wheels Beatnik Bandit,
    1968-71 $10-$20
Hot Wheels Custom Volkswagen,
    1968-71 $10-$15
Hot Wheels Deora, 1968-69 $40-$60
Hot Wheels Red Baron, 1970-79
    $10-$20
Ken doll, flocked hair, 1961 $100

Liddle Kiddle, Bunson Burnie,
    with firetruck $40
Liddle Kiddle, Calamity Jiddle $60
Liddle Kiddle, Peter Paniddle doll $25
Mousegetar Jr., 1950s $125
Skipper doll, straight leg, 1964 $50
Thingmaker/Creepy Crawler, 1964 $80
Vac-U-Form Casting Set, 1962 $65

**MEGO**
Spider-Man, 1972, 8" $20

**MILTON BRADLEY**
Beatles Flip Your Wig Game $125
Beverly Hillbillies Set Back Game $20
Bullwinkle Hide & Seek Game,
    1961 $30
Candy Land, 1949 $50
Captain Video Game, 1952 $80
Dastardy & Muttley, 1969 $40
Go to the Head of the Class,
    various versions $10-$15
Howdy Doody Adventure Game,
    1950s $50
Howdy Doody's TV Game, 1950s $50
Mystery Date, 1965 $75
Mystery Date, 1972 $35
Snoopy & the Red Baron, 1970 $35
The Game of Life, 1960s $40
Twister, 1960s $15-$20

**MINER INDUSTRIES**
Secret Agent 86 Pen Radio, 1960s $70

**MISCELLANEOUS**
**AND UNKNOWN**
**MANUFACTURERS**
Beatles record-shaped gumball
    charms, set of four $30
Cadaco-Ellis Foto-Electric
    Football, 1965 $15
Child-size kitchen $50-$80
Coonskin cap, various mfrs.,
    1960s and 70s, $35-$45
Crayola crayon boxes,
    various sizes, 1960s $4-$8
Honey Wheat Dinosaurs,
    various $5-$10
Hush Puppy, vinyl $35
Klacker-type toys $10-$15
Lamb Chop hand puppet $20
Lincoln Logs, 1950s-60s sets $35-$50
Lone Star Girl from U.N.C.L.E.
    Garter Holster, 1966 $125
Magic Rocks $15
Play-Doh canister, 1960s $5
Play-Doh Wood-Doh Modeling
    Compound, 1959 $25
Pogo figures, miscellaneous $8-$12
Rat Fink ring $15
Silly Putty on original store card
    $25-$35
Space Cadet Field Glasses $60
Space Cadet Flashlight $90
Spoonmen $35-$40
Super Winky Dink TV Game,
    kit #250, 1954 $60
Tinkertoys canister, 1960s $10-$20
Yonezawa Space Saucer
    Mercury X-1 $175
Yoshiya Space Dog, 1950s $250
Zoomer Robot, 1950s $300

**OHIO ART**
Etch-A-Sketch, 1960s $10-$20

**PEZ**
Chick in egg, no feet $20
Spider-Man, no feet $15
Pluto, no feet $10
Penguin (Batman villain),
    soft head $135

**PARK PLASTICS**
Squirt Ray Water Gun $25

**PARKER BROTHERS**
Clue, 1949 $25-$40
Clue, 1960s $15-$20
Davy Crockett Frontierland
    Game, 1955 $40-$50
Disney Mouseketeer Game,
    1964 $50-$60
Howdy Doody's Own Game, 1949 $45
Mary Poppins Carousel Game,
    1964 $30
Monopoly, 1950-60s editions $20-$25

**PETER PUPPET**
Davy Crockett guitar $175
Flub-A-Dub, marionette, 1950s $375
Howdy Doody, marionette, 1950s $150

**PLASTIC BLOCK CITY, INC.**
Block City, 1950s $35-$45

**PRESSMAN**
Groucho's TV Quiz Game, 1954 $45
Winky Dink Paint Set, 1950s $75

**RANGER STEEL**
Space Patrol Cosmic
    Ray Gun, 1954 $75

**REMCO**
Beatles dolls, each $150
Hawaii Five-O Game, 1960s $75
Jupiter 4-color Signal Gun, 1950s $90
Melvin the Moon Man, 1960s $75

**RENWAL**
Doll house mantle clock $10
Doll house radio phonograph $25
Doll house sewing machine $40
Doll house telephone $15
Gasoline Truck, 4-¼" $20
Speed King racer, 3-¼" $20
Speed King racer, 4-¾" $20

**REVELL**
Rat Fink slot car, 1966,
    in original box $250

**RUSHTON**
Chubby Tubby, 17" $50
Zip the Monkey, plush and vinyl $50

**SAALFIELD**
Tom Corbett Space Cadet
    coloring book, 1952 $75
Tom Corbett Space Cadet
    punch-out book, 1952 $95

**SCHAPER**
Cootie, single Cootie on box $15-$25
Don't Spill the Beans, 1967 $15

**SCHMIDT**
Hopalong Cassidy Buck 'N Bronc
    Cap Gun $250
Roy Rogers Gun & Holster Set $500

**SMETHPORT**
Dapper Dan $18
Wooly Willy $12

**STORI VIEWS**
Cinderella Pixie Viewer, 1950s $20

**SUN RUBBER**
Hoppity Horse $45
Squeaker dolls $15-$25

**TEE-VEE TOYS**
Howdy Doody figures, 4" $15-$20

**TONKA**
Carnation Milk Van, 1965 $200
Dump Truck #180, 12", 1949
    $150-$200

Dump Truck #6, 1960 $85-$90
Mini-Tonka Cement Mixer, 1964 $45
Minute Maid Orange Juice truck,
    1955 $300

**TOPPER**
Johnny Astro $75
Johnny Toymaker, 1968 $50
Secret Sam Shooter Pipe $10

**TOYKRAFT**
Winky Dink Magic TV Kit $85

**TRANSOGRAM**
Ben Casey MD Game, 1961 $20-$30
Countdown Space Game, 1959 $50
Disneyland Game, 1965 $25
Dragnet Game, 1955 $50-$60
Eliot Ness and the
    Untouchables Game, 1961 $70
Flintstones Stone Age Game, 1961 $45
Green Ghost Game, 1965 $75
Popeye Score-A-Matic $45
Rin Tin Tin Game, 1950s $50
Rin Tin Tin Paint By Number $60
Yogi Bear Score-A-Matic $35

**TUDOR**
Tru-Action Sports Car Race,
    1950s-60s $25
Tru-Action Electric Football,
    various $10-$25

**UNEEDA**
Pee Wee, doll $5
Pee Wee Doll Box, paper dolls,
    Whitman/Uneeda, 1966 $10
Pee Wee Tote, Ideal/Uneeda $10
Wishnik, hula Troll doll $30
Wishnik, two-headed Troll $50
Wishnik, graduation gown Troll $20

**WATKINS-STRATHMORE**
Man from U.N.C.L.E.
    coloring book, 1965 $35

**WHAM-O**
Cheerios box, Super Ball
    and Frisbee offer, 1969 $30
Frisbee, 1966 $15
Hula Hoop, 1950s-60s $10
Mars Platter $50
Mini Frisbee, 1967, 4" $15
Pluto Platter $225
Super Ball, multicolored, small $5-$10

**WHITMAN**
Adventures of Rin Tin Tin
    coloring book, 1955 $25
Barbie and Ken Paper Dolls, 1970 $35
Bugs Bunny Private Eye
    coloring book, 1957 $20
Family Affair Game, 1967 $35
Fury, frame tray puzzle, 1950s $20
Gene Autry coloring book, 1950 $65
Gumby & Pokey sticker book, 1968 $25
Hot Wheels sticker book, 1968 $10
Hot Wheels T.V. Show,
    frame tray puzzle, 1970 $10
Jetsons, frame tray puzzle, 1962 $30
Krazy Ikes, wood $15-$25
Krazy Ikes, plastic $8-$15
Lassie, frame tray puzzle, 1957 $20
Little Lulu, frame tray puzzle, 1959 $25
Magic Rub-Off Pictures $30
Raggedy Ann coloring book, 1968 $10
Rin Tin Tin, jigsaw, 1950s $20
Ruff & Reddy,
    frame tray puzzle, 1950s $25
Zorro, frame tray puzzle, 1950s-60s
    $20

# ADDITIONAL READING

The following list contains some of the many sources that provide information about the marvelous toys the Boomer generation played with. They range from excellent, well-researched histories of television and pop-culture to pictorial guides focusing on the flashiest toys of the times. Other valuable sources of information include advertisements and articles in consumer magazines, toy-trade magazines and manufacturing publications of the 1940s, '50s and '60s. Although these materials are extremely difficult to locate, several publishers have issued books of toy-catalog reproduction pages.

Ambridge, Geoffrey S. *The Bumper Book of Lone Star Diecast Models and Toys 1948-88.* East Sussex, U.K.: Geesam-Fossicker Publications/Sumfield & Day Ltd., 2002

Byrne, Chris. *Toys: Celebrating 100 Years of the Power of Play.* New York: Toy Industry Association, Inc., 2003.

Cockrill, Pauline. *The Teddy Bear Encyclopedia.* New York: DK Publishing, Inc., 2001.

Davis, Stephen. *Say Kids! What Time Is It?* Boston: Little, Brown & Co., 1987.

Frey, Tom, Jim Douglas, and Dick Brodeur. *Toy Bop.* Murrysville, Pa.: Fuzzy Dice Productions, Inc., 1994.

Fritz, Peter, ed. *The Big Toy Box at Sears.* Leawood, Kan.: Classic Toy Soldiers, Inc., 1997.

Hanlon, Bill. *Plastic Toys: Dimestore Dreams of the '40s & '50s.* Atglen, Pa.: Schiffer Publications, 1993.

Harmon, Jim. *Radio & TV Premiums.* Iola, Wis.: Krause Publications, 1997.

Harry, Lou. *It's Slinky! The Fun and Wonderful Toy.* Philadelphia, Pa.: Running Press, 2000.

Heaton, Tom. *The Encyclopedia of Marx Action Figures.* Iola, Wis.: Krause Publications, 1999.

Hoffman, David. *Kid Stuff.* San Francisco, Calif.: Chronicle Books, 1996.

Holland, Thomas W., ed. *Boys' Toys of the Fifties & Sixties: Memorable Catalog Pages from the Legendary Sears Christmas Wish Books, 1950-1969.* Sherman Oaks, Calif.: The Windmill Group, 1997.

Holland, Thomas W., ed. *Girls' Toys of the Fifties & Sixties: Memorable Catalog Pages from the Legendary Sears Christmas Wish Books, 1950-1969.* Sherman Oaks, Calif.: The Windmill Group, 1997.

Holland, Thomas W., ed. *More Boys' Toys of the Fifties & Sixties: Toy Pages from the Great Montgomery Wards Christmas Catalogs, 1950-1969.* Sherman Oaks, Calif.: The Windmill Group, 1998.

Hultzman, Don. *Collector's Guide to Battery Toys.* 2nd Ed. Paducah, Ky.: Collector Books, 2002.

Huxford, Sharon and Bob Huxford. *Schroeder's Collectible Toys* (various years and editions). Paducah, Ky.: Collector Books.

Kaplan, Louis, and Scott Michaelson. *Gumby: The Authorized Biography of the World's Favorite Clayboy.* New York: Harmony Books, 1986.

Kelly, Douglas R. *The Die Cast Price Guide, Postwar: 1946 to Present.* Dubuque, Iowa: Antique Trader Books, 1997.

Kerr, Lisa, and Jim Gilcher. *Ohio Art: The World of Toys.* Atglen, Pa.: Schiffer Publications, 1998.

Kisseloff, Jeff. *The Box: An Oral History of Television, 1920-1961.* New York: Viking Penguin, 1995.

Klein, Raymond R. *Greenberg's Guide to Tootsietoys 1945-1969.* Waukesha, Wis.: Greenberg Publishing Co., Inc., 1993.

Leopard, Dave. *Rubber Toy Vehicles.* West Columbia, S.C.: David M. Leopard/Wentworth Printing Corp., 1994.

Liljeblad, Cynthia Boris. *TV Toys and the Shows That Inspired Them.* Iola, Wis.: Krause Publications, 1996.

Longest, David, and Michael Stern. *The Collector's Encyclopedia of Disneyana.* Paducah, Ky.: Collector Books, 1992.

McMahon, Jeff. *Where the Frisbee First Flew.* Freestyle Frisbee Page, http://www.frisbee.com. Tom Leitner, site wizard.

Malafronte, Victor A. *The Complete Book of Frisbee.* Alameda, Calif.: American Trends Publishing Co., 1998.

Malloy, Alex G. *American Games, Comprehensive Collector's Guide.* Iola, Wis.: Krause Publications, 2000.

Miller, G. Wayne. *Toy Wars: The Epic Struggle Between G.I. Joe, Barbie, and the Companies that Make Them.* New York: Times/Random House, 1998.

O'Brien, Karen, ed. *O'Brien's Collecting Toys.* 11th Ed. Iola, Wis.: Krause Publications, 2004.

O'Brien, Karen, ed. *Toys & Prices.* 11th Ed. Iola, Wis.: Krause Publications, 2003.

O'Brien, Richard. *The Story of American Toys.* New York: Abbeville Press, 1990.

O'Brien, Richard, ed. *Collecting American-Made Toy Soldiers.* 3rd Ed. Florence, Ala.: Books Americana, 1997.

O'Brien, Richard, ed. *O'Brien's Collecting Toys: Identification and Value Guide.* Various editions, Books Americana and Krause Publications.

O'Brien, Richard, ed. *Collecting Toy Cars & Trucks.* 2nd Ed. Iola, Wis.: Krause Publications, 1997.

O'Connor John E., ed. *American History/American Television.* New York: Frederick Ungar Pub. Co., 1983.

Rich, Mark. *Toys A to Z.* Iola, Wis.: Krause Publications, 2001.

Rich, Mark, and Jeff Potocsnak. *Funny Face! An Amusing History of Potato Heads, Bloc Heads, and Magic Whiskers.* Iola, Wis.: Krause Publications, 2002.

Smith, Ron, and William C. Gallagher. *The Big Book of Tin Toy Cars: Passenger, Sports, and Concept Vehicles.* Atglen, Pa.: Schiffer Publications, 2003.

Smith, Ron, and William C. Gallagher. *The Big Book of Tin Toy Cars: Commercial and Racing Vehicles.* Atglen, Pa.: Schiffer Publications, 2004.

Sommer, Robin Langley. *"I Had One of Those": Toys of Our Generation.* New York: Crescent Books, 1993.

Strange, Craig. *Collector's Guide to Tinker Toys.* Paducah, Ky.: Collector Books, 1996.

Strauss, Michael Thomas. *Tomart's Price Guide to Hot Wheels.* Dayton, Ohio: Tomart Publications, 1993.

Wiencek, Henry. *The World of LEGO Toys.* New York: Harry N. Abrams, Inc. 1987.

# INDEX

## A

A. & E. Tool & Gage Co., Inc., 150–151
A. C. Gilbert Co., 145, 166–167, 204
A. G. Spalding & Bros., 190
Academy Die-Casting & Plating Co., 64
Accessory toys, 14–17
    dolls, 27, 28, 45–46, 49, 106
    Hot Wheels, 50
    Safety-Bake Oven, 35
Acme Merchandise Co., Inc., 77
Action Cars, 98–101, 204
Addams Family, 163–164, 204
Aladdin, 29, 65, 72, 90, 204
Alden's, 138
American Doll & Toy Corp., 47
American Plastic, 141, 204
American Skyline, 143
Arant & Co., Inc., 127
Archer Plastics, 104, 204
Argo Action Cars, 99, 100, 204
Arrow, 178, 204
Atomic Mobile Unit, 120–121
Auburn Rubber Co., Inc., 148–149, 204
Aurora Plastics, 88–91, 204
Automatic Toy Co., 65, 204

## B

Baker, Lynn, 68
Barbie, 10, 12–17, 29, 31
    accessories, 17, 204
    Tammy compared, 45, 47
    toy values, 204, 205
Barclay, 51
Barry & Enright Productions, 97
Bash!, 168, 204
Batman, 78–79, 204
Beany-Copter, 82–83
Bears, 176–177, 200, 204. See also Yogi Bear
Beatles, 76–77, 205
Ben Casey, 169, 205
Ben Cooper, Inc., 77, 79, 192, 204
Best of the West dolls, 28
Betsy McCall, 47, 49, 179
Billy Blastoff, 172, 204
Binney & Smith, 196
Block City, 141, 205
Bob-A-Loop, 194
Boyd, William, 65
Bozo the Clown, 185, 204, 205
Breyer Molding Co., 117, 119, 204
Budgie, 32
Bugs Bunny, 196, 204, 205
Burp Gun, 70
Buzzy Bee, 202, 204

## C

Cadaco-Ellis Foto-Electric Football, 153, 205
Capitol Records, 185, 204
Capp, Al, 37
Captain Action, 29
Captain Kangaroo, 191, 195
Captain Video, 114–115, 204, 205
Carrom Industries, Inc., 111–112
Cartoons, 21, 70–72
Casting sets, 39–41
Catalogs and books, 7–8, 206
Chasse, Paul, 93
Chatty Cathy, 30–31, 205
Chubby Tubby, 176, 177, 205
Clarabell the Clown, 60, 61, 106, 195
Classy Products Corp., 63, 64
Clokey, Art, 105–106
"Clue" game, 112, 205
Colorforms, 46, 57, 179, 204
Connecticut Leather, 72, 204
Coonskin cap, 55–57, 63, 205
Cootie, 11, 73, 205
Cox Manufacturing Co., 167, 204
Crayola crayons, 196, 205
Creeple Peeple, 40, 205
Creepy Crawler, 40, 205
Crounse, Avery, 68

## D

Daisy Mfg. Co., 64, 108
Dam, Thomas, 48–49
Daniel Boone, 55–57, 63, 204
Dapper Dan, 193, 205
Darrow, Charles B., 136–137
Dastardly and Muttley, 164, 205
Davy Crockett, 55–57, 204, 205
Dawson, Velma, 60
De Luxe Reading Corp. See Topper Toys
Dell, 123, 204
Dick Tracy, 98–101
Dillon Beck Manufacturing Co., 62, 102–103, 204
Dinosaurs, 124–126, 205
Disney
    Davy Crockett and Daniel Boone, 55–57, 63, 204, 205
    Disneyland, 70
    Goofy, 87
    Mickey Mouse, 21, 70–72, 77, 204
    toy values, 204, 205
Doepke Model Toys, 68
Dolls
    Barbie. See Barbie
    for boys, 26–29
    for girls, 44–47, 86–87, 191, 204
    houses and furniture, 20, 140, 205
    plastic, 48–49, 61, 62
    talking, 30–31
    toy values, 204, 205
Dowst Mfg. Co., 33, 136–137, 150–151, 167, 204
Dream Pets, 158, 204
DuMont, 114–115
Duncan, 181, 204

## E

Easy-Bake Oven, 34–35, 204
Eldon Industries, 74, 165–167, 172, 204
Elgo and Elgo/Halsam, 143, 204
Emenee Industries, Inc., 40
Erector sets, 145, 204
Etch-A-Sketch, 93, 205

## F

Fairchild Variety Products, Inc., 157
Farm sets and equipment, 66–67, 148, 205
Fischer, Dennis, 85
Fisher-Price Toys, 201, 202, 203, 204
Flatsy doll, 87, 204
Flintstones, 162, 204, 205
Flubadub, 60–61
Flying saucers, 36–37
Football, electric, 152–153
Franscioni, Warren, 37
Frisbee, 11, 36–37, 205
Frisbie Pie Factory, 36, 37, 204
Frosty Sno-Cone Machine, 35
Fury, 118–119, 205

## G

G. I. Joe, 26–29, 204
Game of Life, The, 170, 205
George Schmidt Mfg. Co., 63, 64, 65, 205
Gilbert. See A. C. Gilbert Co.
Gimbels, 58–59
Girder & Panel, 142, 204
Give-A-Show Projector, 92, 204
Glass, Marvin, 42, 84
Gleason, Jackie, 22, 205
Go to the Head of the Class, 134–135, 205
Groucho's games, 112, 204, 205
Gumby, 105–106, 204, 205
Gund, 200, 204
Guyer, Reyn, 81
Gyrofriction car, 146–147

## H

Haas, Eduard III, 180
Halsam, 141, 143, 144
Handler, Elliott and Ruth, 12
Handy Andy, 27
Harmon, Larry, 185
Hartland Plastics, 57, 65, 118–119, 131, 204
Hasbro
    accessories, 46, 72
    Frosty Sno-Cone Machine, 35
    games, 21, 79
    Mr. Potato Head, 11, 18–23, 204
    Son of Flubber, 27
    toy values, 23, 29, 204
Hassenfeld Bros., Inc. See Hasbro
Hawk Model Co., 157
Hopalong Cassidy, 64–65, 113, 204, 205
Hoppity Horse, 182, 205
Hot Wheels, 50–51, 205
Howdy Doody, 53, 60–61, 204, 205
Hubley Mfg. Co., 33, 64, 150, 151
Hula Hoop, 48, 54, 205

## I

Ideal Toy Corp.
    accessories, 140
    Atomic Mobile Unit, 120–121
    dinosaur models, 124
    dolls, 44–47, 64, 65, 78–79, 87, 107
    games, 42–43, 90, 160, 164, 168, 169
    punchos, 197
    robots, 62, 84, 204
    stuffed-toys, 194
    television advertising, 24
    toy values, 29, 42, 47, 204
    Weird-Ohs, 157
Incredible Edibles, 38
Irwin Corp.
    accessories, 140
    cars, trucks and boats, 83, 146–147, 165
    plastic bricks, 141
    toy values, 204

## J

J. Halpern Co., 64, 194
Jack Manoil Co., 150, 151
James, Richard, 58–59
James Industries, Inc., 58–59, 204
Japanese battery toys, 128–129
Jaymar, 72, 119, 204
Johnny Astro, 171, 205
Johnny Lightning cars, 50
Johnny Toymaker, 40, 41, 205

## K

Keeshan, Robert, 60, 195
Kenner Products Co.
    Easy-Bake Oven, 34–35, 204
    Electric Mold Master, 40–41
    Girder & Panel, 142, 204
    Give-A-Show Projector, 92, 204
    Spirograph, 85, 204
    toy values, 35, 204
Kestral, 197, 204
Kilgore Mfg. Co., 53, 63, 64
King Seeley Thermos, 161, 204
Kislevitz, Harry and Patricia, 179
Kitchens and accessories, 34–35, 138–139, 205
Klackers, 173, 205
Knapp Electric Co., 198
Knerr, Richard, 37, 54
Knickerbocker, 176–177, 185, 204
Knievel, Evel, 107
Kohner, 61, 162, 204
Krazy Ikes, 198, 205

## L

Lakeside Industries, 105–106, 204
Lamb Chop, 194, 205
Lee, 113, 204
Lerner, George, 18
Leslie-Henry Mfg. Co., 64
Lesney Matchbox, 32–33, 204
Lewis, Sheri, 194
Liddle Kiddles, 86–87, 191, 205
Lido, 115, 204
Lincoln Logs, 144, 205
Lionel Corp., 34
Livingston, Alan, 185
Lone Ranger, The, 63, 130–131, 205
Louis Marx Co.
    cars and trucks, 72, 99, 100, 121
    figures, 28, 65, 90, 130–131, 162, 177

modern farm, 66–67
Nutty Mads, 157, 205
plastic dollhouse furniture, 140
Prehistoric Times, 124–125, 205
robots, 62, 80
space toys, 83, 110, 114, 115
television advertising, 24
toy values, 23, 29, 57, 61, 204–205
visionary toys, 113
Lowe, 97, 169, 204
Lowell Toy Manufacturing Corp., 111–112, 204

**M**

Maggie Magnetic, Inc., 122–123, 204
Magic Rocks, 186, 205
Magnet Hat & Cap Corp., 77
Man from U.N.C.L.E., 160–161, 204, 205
Marx. See Louis Marx Co.
Mastro Industries, Inc., 77
Matchbox cars, 32–33, 204
Mattel
Beany-Copter, 82–83
dolls, 30–31, 86–87, 185. See also Barbie
Hot Wheels, 50–51, 205
Incredible Edibles, 38
Mousegetar, 71, 72, 205
plastics for toys, 62
spy toys, 161
television advertising, 70
Thingmakers, 39–41, 205
toy values, 17, 41, 51, 205
Maverick, 65
McVicker, Joe, 199
Mego, 29, 205
Melin, Arthur, 54
Mercury Plastics, 109
Metal Ware Corp., 34, 35, 139
Metaltex, Inc., 46
Mickey Mouse, 21, 70–72, 77, 204
Midgetoy, 151
Milton Bradley Co.
games, 76–77, 81, 111, 115, 134–135, 164, 169
Snoopy & the Red Baron, 183–184, 205
toy values, 61, 77, 170, 205
Minamoto Trading Co., 101, 129, 139
Miner Industries, 161, 205
Monopoly, 136–137, 205
Montgomery Ward's
aerial toys, 83
catalog, 7, 56–57
farm sets, 66
life-size kitchen, 139
punchos, 197
Morrison, Fred, 37
Mound Metalcraft, Inc., 68–69
Mouse Trap, 42–43, 204
Mousegetar, 71, 72, 205
Mouseketeers, 70, 71–72
Mr. Machine, 84, 204
Mr. Potato Head, 11, 18–23, 204
Mystery Date, 169, 205

**N**

Newton, Ruth E., 178
Nosco Plastics, 146
Nutty Mads, 157, 205

**O**

Odell, Jack, 32
Ohio Art Co., 93, 205

**P**

Pajeau, Charles H., 190
Palmer Plastics, Inc., 89, 140
Park Plastics, 110, 205
Parker, Fess, 55–57, 204
Parker Brothers
games, 72, 136–137, 170
toy values, 57, 61, 205
Peanuts, 183–184
Peter Puppet Playthings, Inc., 57, 61, 205
Pez, 180, 205
Pipco, 37
Pixie and Dixie Punchos, 197, 204
Plastic material for toys
cap guns, 63
dollhouse furniture, 140
dolls and robots, 48–49, 61, 62
farm sets, 66
history, 20
Hula Hoops, 48, 54, 205
influence on toys, 53
model building, 88–91
polyethylene, 74
restrictions during war, 102
Tenite, 37
vehicles, 20
Plastigoop, 39–40
Play-Doh, 199, 205
Pluto platter, 36, 37, 205
Pogo, 183–184, 205
Pokey, 105–106, 204, 205
Prehistoric Times, 124–125, 205
Premier Products Co., 104
Presley, Elvis, 77
Pressman, 97, 112, 205
Pride Products, Inc., 61
Push puppets, 162

**R**

R. & S. Toy Mfg. Co., Inc., 53, 64
R. Dakin & Co., 158, 204
Rainbow Crafts Co., 199
Rat Fink, 156–157, 205
Remco Industries, Inc.
dolls and robots, 27, 62, 77
games, 164
Jupiter 4-Color Signal Gun, 110
toy values, 205
Renwal Mfg. Co., 140, 146–147, 205
Resources, 206
Revell, Inc., 77, 91, 157, 167, 205
Rin Tin Tin, 116–117, 205
Robert the Robot, 62, 204
Rock 'em Sock 'em Robots, 80, 205
Rocky, Bullwinkle and Boris, 107, 204, 205
Rogers, Roy, 63–65, 204, 205
Roth, Ed, 50–51
Rubber, history of, 182
Rushton Co. (Atlanta Playthings Co.), 61, 176–177, 205

**S**

Saalfield Publishing Co., 17, 77, 113, 205
Safety concerns, 23, 35, 97, 173
Safety-Bake Oven, 35
Santa Maria, 91
Sawyers, Inc., 191

Schaper, 73, 205
Schaper, Herb, 73
School Bus, 201
Schulz, Charles, 183–184
Schwartz Toy Mfg. Corp., 127
Score-A-Matic, 192
Scrabble, 111–112
Sears
catalog, 7–8, 14, 129
dolls, 17, 47, 48, 78
farm sets, 66
Roy Rogers items, 64
Thingmakers, 40
Secret Sam Shooter Pipe, 160, 161, 205
Selchow & Righter Co., 111–112
Silly Putty, 187, 205
Skandia House, 49
Slinky, 11, 58–59, 204
Slot cars, 166–167
Slush-metal casting, 39, 51
Smethport Specialty Co., 193, 205
Smith, Bob, 60–61
Smith, Leslie and Rodney, 32
Snoopy & the Red Baron, 183–184, 205
Space Cadet, 113, 205
Space Patrol, 108–110, 205
Space people, 104
Speed King, 146–147, 205
Spirograph, 85, 204
Spoonmen, 127, 205
Sputnik, 36, 122–123, 204
Spy toys, 160–161
Squeakers, 178, 204, 205
Stori-Views, 92, 205
Strombeck-Becker Mfg. Co., 151, 167
Structo Mfg. Co., 68, 69, 139, 145
Stuart Mfg. Co., 117
Sun Rubber Co., 14–15, 178, 182, 205
Super Ball, 159, 205
Surf Skater Co., Inc., 77
Suzy Homemaker, 34, 40

**T**

T. Cohn, Inc., 108, 115
Tammy doll, 44–47, 204
Teddy Bear, musical, 200
Tee-Vee Toys, Inc., 61, 205
Television
advertisements, 20, 30, 84
Disney, 70
games, 76–77, 81, 111–112, 204, 205
influence on toys, 20–24, 34, 35, 52–53, 80, 132
switch from radio, 52
television kits, 65, 94, 96–97, 204, 205
Tesch, Alvin, 68
Thimbledrome, 166, 167
Thingmakers, 38–41, 205
This Little Piggy, 203, 204
Tin toys, 98–99
Tinkertoys, 190, 205
Tom Corbett, 83, 113, 114, 204, 205
Tonka, 68–69, 205
Tootsietoy, 33, 136–137, 150–151, 204
Topper Toys
Homemaker Super Oven, 34
Johnny Astro, 171, 205
Johnny Lightning cars, 50
Secret Sam Shooter Pipe, 160, 161, 205

Tammy doll, 44
television advertising, 24
Thingmakers, 40
toy values, 41, 205
Toykraft, 97, 205
Toymaster Products Co., Inc., 138–139
Tractors, 67
Transogram Co., Inc.
accessories, 79
games, 72, 90, 113, 162, 164, 169
Rin Tin Tin, 116–117
Score-A-Matic, 192
toy values, 205
Tremax Industries, 74
Trolls, 40, 48–49
Tru-Vue Co., 191
Tudor Metal Products, 152–153
Twister, 81, 204, 205

**U**

U. S. Plastic Co., 108, 110
Uke-A-Doodle, 70
Uneeda Doll Co., Inc., 48–49, 87, 205

**V**

Vac-U-Form casting set, 40, 205
Values of toys, 204–205
View-Master, 191
Visible Woman, The, 91
V-RROOM! boy toys, 31

**W**

Walters, Ed and Iola, 118–119
Wannatoy, 102–103, 204
Ward's. See Montgomery Ward's
Warner Brothers, 196
Watkins-Strathmore, 161, 205
Weird-Ohs, 157
Wham-O, 36–37, 54, 107, 159, 205
What's My Line? Game, 111–112, 204
Whee-Lo, 122–123, 204
Whirly-Whirler, 37
Whitman Publishing Co.
accessories, 46
books, 106, 196
games, 164
Krazy Ikes, 198, 205
puzzles, 65, 117, 118, 119
toy values, 17, 51, 205
Winky Dink, 94, 96–97, 204, 205
Wishnik, 48–49, 205
Withington, 64
Wolverine Supply & Mfg. Co., 52, 138, 139
Wonder Products Co., 118
Wooly Willy, 193, 205
Wright, James, 187
Wright, John Lloyd, 144

**Y**

Yogi Bear, 176–177, 192, 204, 205
Yonezawa Space Saucer Mercury X-1, 129, 205
Yoshiya Space Dog, 129, 205
Yo-Yos, 181, 204

**Z**

Zippy the Chimp, 61, 176
Zoomer Robot, 129, 205
Zorro, 78, 191, 205